I have tramped all over the hills on the south side of the Yangtze,
And whenever I come to another mountain, I can't help lingering there;
Alone, I carry with me a little moon-like lump from heaven,
Always ready to try the second best spring in the world of men.

The stone path winds back and forth like the spines of nine dragons,
The reflections on the water glimmer like the five lakes of heaven;
Hermit Sun Deng spoke not a word, so I returned, empty-handed,
But halfway down the ridge, I heard the sound of the pines
rustling through the myriad ravines.

On Mount Hui I Visit the Recluse Qin and We Boil
a Lump of Little Dragon Tea, then Climb the Highest Peak
and Gaze at Lake Tai in the Distance
Su Dongpo, 11th century

THE TRUE HISTORY OF TEA

VICTOR H. MAIR & ERLING HOH

WITH 82 ILLUSTRATIONS

DEDICATED TO ERLING'S SON NOAH
AND VICTOR'S SON THOMAS KRISHNA

On the jacket: *Front* A tea party in Calcutta, 1890 (see p. 215). *Back,*
clockwise from top left A late Ming-dynasty Chinese blue and white
teapot (Percival David Foundation of Chinese Art, London); the
tea plant (from Franz Eugen Köhler, *Medizinal-Pflanzen*, Germany,
1887); a Dutch East Indiaman (Scheepvaart Museum, Amsterdam);
a Chinese tea laborer (Collection Mainwaring-Robertson).
Half-title: The Belitung tea bowl (see pp. 46–47).
Title page: Chinese Qing-dynasty laborers trample tea into
chests, *c.* 1800.

First published in the United Kingdom in 2009 by
Thames & Hudson Ltd, 181A High Holborn, London WC1V 7QX

www.thamesandhudson.com

British Library Cataloguing-in-Publication Data
A catalogue record for this book is available from the British Library

ISBN 978-0-500-25146-1

Printed and bound in Singapore by Tien Wah Press (Pte) Ltd.

CONTENTS

PROLOGUE

~~~~~~~~~~~~~~~~~

TEA: LEAF OF AWARENESS

~~~~~~~~~~~~~~~~~

On a cold, clear night in December, 1773, a band of freedom-loving Bostonians, barely disguised as Native Americans, made their way to the town's harbor, where the *Dartmouth*, *Eleanor*, and *Beaver* lay moored at the wharf laden with tea. Having boarded the ships, these sons of liberty then broke open the chests stored in the holds and shoveled the tea into the sea. Soon, the harbor was awash with 90,000 lb of fragrant leaves. "This is the most magnificent Movement of all.... This Destruction of the Tea is so bold, so daring, so firm, intrepid, and inflexible, and it must have so important Consequences and so lasting, that I cannot but consider it as an Epocha in History," wrote the Boston merchant John Adams, who was destined to become the second president of the new republic.

The tea that filled Boston Harbor on that historic night had been picked at dawn in the hinterlands of the Fujian province of China, withered, tossed, oxidized, fired, rolled, packed in wooden chests lined with lead, carried by coolies shod in grass-sandals, tasted and haggled over by plump merchants, journeyed four months in the damp storage of an East Indiaman round the Cape of Good Hope to London, broken, warehoused, and then reloaded by stevedores for the final, fateful voyage across the Atlantic. From its humble origins in the Himalayan foothills of Southeast Asia, the salubrious tea plant has been traded by humans to every nook and cranny of the globe, and adopted by every people under the sun. Long before igniting the American War of Independence, it abetted the poets of China in their greatest achievements. It has burrowed itself to the core of the Japanese soul, solaced many a weary Tibetan yak herder, fueled the midnight cogitations of Britain's great inventors, and offered untold numbers of Russian peasants a path to sobriety. Through the centuries, it has provided a safe, stimulating beverage that played a crucial role in reducing human epidemics and making habitation in crowded, bustling cities possible. In the modern world, it marks the day's rhythm for hundreds of millions of people, from the Koryaks of the Kamchatka Peninsula in Russia to the Samburu pastoralists of northern Kenya.

It is precisely the epic nature of tea's odyssey that has always made its history so difficult to write. With its botanical, medical, religious, cultural, economic, anthropological, social, and political dimensions, with its roots in antiquity and utter unconcern for distances and linguistic divides, the task of gathering its many strands into a single story for the general reader has always proved daunting for authors, whether from the West or the East. Yet in the storerooms of the world's libraries, and in the archives of the Internet, lie reams of books and journals that contain the meticulous, passionate labors of poets, historians, scientists, and humanists, each shedding light on a particular aspect of tea history. In *The True History of Tea*, we have endeavored to consult these documents and original sources (in a number of occidental and oriental languages), to distinguish fact from popular lore, to clear up many misunderstandings regarding this beloved beverage, and to distil our research into a tale that can be enjoyed by anybody with an interest in tea and its remarkable place in the history of humankind.

The first chapter surveys an array of the plants apart from tea that humans have experimented with in search of a morning perk, relief from hunger and fatigue, religious experience, and artistic inspiration. In Chapter 2, we introduce the tea plant, tracing its botanical origin to Southeast Asia, its first use as a masticatory and preserved vegetable among the Austroasiatic people who inhabit that region, and how knowledge of the tea plant's properties spread north to the Ba people in the Sichuan Basin of China. Chapter 3 follows the diffusion of tea eastward along the Yangtze river, its adoption by Buddhists, Taoists, and herbal doctors, and its first recorded use as an alternative to alcohol and agent of temperance. In northern China, however, tea was initially rejected by the nomadic Tabgatch rulers, who considered their own fermented horse milk a vastly preferable beverage.

By the middle of the Tang dynasty (Chapter 4), tea had been firmly established as China's favorite beverage, as evinced by the magnificent tea vessels unearthed at the Famen Temple, the first imposition of an imperial tax on tea, and the publication of Lu Yu's *Classic of Tea*. During the subsequent Song dynasty (Chapter 5), the center of China's tea production shifted south to the coastal province of Fujian, and together with firewood, cooking oil, rice, salt, soy sauce, and vinegar, tea became one of the "seven daily necessities." A draconian state monopoly on the tea trade was imposed, and as the Tibetans, Mongols, Uyghurs, and other neighboring peoples fell under the spell of tea, the exchange of tea for horses of war (Chapter 6) evolved as a cornerstone of China's foreign policy.

From China, tea was dispersed around the world along three main paths: firstly, eastward to Japan; secondly, westward by land, initially to Tibet, Mongolia, Central Asia and Iran, and later to Russia and its Slavic neighbors; and thirdly, by the British (and other European nations) around the world by sea: to Western Europe, North and South America, Indonesia, India, Ceylon (Sri Lanka), Australia, New Zealand, the Fiji Islands, Morocco, and East Africa. With the arrival of tea in Japan (Chapter 7), the seeds were sown for a unique tea culture that has come to embody all the idiosyncrasies of that island nation. In the 15th and 16th centuries, the philosophy and esthetics of the Japanese tea ceremony were brought to their apotheosis through the genius of Sen Rikyū (Chapter 8), who in his "one-page testament" boiled ostensibly the most elaborate, circumscribed ceremony invented by humans down to the following pithy statement: "It is simply to drink tea, knowing that if you just heat the water, your thirst is certain to be quenched. Nothing else is involved."

In the Ming dynasty (Chapter 9), loose-leaf green tea became the most common kind in China. Gradually, the art of abetting and controlling the tea leaves' natural oxidation (fermentation) was acquired, which gave rise to the semi-oxidized Oolong and fully oxidized black teas. Today, the world of tea can largely be divided into the green tea cultures of China, Japan, and Morocco, the black tea cultures of Britain, its former colonies, Russia, the Middle East, and East Africa, the Oolong tea culture of Taiwan,

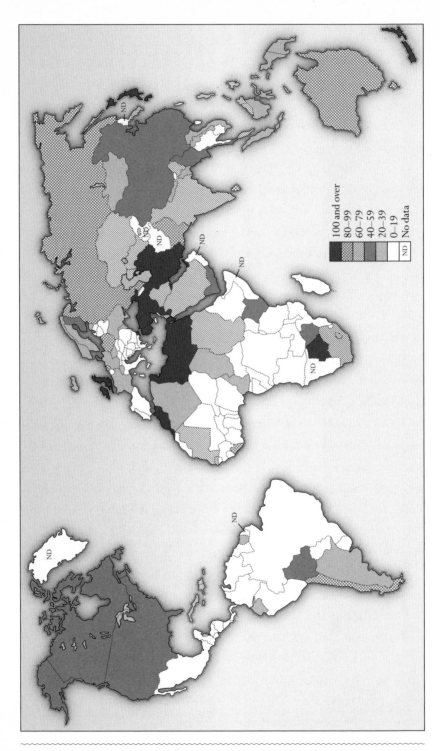

Tea consumption around the globe in liters per person per year (1994–96).

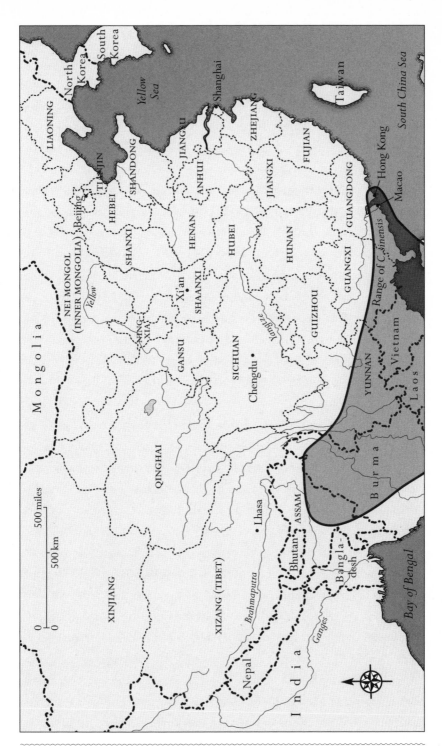

The heartland of tea lay in Southeast Asia, northeastern India, and southwest China.

and the brick tea cultures of Tibet, Mongolia, and Central Asia. Among the Tibetans, with their heavy diet of yak meat and barley, brick tea was prized for its digestive properties, and consumed with butter and salt in copious amounts (Chapter 10). In the 16th century, the "Yellow Hats" emerged as the most powerful Buddhist group in Tibet, and when the Mongols converted to Tibetan Buddhism for the second time toward the end of that century, they also adopted the Tibetan custom of boiling their tea long and well to extract every drop of its flavor and strength, mixing it with horse milk instead of yak butter. At about this time, the Russian people in the city-state of Moscow were emerging from their chrysalis and expanding eastward rapidly (Chapter 11). This inevitably brought them into contact with the Chinese empire, and after a few initial skirmishes, the two countries settled down to a relatively peaceful and prosperous trading relationship. Caravans of camels and ox-carts laden with tea traversed the Gobi Desert to the Mongol border south of Lake Baikal, where the market town of Kyakhta, founded in 1727, grew into one of the wealthiest cities in the Russian empire.

Along the ancient Silk Road that skirted the fringes of the vast Taklamakan desert and continued over the Pamir mountains into the fertile Ferghana valley, tea gradually supplanted silk as the staple commodity, and from the bazaars of Samarqand and Bukhara, the new beverage spread to Persia and Afghanistan (Chapter 12). Islam forbade the drinking of wine and debated the appropriateness of coffee, so that with the advent of affordable Indian tea in the 19th century, the Middle East was gradually transformed into a solid bastion of tea-drinkers. Throughout the first half of the second millennium, horse-borne Mongol and Turkic people continued to press west, and with the rise of the Ottoman Turks in Anatolia, the caravan routes that had conveyed the spices of India to Europe fell into hostile hands. This was the catalyst for the great European age of exploration, as Christopher Columbus sailed west and Vasco da Gama east, both in search of a sea route to India free from troublesome middlemen (Chapter 13). When Portuguese, Dutch, and English ships began appearing in the waters of China and Japan, tea was one of the exotic commodities they returned home with in their holds. In Europe, doctors debated the blessings and vices of the new herb, and after a first flirtation with coffee, England threw itself headlong into a love affair with tea that transformed it into the greatest tea-drinking nation on the planet. During the 18th and 19th centuries, tea consumption in Britain expanded with such speed that national economists began to worry about the amount of silver being spent to procure the leaf (Chapter 14). The famous Swedish botanist Carl Linnaeus made an attempt to cultivate the tea plant, but was thwarted by the harsh Nordic winter. As Britain turned to opium from India as a replacement for silver to pay for its tea, tensions with China escalated, and in 1840, the first cannon balls of the Opium Wars were fired.

Contrary to popular perception, it was not the villainous role of tea in America's road to independence that turned the young republic into a nation of coffee-drinkers, and tea remained a popular beverage in America throughout the 19th century (Chapter 15). But in those days, Americans preferred green tea, which they iced in their newly invented refrigerators and served as tea punches flavored with fruit juices and spiked with spirits. It was around this time that the British initiated tea cultivation on an industrial scale in the Indian province of Assam, which was followed by Ceylon; by the end of the 19th century, India had overtaken China as the world's major tea exporter (Chapter 16). The final episode of Britain's tea trade with China was written by the tea clippers, the most beautiful sailing ships ever to grace the seven seas (Chapter 17). Loading the new season's tea in May off Fuzhou's Pagoda Anchorage, the tea clippers, gleaming with polished brass and teakwood, raced each other every year round the Cape of Good Hope, until the Suez Canal, opened in 1869, cut the passage to London short by thousands of miles and ushered in the age of the steamship.

In Chapter 18, tea in our time presents a picture as varied and intriguing as a Picasso painting. In Australia, the "billy" can is swung three times around the head to settle the tea leaves before the cups are filled. In Japan, the preparation of a bowl of tea is governed by some 1,000 variations of *temae* – the rules of body movement in the Japanese tea ceremony. During World War II, tea played a crucial role in Britain's monumental struggle to defeat the Third Reich. Mao washed his teeth with green tea, and today, the favorite drink among Beijing yuppies is a cocktail of green tea and Chivas Regal. In America, spiced chai is vying with coffee for the new generation of trendy cosmopolitans. The Tuaregs of sub-Saharan Africa, for their part, pour their strong green tea from a height to produce an enticing foam. Such are the hundred diversions of tea in the modern world.

To pay tribute to Lu Yu, the founding father of tsiology (the art and science of tea), we have included a full translation of his autobiography (Appendix A). In the year 1900, Wang Yuanlu, the self-appointed caretaker of the Dunhuang Buddhist caves near the western end of the Great Wall, uncovered a hidden cache of manuscripts dating back a millennium and more. These included the oldest known printed book, a woodblock edition of the *Diamond Sutra* now in the British Library, as well as the delectable *A Debate Between Tea and Beer* (Appendix B). And as a final treat to the language buffs, we here present the most incisive, authoritative, and entertaining treatise (Appendix C) on the genealogy of words for tea ever published.

Tea represents a true triumph of the meek. No other beverage has given rise to such an eclectic wealth of pots, cups, and other paraphernalia. No other drink has been elaborated in such an exuberant variety of rituals, each serving as a mirror of the culture from which it has sprung. The cultivation of tea provides a lucrative commodity for the big multinationals, and a livelihood for millions of farmers and estate workers in East Africa, India, Sri Lanka, Indonesia, China, Iran, Turkey, Georgia, and many other countries. Whether your next cup of tea is made from a sachet of PG Tips, Dongding Oolong, gunpowder, *biluochun,* Earl Grey, or Japanese Gyokuro, it all comes from leaves of the same unassuming bush. So, between sips, take some time to contemplate the hue of your infusion, the road those leaves have traveled both in time and space, their rich history, the confidences they have elicited, the cultural transformations they have caused, and the peace they have brokered, and reflect for a moment on the fact that millions of your fellow human beings around the planet, whether in an office, a tea house, or a desert, are also taking a break from their daily chores to enjoy a moment of the lucid repose that only tea can conjure forth.

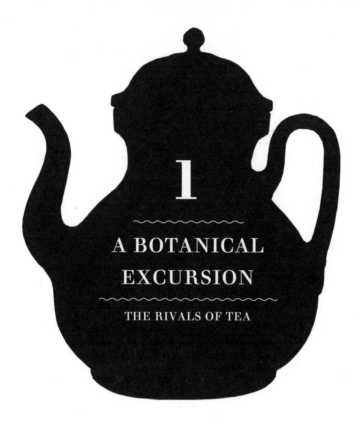

1

A BOTANICAL EXCURSION

THE RIVALS OF TEA

ver since life divided into the animal and plant kingdoms, animals have been putting the roots, stems, leaves, flowers, fruits, and seeds of plants into their mouths. The dinosaurs rose and fell with the gigantic gymnosperms they fed upon. We mammals evolved in a triangular relationship with pollinating insects and flowering plants. At some point, every plant species on this earth has probably been tasted by one animal species or another. Some plants kill us. Some nourish us. Some taste terrible. Some taste good. Some make us hallucinate, others induce a feeling of euphoria. Some stimulate us, dispel hunger and fatigue, make us feel stronger and braver, a little bit more alive.

Tea is the subject of this book, but first, let us take a look at some of the other plants in nature's cupboard that through history have contended for the title of humanity's most popular infusion.

The ancient inhabitants of the Tarim Basin in Eastern Central Asia knew about the medicinal effects of the ephedra plant, which has been found among the grave goods of Bronze Age mummies, buried and freeze-dried in the Taklamakan Desert 4,000 years ago. Millions of laborers in the Andes chew the coca leaf for its stimulating properties, mixing it with lime to free the leaf's active alkaloid compounds. Across the Pacific Ocean, lime is similarly employed to extract the active ingredients and taste of the betel (or areca) nut, a restorative drug popular throughout South and Southeast Asia, where the ingredients are masticated with a paste of lime wrapped in the leaf of the betel pepper (itself a mild stimulant), and where it has given rise to a rich tradition of customs, utensils, and lore.

In Yemen, both men and women chew the fresh leaves of the khat shrub every day for the vitality and pleasure it induces. Native to East Africa, khat was introduced to Yemen in the 13th century by Sufis (members of an ascetic, mystical Muslim sect) and learned sages, who used the plant to lighten the burden of their religious obligations and adhere more closely to their mystical experiences. When Ceylon (now Sri Lanka), Java, and Brazil took over the bulk of coffee cultivation in the 19th century, khat replaced the coffee plant on the land of many Yemeni farmers, and the custom of chewing it spread to all circles of society. Consumed as a social lubricant in special rooms called *mafrag*, khat causes three stages of effect: *tanabbuh* (alertness), *kaif* (well-being), and *qalaq nafsani* (mental anxiety).

While the simple act of chewing leaves, seeds, and roots remains common in some societies, infusing them in water was the next, natural step. And as food came to represent the corporeal body, liquid beverages were connected to the spiritual life, and suffused with ceremonial, social, political, religious, and mystical dimensions. Alcoholic drinks were our first social beverage. Other plants with properties attractive to humans were steeped in water, and the consumption of the infusion elaborated in accordance with the resources and character of that particular society. When James Cook, on his second expedition to find the continent *terra australis incognita*, assumed to exist in the southern Pacific, reached the Society Islands there in September 1773, he observed the Tongan kava ceremony:

Poulaho, king of the Friendly Islands (now known as Tonga) in the south Pacific Ocean, drinking kava.

I had almost forgot to mention the Avā root a kind of Pepper plant on which they make a liquor which is intoxicating.... The manner of Brewing or preparing the liquor is as simple as it is disgusting to a European and is thus; several people take of the root or stem adjoining to the root and chew it into a kind of Pulp when they spit it out into a platter or other Vessel, every one into the same Vessel, when a sufficient quantity is done they mix with it a certain proportion of Water and then strean [strain] the liquor through some fiberous stuff like fine shavings and it is then fit for drinking which is always done immediately; it has a pepperish taste rather flat and insipid and intoxicating.

The custom of drinking kava, which is a relative of the black pepper plant and not alcoholic as Cook believed, persists to this day in the southern Pacific. In Fiji, it is dispensed to military personnel to aid vigilance and reduce anxiety, and is also said to induce a mild euphoria and sense of well-being. But, like tobacco, coca, ephedra, khat, and the betel nut, kava is an imperfect stimulant for daily purposes, in that the drawbacks of its excessive consumption (including skin rashes and liver damage) are as great as or greater than its salutary effects.

The active ingredients of all these stimulants belong to the family of alkaloids, a group of nitrogen-containing, basic (alkaline) compounds of natural origin, that was first isolated and identified by scientists in the early 19th century. While the role of alkaloids in plants themselves is not yet fully understood, their medicinal (or lethal), effects on human beings have been carefully studied and extensively employed. Morphine, strychnine, quinine, ephedrine, mescaline, cocaine, and nicotine all belong to the alkaloid family. To date, over 10,000 alkaloids in more than 4,000 plants have been identified, and biochemists are constantly scouring the vegetable kingdom in search of new varieties with medicinal properties.

Of all these 10,000 alkaloids, one has become the beloved daily companion of humans – caffeine. The substance was first identified in 1820 by the German chemist Friedlieb Ferdinand Runge, after the poet Goethe had presented Runge with a handful of coffee beans and asked him to analyze them. Seven years later, the French chemist Monsieur Oudry discovered the identical substance in tea. For the more than 100 plants known to contain this alkaloid, caffeine is thought to act as a chemical defence, by repelling or killing invaders, whether insects, fungi, or other plants growing nearby. On humans, its effect is comparatively mild. It stimulates the nervous system and blood circulation, and is not harmful in moderation. Remarkably, wherever caffeine plants exist around the globe, humans have been able to identify them and put the caffeine to good use.

Among the Igbo of Nigeria, sharing a cola nut (containing some 2.5 percent caffeine) with one's guests is considered an indispensable part of hospitality. Early every morning in the most inaccessible Amazonian jungles in northern Peru and neighboring Ecuador, the men of the Achuar Jíbaro tribe are said to drink between two and four pints of the world's strongest caffeine drink, an infusion of leaves from the colossal guayasa holly tree, *Ilex guayasa*; one plant was found to contain 7.6 percent caffeine. According to ethnologists, this custom has as much to do with male bonding as it does with getting ready for the day's work, for about 45 minutes after the first sip the Achuar men vomit the drink to reduce the amount of caffeine to a more reasonable level.

In the 18th century, the American naturalist William Bartram observed a similar custom among the Creek Native Americans in the Carolinas, who consumed a black drink containing caffeine – made from an infusion of the leaves and shoots of the yaupon holly, *Ilex vomitoria*:

> Their mode of disgorging, or spouting out the black drink, is singular, and has not the most agreeable appearance. After drinking copiously, the warrior, by hugging his arms across his stomach, and leaning forward, disgorges the liquor in a large stream from his mouth, to the distance of six to eight feet. Thus, immediately after drinking, they begin spouting on all sides of the square, and in every direction; and in that country, as well as in others more civilized, it is thought a handsome accomplishment in a young fellow to be able to spout well.

The black drink was consumed not only by the Creek, but also the Cherokee, Choctaw, Ai, and other Native Americans during their daily village

Native American women prepare black drink in earthen vessels. The drink was also used as a substitute for coffee and tea by European colonists, who called it cassine.

councils, purification rituals, and religious ceremonies. Among the Cherokee, it was the Blue Holly clan, which represented the fifth level of spiritual
attainment – purity of mind, body and spirit – that was responsible for
preparing the black drink for ceremonial purposes, before the Cherokee
were removed to Oklahoma. The Creek believed that black drink purified them from all sin and left them in a state of perfect innocence, that it
imbued them with invincible prowess in war, and was the only true agent of
benevolence and hospitality.

In the 17th century, the use of guarana (with some 5 percent caffeine) was recorded among the Andiraz, Maue, Piapoco, and the Yavita
on the Atabapo river of southern Venezuela. The seeds of this climbing
vine, *Paullinia cupana*, were roasted and ground, mixed with cassava flour
and kneaded to a paste, which was shaped into long rods and dried. To
prepare the drink, they scraped this paste with the tongue of an Amazonian fish, the pirarucu, and dissolved the powder thus produced in cold or
hot water. According to one anthropologist, the Andiraz believed that
guarana bestowed the power to hunt for long stretches on end without
being tormented by hunger and fatigue. Growing in Venezuela and northern Brazil, the guarana seed today forms the basis for a number of energy
drinks, including Full Throttle, No Fear, and SoBe Adrenaline Rush. In
Brazil, Guarana Antarctica is said to be the second most popular drink after
the colas.

When the Spanish adventurer and explorer Juan Díaz de Solís sailed
up the Rio de la Plata in 1516, he came into contact (surviving crew
members reported that he was eaten) with the Guaraní tribe, which
since time immemorial had been preparing a decoction from yet another
member of the holly family, *Ilex paraguariensis,* mainly for shamanistic
rituals. The refreshing brew, known as yerba maté, became popular among
the conquistadors who followed in his wake, and when Jesuit missionaries
arrived they cracked the secret that made it possible to cultivate the seeds
of the wild yerba maté tree: in order to sprout, the seeds must first pass
through the digestive tract of the colorful, large-beaked toucan bird. With
the cultivation and trade subsequently made possible by this discovery,

yerba maté spread to many different parts of South America, and it remains a popular social drink today, prepared in gourds, often ornamented with silver, and shared with a metal straw, a *bombilla,* that filters out the dregs of the pounded leaves.

Cacao, a popular hot and restorative drink that contains only a small amount of caffeine (but a higher level of theobromine, an alkaloid with similar effects), comes from the seeds of the *Theobroma cacao,* a relative of the cola tree. The cacao tree originates in Amazonia, but it was taken into domestication in Mesoamerica. Residues of cacao have been detected on Olmec potsherds, dating to as early as

Yerba maté is a species of the holly genus (Ilex paraguariensis), *and a popular caffeine drink in South America.*

1750 BC, from the Pacific coast of Mexico. The Maya, who flourished in eastern Mexico and the northern part of present-day Guatemala between AD 250 and 900, saw the close resemblance in texture between blood and the chocolate drink, adopted it in sacrificial rituals, and revered the cacao bean as "food of the gods." The Aztecs used cacao beans as money, collected them as tax, and mixed them with maize and red pepper for a drink used in their religious ceremonies.

In 1585, the first trade shipment of chocolate from the New World reached Europe, where the spices were replaced by sugar. In 1657, a Frenchman opened the first cocoa house on Bishopsgate Street in London, and the hot sweet drink became all the rage in Europe. Fry's chocolate factory in Bristol, England, made the first mass-produced chocolate bar in 1847. As chocolate candy conquered the Western world, the confectionary industry sucked up the world's cacao bean production, and the hot cocoa drink subsided from everyday use in most of Europe. In the cafés of Barcelona, Madrid, Mexico City, and Buenos Aires, however, they still take their dark, hot, thick chocolate drink very seriously, with milk and sugar.

The story of coffee, along with tea by far the most popular caffeine beverage, began in the 9th century in the highlands of its native Abyssinia (present-day Ethiopia). From there, the coffee plant (the two most commonly grown species today are *Coffea canephora* and *Coffea arabica*) spread across the narrow Bah el Mandeb straits to Yemen in the southern corner of the Saudi Arabian peninsula, where it was cultivated in the mountains above the coastal town of Mocha. Coffee was adopted as a stimulant by the Sufis, and by the 16th century there were coffee houses in Cairo, Istanbul, and all the other major Middle Eastern cities. It is said to have been introduced to Italy in 1614, reaching France in 1644. By 1720, there were 380 coffee houses in Paris. "Great is the vogue of coffee in Paris. In the houses where it is supplied, the proprietors know how to prepare it in such ways that it gives wit to those who drink it. At any rate, when they depart, all of them believe themselves to be at least four times as brainy as when they entered the doors," wrote the incisive French social commentator Charles Montesquieu.

Ever since tea and coffee first met in the Middle East and in Europe in the 17th century, they have accompanied each other like *yin* and *yang,* all the way to the obligatory "coffee or tea?" of in-flight meals. In the Western world, coffee has assumed the masculine role, tea the feminine. But in the sub-Saharan nation of Mauretania, the men will tell you that they drink green tea instead of coffee because they believe coffee makes you impotent – a charge also leveled in 19th-century Europe – and in Central Asia, drinking copious amounts of tea is considered part of the business of being a man. In 2004–05, world production of coffee stood at 7.2 million tons, compared with 3.2 million tons of tea. Sticklers for statistics, however, note that while 15 grams of ground coffee is required to infuse a decent cup, 5 grams of tea will suffice. And while coffee can only be drawn once, tea leaves can be drawn at least twice – in the case of Oolong tea, up to six times. In this manner, they reach the conclusion that tea, in its different forms, is the world's most widely consumed beverage after water. Here is its story.

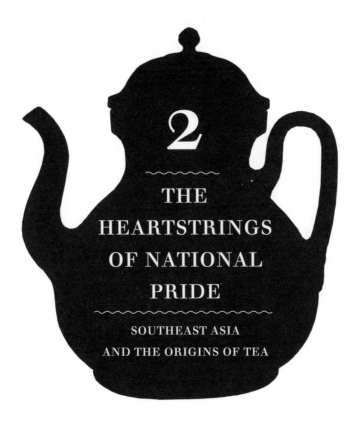

2

THE
HEARTSTRINGS
OF NATIONAL
PRIDE

SOUTHEAST ASIA
AND THE ORIGINS OF TEA

Who says tea is bitter? It's as sweet as Shepherd's Purse
Book of Odes

I n the language of a botanist, the tea leaf is either elliptic-lanceolate, which means that it has the symmetrical shape of an ellipse – a flattened circle – with tapered, pointed ends, or it is obovate-lanceolate, the shape of an egg tapered at both ends, with the narrow end connected to the stalk, and the wide end at the tip. Its edge is serrated, and its texture smooth and leathery. Dark green and evergreen, the leaves alternate along the stem. The diminutive, white, slightly fragrant flowers, an inch across, have five to seven petals arranged in a ring, protected by five leafy, green sepals. The tea flower has numerous stamens (male organs), and a pistil (female organ) with three or four stigma, the part that receives the pollen during pollination. The shelled fruit is smooth and brownish green; the seed dark brown and round or flattened.

In the wild, depending on the variety of the plant, soil, rainfall, humidity, light, temperature, altitude, latitude, and other factors, the tea plant grows into a shrub or tree, up to 45 feet high. Its precise native region has plucked the strings, even agitated the gall, of national pride, but botanists now place the center of its natural distribution in the upper reaches of the Brahmaputra river in the Indian province of Assam, the northern parts of Burma and Thailand, Indochina, and southwest China. This is the region – the foothills of the Himalayas – where a wedge of the Indian subcontinent that collided with Eurasia 50 million years ago has puckered the face of the earth into a series of mountain ranges, valleys, and plateaux that resemble the convolutions of the large intestine. The climate in this area is subtropical – the temperature never falls below freezing and the rainfall is distributed evenly throughout the year – and its vegetation is lush and exuberant. In addition to tea, some of humanity's most economically valuable plants, such as rice and citrus fruits, are thought to have originated here.

In his 1753 *Species plantarum,* the great Swedish botanist Carl Linnaeus, who had not yet seen a live tea plant, named it *Thea sinensis*; in the second edition of 1762, he further described different forms of tea as *Thea bohea* and *Thea viridis*. All are now recognized as one species in the camellia genus, *Camellia sinensis*. The beautiful camellias, which get their name from the Czech botanist and Jesuit missionary G.J. Camel, consist of 120 species, each with a dense bouquet of conspicuous stamens in the flowers. Curiously, early Chinese botanists roaming the hinterlands of Yunnan in the 15th and 16th centuries also grouped the tea plant with the camellias by calling the

The tea plant belongs to the camellias, with their characteristic dense bouquet of yellow stamens. It thrives in sedimentary soils derived from gneiss or granite, prefers a bit of shade, and requires abundant rainfall. In China, the oil from its seeds is used for cooking, while powder from ground seeds was used as a shampoo in the old days. In Vietnam, the French produced fleur de thé, a delicate tea from the white flowers of the plant. Tea plants cultivated at high altitudes, such as in Darjeeling and central Taiwan, produce the finest leaves, and the most complex, shifting infusions.

latter *shan cha* ("mountain tea"). One camellia popular with Yunnanese gardeners early on was *Camellia reticulata,* with its opulent flowers, up to 6 inches across, in various shades of red. In 1453, Zhao Bi wrote a study on camellias that has since been lost, and in the late 16th century, Feng Shike published his *Notes on the* Shan Cha *of Yunnan*, in which he listed 72 different camellia varieties, mostly of *Camellia reticulata*. Another prominent camellia is the *Camellia oleifera*, cultivated in China for the oil in its seeds, used for cooking and not to be confused with "tea tree oil," which is pressed from a species of melaleuca tree known as the "Ti tree." In terms of beauty, the tea plant is also overshadowed by another of its sisters, *Camellia japonica*, of which there are more than 2,000 mainly man-made varieties. The camellias even have their own society, the American Camellia Society, solely dedicated to camellia flower fairs and the promotion of the flowers.

While *Camellia sinensis* is a bit of a wallflower compared with its sisters, the caffeine it contains has made it one of the world's most desirable plants. Botanists distinguish between two main varieties of the tea plant, *Camellia sinensis sinensis*, which grows wild throughout southern China, and *Camellia sinensis assamica*, which grows wild in wetter parts of south and southeast Asia, and is cultivated in China, Assam and Sri Lanka. The *sinensis* variety is a hardy shrub or small tree that grows from 3 to 18 feet high, has stout branches, short stalks, and smallish, slender leaves, and

Parts of Plant	Caffeine
First and second leaves	3.4%
Fifth and sixth leaves	1.5%
Stalk between fifth and sixth leaves	0.5%
Tea flowers	0.8%
Shell of green fruit	0.6%
Seed	0.0%
Hairs of young leaves	2.25%

The caffeine content in constituent parts of the tea plant. Caffeine is believed to function as a natural pesticide, protecting it against parasites, insects, and other predators.

is found wild in forests, thickets, and open shrub, and on rocky slopes and dry, stony hillsides. As it is able to withstand brief periods of frost, it can be cultivated at high altitudes, such as in Darjeeling in the foothills of the Himalayas, the mountains of Taiwan, and in central Ceylon. Paradoxically, the leaves that come from this variety are more delicate, which makes them suitable for the production of green tea, Oolong tea, and fine black tea. The *assamica* variety can grow much taller (up to 45 feet), cannot tolerate frost, and has large, leathery leaves, which give a high yield and provide a strong, robust infusion.

As our species, *Homo sapiens*, began its emigration out of Africa some 60,000 years ago, it slowly made its way eastward across present-day Saudi Arabia, Iraq, Iran, Pakistan, and India, hunting, fishing, gathering, sewing clothes, multiplying, and displacing older forms of our genus with its sharper wit and better tools and weapons. Its very bones were steeped with an encyclopedic knowledge of the plant world. Either by observing other animals, or by their own hard-won experience, early humans knew which vegetables they could eat, and which not. As *Homo sapiens* is thought to have reached Australia around 50,000 years ago, and northern Burma lies halfway, we may speculate that it arrived in the lands where the tea plant grows some 55,000 years ago.

In China, there is an apocryphal story, often bandied about as history, according to which the mythical Shennong ("Divine Farmer"), China's second emperor and first agriculturist, who is alleged to have ruled from 2737 to 2698 BC, tasted 100 plants. Some 72 of them (a magic number throughout Eurasia) made him ill. Only one cured him of these illnesses – the tea plant. Curiosity and gluttony being two hallmarks of our species, it is easy to surmise that humans discovered the nourishing, salubrious effects of the tea leaf much earlier than the Shennong myth claims. And when they did, it was certainly by chewing the raw leaf – a custom practiced to this day by people in its native region.

The homeland of tea is populated by a large number of different people – the Hani, Yi, Bai, Dai, Bulang, Wa, De'ang, and scores of others – many of whom retain ancient ways of collecting, preparing, and consuming the tea leaf. In 1823, the British merchant Robert Bruce traveled up the Brahmaputra river, where he came into contact with the Singpho people, who preserve their tea leaves either by drying them over a fire in the hollow of bamboos, or by fermenting the boiled leaves in holes dug in the ground. At the end of the 19th century, Walter Armstrong Graham described how the traditional Burmese dish of *letpet*, fermented tea leaves, is prepared: the fresh tea leaves are boiled in large, narrow-necked pots made especially for the purpose, and then placed in holes in the ground lined with plantain leaves, covered and left to ferment for a few months. Consumed at important ceremonies, *letpet* is taken as a solid food, dressed with oil, and eaten with garlic, dried fish, and other dishes. Among the Wa, tea leaves are used in sacrifices to ancestors, and placed by the dead in their graves. The matriarchal De'ang worship tea as one of their totemic objects, issue invitations with packets of tea bound with red thread, and offer tea as a conciliatory gesture in disputes between families. And in the 1930s, the Swedish anthropologist Karl Gustav Izikowitz, conducting fieldwork among the Lamet, a Mon-Khmer speaking people in northern Laos, made this observation:

> The Lamet take a pinch of fermented tea leaves, sprinkle a little salt on it, and then chew this quid. The saliva becomes dark brown, and the tea really tastes excellent and has a beneficial, stimulating effect. The Lamet say that if one is not used to chewing this fermented tea, which is called *meng*, and take it late in the evening, it will keep one awake. *Meng* is a highly prized stimulant, and is used almost as much as betel.

The intrepid French ethnographer Jean Berlie, working recently in the Sipsongpanna (Xishuangbanna ("12,000 rice fields")) area along the Chinese border with Burma, writes that to this day, the women of the Hani people, a Tibeto-Burman group, gather wild tea leaves in the surrounding forests between February and May every year, picking up to 8 lb in a day in an area where some of the oldest and largest tea trees have been found. Since the Hani are the earliest known inhabitants of the area, Berlie asks if it is not to this people that we should trace the first human knowledge of the tea leaf.

Due north of Yunnan lies China's Sichuan province, divided into two distinct geographical regions – the Himalayan foothills in the west and the fertile Red Basin in the east. In ancient times, this region was dominated by two peoples: the Shu, whose ancestors created the stunning 3,000-year-old bronze masks found at the Sanxingdui site northeast of Chengdu, and the Ba, who laid their dead to rest in cliff graves with wooden coffins that are still found wedged into the vertical rock walls of the Yangtze river, several hundred feet above the ground. The Ba were a martial people who worshiped the tiger as their totem, possessed a pictographic script that has yet to be deciphered, cultivated rice, produced silk, extracted salt from wells and springs, and hunted the rhinoceros. They also have the distinction of being the first people recorded in written history to have used tea.

The *Huayang Guozhi* ("Gazetteer of the Region South of Mount Hua"), China's first gazetteer, written by Chang Qu during the Eastern Jin dynasty (AD 317–420), describes the history, geography, and notable persons of southwestern China. In his chapter on the Ba state, Chang Qu notes the military assistance provided by the Ba to the northern state of Zhou at the battle of Mu Ye ("Shepherd's Wild"), when Di Xin, the lascivious, cruel last ruler of the Shang dynasty (*c.* 1700–1045 BC) was defeated and his dynasty overthrown. After the war, the Ba became a loyal vassal state to the Zhou, and the *Huayang Guozhi* lists the tribute they presented to the Zhou king: mulberry, silkworms, hemp, ramie (a plant of the nettle family), fish, salt, copper, iron, cinnabar, lacquer, honey, sacred tortoise, giant rhinoceros, pheasant, white chicken, fine yellow cloth, colorful powder, and a vegetable denoted with the character 荼 (pronounced *tu* in modern Chinese), which differs from the acknowledged character for tea, 茶 (*cha* in modern Chinese), only by a single horizontal stroke. The question of whether or not the character 荼 represents an old form of 茶, and thus if it really was tea that the Ba presented to the Zhou, has vexed generations of Chinese etymologists, and bedevils the study of Chinese tea history all the way up to the Tang dynasty. (For a detailed discussion of the ongoing debate, and on the different characters used to denote tea, see Appendix C, pp. 262–68.)

Tea was also produced by the Shu 100 miles south of Chengdu in the Leshan area. In the 5th century BC, the Zhou dynasty disintegrated into an era of internecine fighting called the Warring States period (475–221 BC), during which the northwestern state of Qin grew in strength, devouring weaker states like a silkworm devours a mulberry leaf. In 316 BC, the Qin conquered the lands of Shu and Ba, and with its granaries full of their bountiful produce, went on to conquer the entire region and, under Shi Huangdi (the First Emperor), create the first Chinese empire in 221 BC. In his *Ri Zhi Lu* ("A Record of Knowledge Gained Day by Day"), Gu Yanwu, a brilliant 17th-century scholar, opined: "It was after the Qin had taken Shu that they learned how to drink tea."

The earliest known reference to boiling tea appears in "The Contract for a Youth," written by the noted imperial panegyrist Wang Bao in 59 BC. The entertaining essay relates the fate of a certain slave named Bian Liao, whom Wang met after he had traveled to the Jian river on business and was visiting the widow Yang Hui in her home. When Wang asked Bian to go and buy some wine, the plucky youth picked up a stick, climbed the grave mound of his dead master, and replied: "When my master bought me, Bian Liao, he only contracted for me to take care of the ancestral graves, and did not contract for me to buy wine for some other gentleman."

Wang asked the widow why she didn't sell the slave. She replied that nobody wanted him, whereupon Wang decided to purchase him.

"Enter in the contract everything you wish to order me to do. I, Bian Liao, will not do anything not in the contract," said the slave.

"Agreed!"

When Wang had finished writing and reading aloud the long, exceedingly detailed contract, specifying numerous demanding tasks, the slave beat his head wildly on the ground and cried, as the drivel from his nose hung a foot long.

Among the exasperating litany of tasks, we find "he shall boil tea and fill the utensils" and "he shall buy tea at Wuyang," a market town located near Chengdu, the second largest city in China at the time. The first recorded cultivation of tea is also dated to this period, during the Ganlu era of Emperor Xuan of Han (53–50 BC), when a certain Master Wu Lizhen is said to have planted seven tea bushes on Meng Mountain east of Chengdu. Scores of Buddhist monasteries were founded among its five misty peaks, and for more than a 1,000 years, from the Tang to the Qing dynasties, the fabled "auspicious pistil tea" manufactured by the monks there was dispatched to the capital as imperial tribute, with the first 360 leaves picked each spring prepared specially for the emperor. Li Shizhen, who compiled the monumental pharmacopoeia *Bencao Gangmu* ("Compendium of Materia Medica") in the 16th century, noted that while tea is generally cool in nature, only that produced on Meng Mountain is "warm and able to take charge of disease," and to this day, the green and yellow Meng teas are among the most sought after in China. Firmly and lastingly, the distant southwest had planted the seedbed for the wedding of China to tea.

3

A SLAVE OF YOGHURT

TEA IN THE 1ST TO 6TH CENTURIES

I n the 1st century AD, the Chinese emperor Ming Di is said to have had a dream. He saw a tall man, all in gold, with a bright light emanating from his neck, and a face "as clear and as radiant as a full moon." It was the Buddha. To learn of his doctrine, Ming Di dispatched envoys to India and present-day Afghanistan. They returned with statues, Sanskrit Buddhist texts, and two Indian holy men, Kasyapa Matanga and Dharmaratna, who became the first translators of Buddhist texts from Sanskrit into Chinese.

As the Eastern Han dynasty (AD 25–220) began to fall apart due to malcontent among the country's peasants, the palace eunuchs and mandarin bureaucrats, who despised the eunuchs for their conniving ways and lack of learning, clashed in a struggle for power. The massive civil unrest was further fueled by an array of immortality cults, millenarian rebels, and other Daoist groups, such as the "Yellow Turbans" and "Five Pecks of Rice

Sect" (five pecks of rice being the annual membership fee), which attracted followers with populist programs that offered general amnesties, miracle healings, and eternal life. In AD 184, the "Yellow Turbans" launched a general uprising in the capital Luoyang, but were soon defeated. Outright civil war followed. China divided into the Three Kingdoms (Shu, Wei, and Wu), and the northern part of the empire was carved up by Huns, Tanguts (related to Tibetans), proto-Mongols, and other nomadic tribes. It was a period of great upheaval and mass migrations, during which China's population is said to have shrunk from 56 to 16 million people, providing fertile ground for a new religion, Buddhism, holding forth the lure of complete liberation from the travails of existence.

During these centuries, the knowledge, consumption, and cultivation of tea spread downstream along the Yangtze river valley. Archaeologists disagree on whether tea was among the grave goods that accompanied the Marquis of Dai, who died 186 BC, in his fabulous tomb unearthed in 1972 at Mawangdui in Hunan province, the heart of south China, but from the local gazetteers, we know that a county called *Chaling* (originally pronounced *Tuling* ("Tea Ridge," see p. 29 and Appendix C)), was established in Hunan in AD 168, and that tea was produced as far east as Lake Tai in Jiangsu province, not far from present-day Shanghai. The manner of processing, preparing, and consuming the leaves at the time was described in the Guangya dictionary, written in the 3rd century AD:

> In the region between Jing and Ba [the area between modern eastern Sichuan and the western parts of Hunan and Hubei] the people pick the leaves and make a cake. If the leaves are old, rice paste is used in forming the cake. [People who] wish to brew the tea first roast [the cake] until it is a reddish color, pound it into a powder, put it into a ceramic container, and cover it with boiling water. They stew scallion [spring onion], ginger, and orange peel with it.

As we can see, the step of firing – stopping the natural oxidation of the leaves by heating them to a high temperature – which is crucial for preserving the tea's freshness, had not yet been introduced.

The main social drink in China at the time was alcohol, indispensable at both ancestral rituals and wanton feasts. The ancient Chinese drank *jiu* and *li,* rice beers which were served in two different beakers during a Han-dynasty banquet (for an explanation of the complexities involved in the translation of the word *jiu*, see Appendix B, Note 1 on p. 261). Both made of fermented rice, the *li* was white and sweet (and low in alcohol), while *jiu* was clear and strong. Along with its important role in rituals, the written records abound with stories about the dark underbelly of alcohol, that most expedient gravedigger of dynasties. The first historical record of tea as an alternative to alcohol and an agent of temperance is found in the biography of Wei Yao (d. AD 273) in the *Annals of Wu*. Wei Yao was a respected minister under Sun Hao (AD 242–83), the final ruler of the state of Wu during the Three Kingdoms period and infamous for his cruelty, extravagance, and drunken debauchery. At Sun's banquets, every guest was required to pour at least seven *sheng* (1 *sheng* is ⅔ pint) of *jiu* from their pitchers into their cups, "although it didn't necessarily all have to end up in their mouths." Only the learned Wei Yao, highly thought of by Sun Hao and unable to drink more than two *sheng*, was accorded preferential treatment, and "secretly given tea to replace the alcohol."

Another popular, somewhat mystifying tea anecdote from the period, included in the chapter entitled "Crudities and Slips of the Tongue" in the 5th-century work *Shishuo Xinyu* ("A New Account of Tales of the World"), recounts the story of Ren Zhan, an outstanding young man of whom it was said that "even his shadow was good." Renowned for his spirit and intelligence, Ren Zhan was selected as one of the 120 pallbearers at the funeral of Emperor Wu in 290, and was a candidate to become the husband of Wang Rong's daughter. But after crossing the Yangtze river (in *c.* 307–12), something happened to Ren Zhan, and it appeared that he had lost his ambition. At a reception held to his honor by the Chancellor Wang Dao, Wang could sense this change in Ren Zhan's character. During the concluding toasts, out of the blue, Ren suddenly asked: "Is this *jia* ('early tea') or *ming* ('late tea')?" Prompted by the puzzled looks of the other guests, he hurriedly explained himself: "What I meant is whether it should be taken hot or cold."

The Three Kingdoms was followed by a brief period of unification under the Western Jin dynasty, ruled by members of the Sima family from the former state of Wei. Dissenting warlords and social unrest resulted in the capture of both the capital of Luoyang (in 311) and the city of Chang'an (in 316), which led to a massive move to the south and the establishment there of the Eastern Jin dynasty in 317. The Southern and Northern dynasties (420–589) followed. Magic potions and immortality balls concocted by the Daoist sages were all the rage during these centuries, with precious metals and minerals being the most valued drugs. The famous 4th-century Daoist Ge Hong wrote in his *Shenxian Zhuan* ("Biographies of Celestial Immortals"):

> Everyone who takes them [precious metals] immediately ascends to heaven, and does not accumulate days and months. Second to these are *yunmu* [mica – a shiny silicate mineral], and *xionghuang* [realgar – an arsenic sulphide mineral that we now know to be highly toxic]. Although they will not enable you able to ride clouds and drive dragons, they can serve the spirit, and abet longevity. After these are the vegetable medicines. They can cure the hundred diseases and replenish deficiencies... but they will not make people not die.

But these immortality balls of metal and stone, usually ingested with large amounts of alcohol, were rare, expensive, and dangerous, the preserve of the upper classes. Herbal medicines, by contrast, were cheaper and readily available, and fulfilled the needs of the common people. As one of these herbs, tea was readily adopted by the Daoists, who in their free and easy wanderings across the land roamed remote mountains and forests in search of its most tender buds, advertised its medicinal properties, and disseminated the custom of its consumption. "Tea lightens the body and changes the bones," the Daoist master Tao Hongjing wrote in his *Za Lu* ("Records of Micellanea"). "This is sweet dew. Why call it tea?" Prince Zishang said to the Daoist priest Tan Ji, when the latter prepared tea for him in the Bagong Mountains during the Southern Song dynasty of the house of Liu (420–79).

During the Three Kingdoms, Jin dynasties, and Southern and Northern dynasties (220–589), tea was both cultivated and picked in the wild. The leaves were steamed, pounded, and patted into cakes, which were then baked, pierced, strung together, sealed, stored, brewed, and drunk. In his poem "Chuan Fu" ("Rhapsody on Tea"), the first in praise of tea, the Jin-dynasty poet and scholar-official Du Yu (222–84) describes how the powder of a freshly brewed cup of tea gravitates to the bottom as bubbles float to the top, sparkling like snow. Dating to the same period, the *Tong Jun Cai Yao Lu* ("Records of Prince Tong Collecting Medicine") specifically refers to the purported medicinal properties of these bubbles. And although whisking tea did not become the fashion until the much later Song dynasty (960–1279), there is evidence that it may have been practiced already during the Northern Wei dynasty (424–535): in the 6th-century *Qi Min Yao Shu* ("Essential Techniques for the Subsistence of the Common People"), Jia Sixie explains how to ferment mellow rice beer, advising that one should "take fish-eye soup and steep two *dou* of rice water, boil six *sheng*, pour it in an earthen jar and whisk it with a bamboo brush, just like the froth of tea."

At this time, the various rulers of China were often great patrons of the Buddhist religion, which grew rapidly in strength as impoverished peasants fleeing press gangs flocked to the temples for sustenance and safety. At the end of the Northern Wei dynasty, there were some 40,000 monasteries housing 2 million monks and nuns in that empire, which encompassed present-day China north of the Yangtze. South of that river, there were 2,846 monasteries and 82,700 monks and nuns in the realm of the Liang dynasty (502–57). The monasteries were given money, land, and the right to tax, engaged in agriculture, trade, handicrafts, fortune-telling, and medical practice, and some of them grew enormously wealthy.

Wandering was an integral part of the Buddhist monk's life, and probably a welcome respite from the daily monastic regime, with its long hours of soporific chanting, vexing translation tasks from Sanskrit into Chinese, and endless internecine squabbles. Roaming far and wide, meeting with both mandarins and peasants, these spiritual mendicants served as important cultural agents, bringing news and novel customs from one end of the land to the other. A brick of tea would have fitted nicely in a monk's knapsack, and been the perfect excuse for a break by a clear stream along some steep and winding path on a sultry summer day.

One of these itinerant men was the Indian prince Bodhidharma, a major, albeit semi-mythological, figure in the early history of Chinese Buddhism, easily recognized in innumerable depictions by his broad girth and the fierce scowl on his brow. Among the lore of Bodhidharma is the legend that he crossed the Yangtze river on a single bamboo reed. After arriving in the capital of Luoyang just south of the Yellow river's middle reaches, he is said to have founded the Zen (or Chan) sect of Buddhism at Shaolin Temple, where he also invented the exercises that evolved into the famous Shaolin style of kung-fu fighting, and meditated in a cave for nine years – until his shadow stuck to the wall. The rock to which it clung was later removed from the cave, and is displayed on the temple grounds to this very day. In the most famous legend, which first appeared in Engelbert Kaempfer's *History of Japan* from 1727 and is thus very likely to be apocryphal, the austere Bodhidharma (or "Darma" as he was known in that text) once fell asleep during his long years of meditation. When he awoke the next morning, "full of Sorrow for breaking his solemn Vow, he cut off both his Eye-brows,

According to legend, tea, the drink of wakefulness, sprang from the sleepy eyelids of the Buddhist holy man Bodhidharma.

those Instruments of his Crime, and with Indignation threw them to the Ground: Returning the next Day to the same Place, behold, out of his eyebrows were grown two beautiful *Tea* Shrubs. *Darma* eating some of the Leaves, was presently filled with new Joy, and Strength to pursue his divine Meditations."

But while tea was readily adopted by the Buddhists, it initially encountered resistance elsewhere in northern China, as recounted by Fu Xian (329–94) in his "Report of the Chief Administrator of the Capital": "I have heard that, in the Southern Market [of Luoyang], old women of Shu (Sichuan) make a gruel of tea and sell it. Following an investigation, their utensils and implements were smashed and destroyed. They also sell cakes in the market. What is the reason for prohibiting the sale of tea gruel and troubling these old women of Shu?" he writes.

In the 5th and 6th centuries, northern China was ruled by the Tabgatch nomads, whose homeland was what is now Inner Mongolia. To assert their political control over the Han Chinese (the ethnic group that comprises more than 90 percent of China's present population), the Tabgatch rulers adopted the Chinese language, their dress, and their customs, to the point where one of the kings, Xiao Wendi (r. 471–99), condemned his own son to death for preferring nomadic dress and refusing to live in the hot and humid capital in Luoyang. This policy, however, did not stretch to food and drink, and the Tabgatch rulers, whose staple diet was mutton and fermented mare's milk, routinely mocked Han Chinese southerners for preferring such effete fare as water lily soup, crab spawn, lotus root, frogs, turtles, and tea.

Assistant Archivist Wang Su, whose father and four brothers had been killed for no good reason by the emperor of the southern state of Qi in 493, was a southern official who had surrendered to the Tabgatch and taken up residence in Luoyang. Entertaining the idea of revenge, Wang Su wore undyed cloth and refrained from listening to music to mourn his dead father and brothers. When he first arrived in the state of Wei, he did not eat northern fare such as mutton and goat's milk. Instead, he preferred southern delicacies such as carp soup, and drank so much tea that the men of letters in the capital nicknamed him "Leaky Goblet." But a few years later, at a banquet hosted by the Tabgatch emperor Gao Zu, Wang Su ate mutton and yoghurt gruel like a northerner.

"Of the foods of China, how does mutton compare with boiled fish or tea with yoghurt?" asked the emperor, astonished.

"Mutton is the finest product of the land and fish is the best of the watery tribe. Because people have different preferences, both may be considered delicacies. If we are talking about flavors, then there is a difference in quality between them. Mutton is like a big state the size of Qi or Hu, whereas fish is like a small country the size of Zhu or Ju. Tea, however, is off the mark, the very slave of yoghurt," Wang Su replied.

As the knowledge, cultivation, and consumption of tea spread downstream along the Yangtze river valley, it was by adopted as the preferred beverage by scholar-officials seeking an alternative to alcohol, and by Buddhists preparing their minds for enlightenment. But the nomads who ruled northern China still scoffed at the insipid infusion, much preferring their traditional kumiss, fermented horse milk. Under the Sui dynasty, southern and northern China were reunited and linked by the Imperial Grand Canal, on which tea was transported to the Yellow river valley, and on upstream to the capital Chang'an (present-day Xi'an). Here, the Sui were soon ousted by the house of Tang, the flowering of Chinese civilization and the dynasty which anointed tea as the country's national beverage.

4

~~~

GO HAVE SOME TEA!

~~~

THE TANG DYNASTY

I n the year 610, the Imperial Grand Canal, connecting the Yangtze and Yellow rivers, and thereby southern and northern China, stood completed: 1,100 miles long, 100 feet wide, with roads running along each embankment. Along this bustling artery, the grain, salt, and exotic delicacies of the lush south – ginger, oranges, lychees, and tea – could now be expeditiously transported to the markets and armies of northern China. The canal integrated the country's two major regions, thus creating a huge, unified national market and laying the foundation for the Tang dynasty (609–907) – the golden age of Chinese civilization.

The Tang emperors made their capital in Chang'an, where China's founding father, Qin Shi Huangdi (259–210 BC), lay buried in his pharaonic mausoleum on the outskirts of the city, guarded by legions of subterranean terracotta warriors. With a population of more than one million inhabitants, and enclosed by a rectangular wall 6 miles long and 5 miles wide, Chang'an was one of the world's greatest metropolises at the time, teeming with Persian, Arabic, and Jewish merchants, Buddhist and Daoist mendicants, and Nestorian Christian missionaries. The boiling of water to make tea may have partly contributed to the growth of Chang'an and other large towns and cities, where enhanced sanitation, especially with regard to drinking water, is required. From their imposing capital, the Tang emperors presided over a vast empire that stretched from the Pamir Mountains of Central Asia in the west to the Korean Peninsula in the east, and from Manchuria in the north to Vietnam in the south. A well-oiled bureaucracy kept close tabs on the country's 50 million inhabitants, collecting taxes that allowed the emperor to realize great public works while leading a life of untold elegance and luxury. It was a period of vibrant artistic efflorescence, as China's poets penned the poems that the country's schoolchildren toil over to this day, and its artisans crafted wondrous silk fabrics, porcelain, and lacquerware. Such luxuries traveled with camel caravans across Eurasia and in Arab dhows round the tip of India, into the homes of wealthy Persians, Mesopotamians, and Egyptians, imbuing the name of China with that sense of distant mystery and otherness which still colors its place in the modern world.

During the early Tang, Buddhism and tea continued their fortuitous coalition. From Chang'an, the two were transmitted southwest to the Tibetan Plateau, where the nomadic tribes, unified under the leadership of Srong-tsan Gampo (605–50), had begun making incursions into Chinese territory. To pacify the martial Tibetan king, the Chinese emperor, Tai Zong (r. 627–49), accepted Srong-tsan Gampo's request, accompanied by hundreds of pounds of gold, for a spouse of royal blood. In 641, the princess Wencheng arrived in the Tibetan capital Lhasa with silkworm eggs and a Buddha statue in her wedding basket. She became a good queen, revered by the Tibetans as national benefactress, who is said to have converted the country to Buddhism, and persuaded her husband to exchange his apparel of felt and animal skins for silk underwear. And among the yak loads of her dowry, according to the history books, were strings of tea cakes.

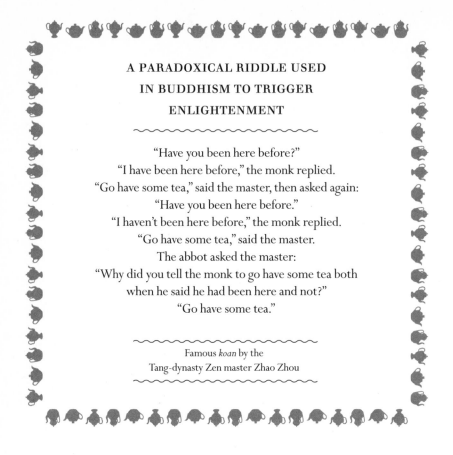

A PARADOXICAL RIDDLE USED
IN BUDDHISM TO TRIGGER
ENLIGHTENMENT

"Have you been here before?"
"I have been here before," the monk replied.
"Go have some tea," said the master, then asked again:
"Have you been here before."
"I haven't been here before," the monk replied.
"Go have some tea," said the master.
The abbot asked the master:
"Why did you tell the monk to go have some tea both
when he said he had been here and not?"
"Go have some tea."

Famous *koan* by the
Tang-dynasty Zen master Zhao Zhou

During the rule of the usurper empress Wu Zetian (r. 684–704), Buddhism enjoyed unprecedented imperial patronage in China. While systematically killing off her political opponents, Wu Zetian built huge Buddhist temples in Chang'an and, in a special display of her pious fervor, issued a nationwide edict prohibiting the consumption of meat and fish which remained in effect for eight years. By this time, tea had become an integral part in the lives of Buddhist monks, who were not allowed to drink alcohol, or eat solid food after noon. The monks cultivated tea, drank it for meditation, while studying, and during ceremonies, offered tea to the Buddha, presented it as a gift to visitors, sold it, and sent it as tribute to the imperial court, which in turn reciprocated. When the emperor Dai Zong (r. 762–79) convened Buddhist monks at his palace to write a new commentary to the

The most complete set of tea utensils in stone from the Tang dynasty. Made of granite, the set includes a stove, grinder, pot, ewers, bowls with stands, and a tray.

Dharmaguptakavinaya (a codification of monastic rules), he provided them with paper, ink, a 90-day supply of vegetarian food, and 25 strings of tea.

The place of tea in Buddhist life is attested by the following account, found in *A Record of Things Seen and Heard by Mr. Feng* (compiled in around the year 800):

> During the Kaiyuan period [713–41, the early part of the reign of Xuan Zong], the Demon-Quelling Master caused a great vogue for Chan Buddhism at the Lingyan Temple on Mount Tai. He and those who studied under him devoted themselves to not sleeping and not eating after noon, but were all allowed to drink tea. They carried it with them, boiling and drinking it everywhere. This habit was in turn imitated by others, and became a custom. From Zou, Qi, Cang and Di [places in Shandong province, where Mount Tai is located, and neighboring Hebei province] it gradually spread to the capital. Many shops making and selling tea opened in the markets, and people, whether religious or lay, pay money to drink it. The tea arrives in a constant stream of boats and carts from Jiang and Huai [in the south], and is piled up in mountains, with many different types. . . .

It was also in the Tang that tea spread with Buddhism to Japan. Two of the most famous Japanese Buddhist monks were Saichō and Kūkai, who in the summer of 804 traveled to China as part of an official embassy, seeking to learn more about Buddhist texts. Having endured a 50-day, storm-thrashed voyage across the Yellow Sea to the Chinese port of Ningbo, Saichō settled in at Fulong Temple on Mount Tai. There he studied the "ox head" method of meditation and the scriptures of the Tiantai Sect under the temple's abbot Xingman, who had formerly been its Tea Master, in charge of offering tea to the Buddha, presiding over official tea ceremonies, and offering gifts of tea to guests. At Saichō's farewell party in the spring of 805, tea was served instead of rice beer, and upon his return to Japan, Saichō planted the tea seeds he had brought with him at the Hiei Shrine by the foot of Hiei Mountain near the capital Kyoto – the first recorded cultivation of tea in Japan.

For his part, Kūkai traveled to the Ximing Temple in Chang'an, which offered preparatory language courses for foreign monks. During his stay in China, Kūkai studied the scriptures of Esoteric Buddhism, the main sect in Tibet, before returning to Japan in 806 laden with Buddhist sutras, statues, mandalas (concentric schematic representations of the cosmos), and calligraphy, which he presented to the Japanese emperor Saga in 809. "When I am not busy presiding over rituals, I study the language of India with tea by my side," he wrote. While Kūkai and Saichō were considered the greatest Buddhist spirits of the Heian period of Japanese history (794–1185), the two seem to have fallen out after Saichō's disciple Taihan left him to study under Kukai. Saichō later attempted to win Taihan back by sending him 10 catties (13 lb; 1 catty is 1⅓ lb) of tea, but the gift failed to change the disciple's mind.

Under the emperor Xuan Zong (r. 712–56), the Tang reached its greatest prosperity and territorial expanse, before the sudden reversal of fortune of 751, when Arab and Chinese forces, for the first and only time in history, clashed by the city of Atlakh, near Djambul in present-day Kazakhstan. During the momentous five-day battle, the Chinese army, betrayed by Turkic Qarluq soldiers who defected to the Arabs, was soundly defeated and routed from Central Asia, not be seen there for another millennium. In the ensuing years, China came under attack from all directions: by Tibetans in the east, Turkic people in the north, Koreans in the east, and the Tai-dominated kingdom of Nanzhao in the south, which defeated a couple of the emperor's armies.

It was at this precarious moment that the singular personage of An Lushan appeared on the stage of East Asian history. Of Sogdian-Turk extraction, the enormously fat An Lushan was the favorite of Xuan Zong's cherished concubine Yang Guifei. Condemned to death for losing the forces under his command through rash conduct, An Lushan was subsequently reprieved by the emperor, only to launch one of the most devastating civil wars in Chinese history. It took eight years and the assistance of the Turkic Uyghur nation to defeat An Lushan and restore order. As for the fabled Yang Guifei, she was denounced as a traitor, forsaken by her emperor when he fled to Sichuan, and strangled to death by the chief eunuch.

During An Lushan's siege of Suiyang, southeast of Kaifeng on the Yellow river's lower reaches, the defenders kept themselves alive by eating paper, tree-bark, and their stocks of tea. Refugees fled south to the coastal province of Fujian, where the population surge spurred a flourishing tea industry. Among the millions of people uprooted by the An Lushan rebellion was a reclusive poet by the name of Lu Yu, born in 733 in Jingling, Fuzhou, some 60 miles west of the city of Wuhan in Hubei province. Orphaned at a young age, Lu Yu was raised as a foundling by the abbot Ji Chan in Dragon Cloud Monastery, before he ran away to join the theater. According to *The Autobiography of Instructor Lu* (see Appendix A for the complete text), written in 760 at the height of the rebellion,

A 10th-century Lu Yu figurine.

> Lu Yu built a hut by the bank of the Grandiflora stream. He closed his door and read books; he refused to mix with rogues, though he would spend whole days chatting and convivializing with eminent monks and lofty scholars.

THE BELITUNG TEA BOWL

This unique Tang-period tea bowl was recovered by German explorers Tilman Walterfang and Mathias Draeger in 1998 from a 9th-century AD shipwreck off Belitung Island in the Tanjung Pandan region of Indonesia (between Sumatra and Borneo). The ship was of Indian or Arab-Persian construction (judging from the timber used, more likely Indian) and was evidently bound for a destination in the Middle East, perhaps somewhere in the Persian Gulf. The cargo included a total of over 53,000 items: of these, 44,000 were bowls made in kilns at Changsha in Hunan province, China. Several of the bowls bear inscriptions dating them to the year 826.

On this particular bowl are found three Chinese characters. Although the inscription is short, it offers a wealth of precious information about the culture of tea-drinking in the 9th century. In Modern Standard Mandarin pronunciation, the characters are read as *chazhanzi*, which means simply "tea bowl." Linguistically, there are two significant features of the term *chazhanzi*. Firstly, the character used to write the syllable *cha* ("tea") actually appears in the old form that is pronounced *tu*, not the new Chinese character designed specifically to indicate the Sinitic word for tea that had recently been invented (see Appendix C). Secondly, the noun suffix *–zi* is rare in written records dating to this time, since the usual literary expression for this type of tea bowl would simply have been *chazhan* (*zhan* meaning "bowl"). The addition of the *–zi* suffix is a sure sign of colloquial usage (it is not used in this way in Classical Chinese). Furthermore, it is particularly in the records of the dialogs of Zen masters that this colloquial suffix begins to appear with conspicuous frequency.

In their teaching, Zen masters would often pick up an object used in their daily life: fly whisk, fan, monk's staff, or walking stick, spade, spoon, flatcake, cushion, sandal, and – not unexpectedly – tea bowl. The particular item raised by the master was not as important as the sheer act of picking up a prosaic object. This is meant to remind the student not to go astray while pursuing his task of grasping the way, which does not require any seeking for things outside of the here and now. On the other hand, although the particular object raised by the master might not be an essential part of the gesture, the gesture of raising something in this way is recognized in Zen circles as significant to such a degree that sometimes the master does not say anything and yet he is understood.

There are roughly a hundred instances in recorded Zen dialogs of monks picking up a tea bowl as part of their discourse. Even in these dialogs, however, the use of the highly colloquial form *chazhanzi* is infrequent, *chazhan* alone normally being used. Probably the earliest occurrence of the tea bowl gesture is in the biography of a monk called Yongquan ("Surging Spring") in *Zutang Ji*

("Collection from the Hall of Patriarchs"), the first book to include extensive records of the words and deeds of the Zen masters. It is noteworthy that in this passage the colloquial expression *chazhanzi* is used.

Picking up a tea bowl as a pregnant Zen gesture appears to have become popular among the group of disciples centered around Master Xuefeng (822–908), who taught in the Min region, near Fuzhou in Fujian province, in particular Xuansha (835–908) and Yunmen (864–949). This complements the evidence about the location and time of the early use of the term *chazhanzi* by the monk Yongquan mentioned above. Indeed, the *Zutang Ji* was produced in the same environment (Fuzhou area during the Five Dynasties (907–60)).

All of these data provided by the inscribed tea bowl from the Belitung shipwreck reinforce our findings for the sudden popularity of tea in 9th-century China. Namely, tea-drinking was characteristically southern and was closely associated with Buddhism, especially Zen Buddhism, and it was primarily through Buddhist channels that tea was transmitted to the north.

While this may not suffice to prove that Indians and Arabs were drinking tea in the Tang, is does provide firm, long-sought evidence of maritime trade between the Arab and Chinese empires in the 9th century, first described in 851 by the Arab merchant Suleyman, who presumably sailing with such a dhow, voyaged from Siraf on the coast of present-day Iran to Canton, which at the time was a city of some 200,000 inhabitants, with boats from Southeast Asia, India, Persia, and Arabia thronging its port. The main commodities carried by these vessels were aromatics such as frankincense and myrrh, which the Chinese used to make incense. As for the things to be found in the Chinese port, Suleyman mentions the two new commodities that, together with silk, were to form the pillars of Chinese export trade until the modern era: "a clay of highest quality used to make bowls as thin as glass, so transparent that the liquid inside them is visible," and "a certain herb which is drunk infused in hot water. This herb is sold in all the towns at high prices, it is called *sākh*, a kind of dried herb that the Chinese drink in hot water. It has more leaves than ratb'ah (possibly *Medicago sativa*) and something more of aroma, but its taste is bitter. The drink so made is serviceable under all circumstances."

This may have been the very hut were Lu Yu completed the first draft of his famous founding treatise on tsiology, later dubbed *The Classic of Tea*, which was written and circulated in three editions between 758 and 775. In some 7,000 terse characters, Lu Yu provides a succinct yet panoramic overview of tea culture in the Tang: its origins, the tools and utensils needed to manufacture and prepare tea, the process of manufacturing and preparation, what water to use, how to boil the tea, references to tea in Chinese history, tea cultivation districts, which utensils could be dispensed with if absolutely necessary, and last but not least, instructions to people who care about tea to copy his book on four or six silk scrolls and hang them on the wall for instant and constant edification.

With Lu Yu's work, tea finally emerged from its chrysalis and strode upon the main stage of life in China. As the drink spread to every nook of the land and stratum of society, Lu Yu was elevated to the status of demigod, especially among tea merchants and pottery makers. "Many of the potters in Gong county make porcelain idols. Those who buy a few scores of tea utensils are presented with one figure of Lu Yu in reward. People selling tea in the market who do not make a profit usually pour libations upon it," says the 9th-century *Supplement of the History of the Tang*.

In the first chapter, Lu Yu wrote that "tea grows best in a soil that is slightly stony, while soil that is graveled and rich is the next best." To manufacture cake tea, the most common type during the Tang, the following implements were required: a bamboo basket for picking; a screen of bamboo strips to grade the leaves; a furnace and cauldron for steaming; a pestle and mortar to pound the steamed leaves; an iron mold to form the pounded tea into cakes; a platform of stone or wood covered by an oil cloth where the cakes could be allowed to set in their molds; an awl to pierce eyes through the cakes; a bamboo rod to move the cakes from place to place; a drying furnace with a wooden rack to hold the cakes some 4 feet above burning charcoal; long strips of bamboo to string the cakes together for a final airing; and a wooden storage chamber covered with bamboo mats.

"Tea has a myriad shapes. If I may speak vulgarly and rashly, tea may shrink and crinkle like a Mongol's boots. Or it may look like the dewlap

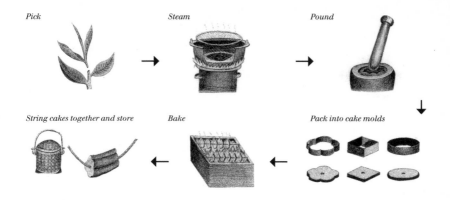

Pick   *Steam*   *Pound*

String cakes together and store   *Bake*   *Pack into cake molds*

Tang-dynasty tea processing. "All there is to making tea is to pick it, steam it, pound it, shape it, dry it, tie it, and seal it," wrote Lu Yu.

of a wild ox, some sharp, some curling as the eaves of a house. It can look like a mushroom in whirling flight just as the clouds do when they float out from behind a mountain peak," wrote Lu Yu, a purist who denounced all the popular condiments that were used to spice up the tea: scallion (spring onion), ginger, jujube, tangerine peel, cornel (dogwood) berries, peppermint, and so on. "Such preparations are the swill of gutters and ditches, and a common custom no end!" Condoning only the use of salt, Lu Yu was also a pioneer in the art of appreciating and evaluating water. Indeed, if one does not care for the taste of water, how can one care for the taste of anything else? "Water from the slow-flowing streams, the stone-lined pools or milk-pure springs is the best mountain water. Never take tea made from water that falls in cascades, gushes from springs, rushes in a torrent or that eddies and surges as if nature were rinsing its mouth," he wrote.

Among the 24 tea utensils listed in *The Classic of Tea* for making tea was the *lüshuinang* ("water-strainer"), a device brought to China by Buddhist monks who used it to avoid the accidental killing of living creatures in their drinking water. As for tea bowls, according to Lu Yu the best came from the Yue kilns of Zhejiang province (the site of one kiln was discovered by Tsuneo Yonaiyama, the Japanese consul to Hangzhou, in 1930). The Yue kilns mainly manufactured pale green, semi-porcelaneous ware (known as

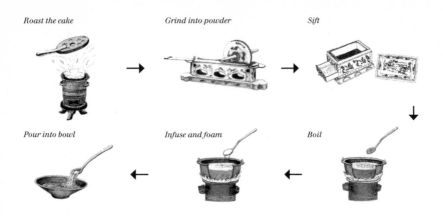

Roast the cake → *Grind into powder* → *Sift*

Pour into bowl ← *Infuse and foam* ← *Boil*

Tang-dynasty tea preparation. For true connoisseurs, even the choice of firewood mattered. Charcoal was best, while oily wood and worn-out utensils were taboo.

celadon), which Lu Yu wrote enhanced and deepened the natural color of the tea. Special *mise* ("secret color") celadon ware from Yue was reserved exclusively for the emperor. In 1913, the German Orientalist Friedrich Sarre discovered fragments of a Tang-dynasty Yue celadon in Mesopotamia by the Tigris river at the site of Samarra, the capital of the Abbasid Caliphs from 836 to 883.

To prepare the tea, Lu Yu wrote that one should cure the cake over a fire until "the stems are as tender as a baby's arm," store the cake in a paper sack until cool, and then grind it with a roller. The water in the cauldron should be brought to the boil in three stages: "fish eyes," "pearls from a gushing spring along the rim," and "galloping waves." "Any more and the water will be boiled out and should not be used," wrote Lu Yu, an observation that accords well with modern science, since water that has been boiled too long loses its oxygen and carbon dioxide, which assist the decomposition of certain proteins and acids that enhance tea's aroma. At the "fish eyes" stage, a measure of salt is added. At the second stage, the tea is put into the boiling water, and at the stage of "galloping waves," it is ladled into the cups "so that it will come out frothy." "The first cup should have a haunting flavor, strange and lasting.... But when you drink it, sip only. Otherwise you will dissipate the taste," Lu Yu wrote.

Before the mid-Tang, Meng Mountain tea (which we first encountered at the end of Chapter 2) was so rare and precious that a bolt of silk was not enough to pay for one pound of it. But as demand for tea in the north grew, the farmers on Meng Mountain planted tea bushes as fast as they could, and within a few decades, the markets were burgeoning with their tea. In villages all over the land, "west of the pass and east of the mountains," the common people were said to be able to go for days with no food, but not one without tea. Among peasants in the south, who cultivated tea bushes on hills and mountainsides unsuitable for other crops, the saying "one tea bud is worth seven grains of rice" was coined. Tea was light, easy to transport and non-perishable, a ready commodity.

Another major tea production area was the Fuliang region in Jiangxi province, east of Lake Poyang, which was said to produce some 7 million mule loads of tea per year. In Bo Juyi's 9th-century poem "Pipa ji" ("Record of the Lute"), a tea merchant, taking "profit seriously and separation lightly," leaves his wife on a boat in Xunyang at the north end of Lake Poyang to go to Fuliang 75 miles away to jostle with the other merchants in the tea market. During the late Tang, some 70–80 percent of the 5,400 households in the county of Keemun (Qimen) in the Fuliang region cultivated tea, using the income to buy clothes and food and to pay off corvée labor impositions.

The expanding trade spurred new developments in the cultivation of tea. In his *A Compendium of Essentials for All Seasons,* the Tang author Han E states that the best place to plant tea shrubs is in rich and loose soil on mountain slopes facing south, but under the shade of mulberry, bamboo, or other plants such as hemp and millet, as the delicate tea plant is sensitive to direct sunlight. If tea is planted on flat land, a ditch to drain the water must be dug, because the shrub will die if the roots are inundated with water. To protect the seeds from the winter cold and hasten their germination in the spring, they should be mixed with wet sand and stored in baskets covered with grain stalks. In the second month of the lunar year, pits should be dug 1 foot deep and 2 feet apart, filled with a bit of night soil, then planted with 60 to 70 seeds in each pit and covered with an inch of earth. To avoid disturbing

FAMEN TEMPLE

Near present-day Xi'an lies the Famen Temple, originally built during the Eastern Han Dynasty. In 1987, during the reconstruction of the temple's octagonal, 13-story pagoda that had housed a precious relic, a secret underground chamber was discovered. The chamber contained a trove of some 600 treasures, all carefully recorded on a stone tablet, bestowed in 869 by the emperor Yi Zong to bless the relic – a finger bone of the Buddha. Among the items was an imperial tea set in gilded silver, including a magnificent grinder, a sifter decorated with two flying *apsaras* (celestial nymphs in Hindi mythology), a turtle-shaped tea box, spoons, a *mise* celadon tea bowl and a rare glass tea bowl. There was also a salt dish decorated with four *makara* fish, another creature from Hindi mythology. It was an exhilarating find, especially for tsiologists. Here were the very utensils described by Lu Yu, not in common materials such as wood, bamboo, copper, or iron, but in precious metals and glass, made by the finest craftsmen in the land.

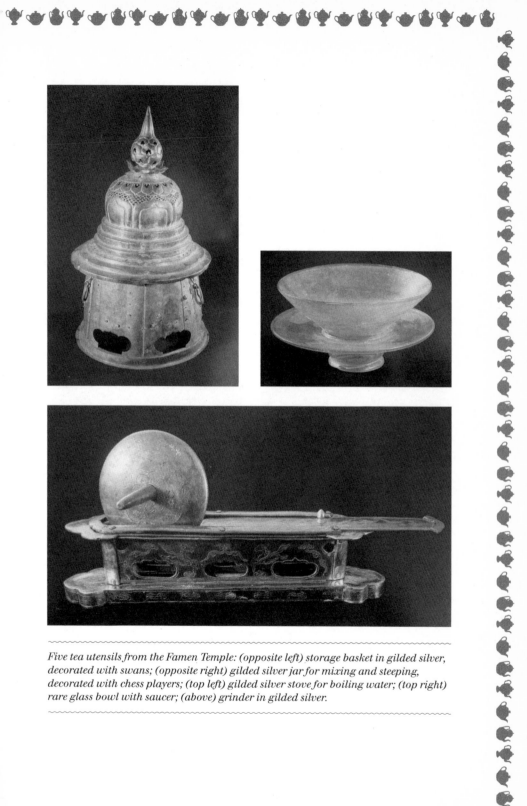

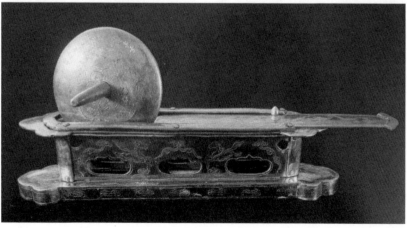

Five tea utensils from the Famen Temple: (opposite left) storage basket in gilded silver, decorated with swans; (opposite right) gilded silver jar for mixing and steeping, decorated with chess players; (top left) gilded silver stove for boiling water; (top right) rare glass bowl with saucer; (above) grinder in gilded silver.

the seeds, weeding should not be undertaken. And if it is dry, the water of washed rice can be used to irrigate the seeds.

One of Lu Yu's favorite teas was grown on Guzhu Mountain near Yixing on the western side of Lake Tai, and in 771, the Tang emperor Dai Zong (762–79) established China's first imperial tea garden at this site. From a humble beginning of 10,000 *liang* (833 lb; 16 *liang* are 1 catty), the production of its purple-shoot tea grew to some 18,408 catties (24,543 lb), and by the year 785, some 30,000 corvée laborers were conscripted at the time of harvest to pick and prepare the leaves.

The impositions of the Guzhu Mountain "tribute tea," as it was known, were a heavy burden on the people of Yixing, as depicted in Yuan Gao's poem "Tea Mountain":

> I've come to survey Islet Springs,
> So that I'm able to gain a personal understanding of tea affairs;
> The peasants have abandoned their plowing and hoeing,
> And gone off to the truly bitter labor of tea-picking.
>
> Once a man is taken for corvée duty,
> His entire household is affected;
> They grasp vines, pulling themselves up the slanting cliffs,
> Hair disheveled, they enter the wild brambles.
>
> The whole morning long they barely pick a handful,
> Yet their hands and feet are covered with sores.
> Sad laments echo through the empty hills,
> Even for the grasses and trees there's no springtime.

While the people were forced to neglect their own fields and press-ganged into work in imperial gardens, the regional inspectors, who had all their documents ready to be stamped even before the first buds had appeared, amused themselves with harlots in gaily painted pleasure boats on Lake Tai. And when the first purple-shoot tea had been harvested and prepared, it was dispatched by pony express day and night for ten days to the imperial court in Chang'an, and presented to the emperor just in time for the

Qingming (Grave Sweeping) Festival, held on the 5th day of the 4th month each year, 104 days after the winter solstice, when all fires are put out and then rekindled, the dead honored and their graves decorated.

In 782, the trade in tea, together with bamboo, wood and lacquer, had become lucrative enough for the imperial authorities to impose a 10 percent levy. Three years later, the Zhu Ci Rebellion forced the emperor De Zong (r. 779–805) to flee the capital. To reduce the burden on the common people, he abolished the new taxes, but when floods devastated the country in 793, the tea tax was soon reinstated to supplement the two ancient monopoly taxes on salt and iron. During De Zong's reign, tea tax revenue was some 40 million bronze coins per year. By 821, Wang Bo, the salt monopoly commissioner, citing the empty state coffers, pushed through a heavy hike in the tea tax which increased the revenue to 60 million coins.

Wang Ya, prime minister under the emperor Wen Zong (r. 827–40), took the state's rapaciousness beyond the pale by establishing a virtual government monopoly on the cultivation and sale of tea. Farmers' tea bushes were forcibly transferred to state plantations, and their stocks of tea burned. Merchants were only allowed to purchase tea from the state plantations, and the sales tax was raised even higher. The people rose in revolt, Wang Ya was executed by *yaozhan*, that is, cut in two at the waist, and the government monopoly eventually broken. But in 841, the tea tax was raised yet again. Under these chaotic circumstances, smuggling naturally grew rampant, before the salt and iron commissioner Fei Xiu clamped down and promulgated a 12-clause tea law that stipulated the death penalty for anybody caught smuggling above 300 catties more than three times.

In the 9th century, according to the Tang poet and scholar-official Du Mu's "Commander Shang Li Discusses River Bandits," large gangs of river bandits operated on the middle reaches of the Yangtze. Having plundered vessels on the river or towns along it, these bandits moved their ill-gotten loot up into the mountains to the south. "As they do not dare to trade their contraband in the towns, the tea mountains are the only place where they can sell it. When the tea is ready, merchants from far and near [the bandits] take their beautiful silk brocades, gold hairpins, and silver bracelets to the mountains and exchange them [for tea]. The women and children [of the tea farmers] wear beautiful clothes, but the officials ask no questions, and people are not surprised," wrote Du Mu. Having entered the mountains as thieves, the river bandits "became ordinary people after obtaining tea," which they brought to the north and sold, before plundering another boat.

In the late Tang, Lu Yu's *Classic of Tea* was followed by several other works that offer a glimpse into the hyper-esthetic universe of these wandering tea connoisseurs. Zhang Youxin's *A Record of Water for Decocting Tea*, from the first half of the 9th century, provides a list of the 20 best water sources in China, purportedly compiled by Lu Yu, which ranks the spray from water in the Kangwang valley on Mount Lu in Jiangxi province on the northwest edge of Lake Poyang number one, and water from melted snow last. Furthermore, "if you make tea with water from the place where it is cultivated, it will invariably be excellent, because the water and the land are suited to each other. If you go away to another place, the water will contribute half, while skill in preparation and clean vessels will complete the effect."

Sixteen Types of Hot Water for Tea by Su Yi describes different kinds of hot water according to how long it is boiled, the briskness of the boil, the vessels it is boiled in, and the types of fuel used. There is *infant water* and *great robust water*, while *rule water* is accorded the following definition: "All wood can be used to boil water, not only charcoal. Only the water for *rich tea* must be boiled with charcoal. Tea shops also have a *rule*: the water must not be stopped, and the fuel must not be smoked. If these *rules* are violated, the hot water will be perverse, and the tea will be *dangerous*."

During the Tang, tea was canonized by the errant scribe Lu Yu, taxed by the emperor, and transmitted to both Tibet and Japan. The magnificent tea vessels from Famen Temple, and the spectacular discovery of the Belitung shipwreck, with its cargo of mid-9th century tea bowls, both attest to the prominent place held by tea in Chinese society at the time. In the subsequent Song dynasty, tea production expanded to virtually all of southern China, a harsh government monopoly was imposed, and the fashions of tea preparation and drinking continued to evolve.

5

CLOUDY FEET IN HARE'S FUR CUP

THE SONG DYNASTY

In the 10th century, the average temperature in China dropped by 2–3 °C (3½–5½ °F), causing Lake Tai in Jiangsu province to freeze over in winter. The tea bushes of the imperial tea estate on Guzhu Mountain died in large numbers, while the buds on those that survived sprouted later each year, making it almost impossible to have the imperial purple-shoot tea ready and delivered to the court in time for the Qingming (Grave Sweeping) Festival. In 977, as a direct result of this so-called "little ice age," the emperor's tea estate was officially moved from Guzhu to the Northern Park, situated in the southeastern coastal province of Fujian.

Made up of 25 tea gardens, with names like Flying Squirrel Burrow, and some 30 processing workshops, the Northern Park tea estate stretched for 5 miles on the hillsides along the eastern branch of the Jian river. A large central factory managed the final manufacturing process, and was

Traditionally attributed to the artist Liu Songnian (c. 1174–1224), this detail from Preparing Tea *depicts two servants getting the tea ready for their masters.*

also provided with dormitories for the skilled workers – millers, peelers, mold-makers and expert graders. Early each spring, gongs up in the mountains sounded at the 5th watch (3–5 a.m.) awakening the tea-pickers to their work, which was to be finished by sunrise.

The tea produced at the Northern Park was a new kind, known as *la cha* ("wax tea"), the finest of all the Song teas. To make wax tea, the freshly picked leaves were graded, washed, steamed, pressed, ground, placed in molds of various forms, roasted over a slow fire, and sealed with an aromatic ointment of Borneo camphor, whereupon a decorative insignia was pressed into the surface. With its labor-intensive manufacturing process and imperial prestige, wax tea was the most expensive variety on the market, and the price of 40,000 copper coins for a single cake has been recorded in the historical annals. "When it comes to the color of tea," wrote the 11th-century official Cai Xiang, author of *A Record of Tea*, "a premium is placed on white, and tea cakes often have precious oils applied to their surface. Thus, there is a distinction between green, yellow, purple and black tea cakes. It is just like when a physiognomist examines the complexion of a person and subtly assesses their inner qualities, with those having lustrous lines being considered superior."

The Northern Song dynasty (960–1126), having re-established a central government after the Tang's collapse and the unrest of the Five Dynasties (907–60), never managed to retake the northern provinces from the nomadic Khitans. In 1126, another tribe of fierce fighters, the Jurchens, forced the Northern Song court to flee south to Hangzhou, which was established as the capital of the Southern Song dynasty (1126–1279), until a third wave of horse-borne warriors, the Mongols, conquered all of China. Despite the warfare and territorial setbacks, the Song has gone down in history as a dynasty of plenty, when Chinese cookery evolved enough style and character to be dubbed a *cuisine*, complete with three kitchens: the northern, southern, and Sichuanese. In agriculture, advances in irrigation and the introduction of a new rice variety from Vietnam made it possible to harvest two crops per year, fueling a surge in the country's population from 50 to 100 million, and giving the peasants the time, energy, and financial resources to cultivate cash crops such as sugarcane, cotton, and tea, further raising standards of living. To facilitate far-flung business transactions, paper money came into widespread use, while transportation was improved by inventions such as the pound lock – a water chamber with gates at both ends – which made it possible for boats carrying more than 100 tons of goods to move on waterways such as the Grand Canal.

In major commercial centers such as Yangzhou, strategically situated at the junction of the Yangtze river and the Grand Canal, there were large communities of foreign merchants, many of them Persians, who are traditionally depicted in Chinese literature as immensely wealthy, mysterious, and in possession of magical powers. While there is no evidence of tea-drinking in Persia at the time, the polymath al-Biruni includes an interesting view of Song tea in his encyclopedic mid-11th-century *Book on Pharmacy and Materia Medica,* which he presumably culled from fellow countrymen traveling to China. "A big river like the Tigris traverses through this city. Both sides of the river are studded with wine sellers' tenements, kilns, and shops. People flock there to drink tea, and do not take Indian cannabis clandestinely. He who transacts business in salt and tea without the king being aware of it is awarded the punishment due to a thief. And the people there slay the thief and eat his flesh." Tea, reports al-Biruni, grew at high altitudes in China, Nepal, and a place called Khatā, and came in several varieties distinguished by its color: white, green, purple, gray, and black. Of these, white was the finest and rarest, and exerted its effect on the body more swiftly than the other varieties. The Tibetans drank tea as an antidote to their excessive alcohol consumption, and acquired it from the Chinese by bartering musk. It was drunk with hot water, and believed to be a *cholagogue*, a medicinal agent which promotes the discharge of bile from the system, as well as a blood purifier.

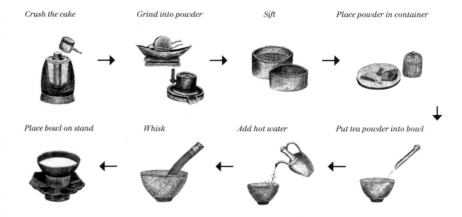

Crush the cake · Grind into powder · Sift · Place powder in container

Place bowl on stand · Whisk · Add hot water · Put tea powder into bowl

Song-dynasty tea preparation: whisking the powdered tea in a cup replaced boiling tea in a pot as the preferred method.

TEA FOR THE AFTERLIFE

In the 1970s, one of the most important archaeological discoveries in the history of tea was made on former Jurchen (Jin) territory, near the town of Xuanhua 75 miles north of Beijing. Dated to the late Liao-early Jin period (1093–1117), the tomb complex of Zhang Shiqing, a member of the local Chinese gentry, was found adorned with scores of wall-paintings showing, in addition to astronomical charts, banquets, and children at play, how tea was prepared and served at the time. The method depicted is basically in the Song fashion, with vestiges of some Tang elements. The water is boiled in a tall, slender ewer, the tea powder ground and placed into a large bowl, where it is whisked with water, then ladled into conical white cups with saucers. Evidently, the fashion for black-glazed hare's fur cups had not yet caught on this far north.

This painting shows two servants preparing tea while children look on.

During the Tang, ground tea had been boiled with a pinch of salt in an iron pot and then ladled into the bowls with a gourd dipper. In the Song, the iron pot was replaced by a porcelain ewer with a lid and a slender spout, used only to boil the water. The cakes of tea were crushed in a silk bag, ground into a fine powder, sifted, and placed directly in the bowls. When the water in the ewer had been brought to boil, it was poured onto the tea, and the liquid in the bowl beaten into a rich froth with a bamboo whisk. This was the most common way of preparing tea in the Song, whether for serving guests or making offerings to the Buddha. Japanese monks studying in China brought the custom of whisked tea with them back to Japan, where it was enshrined in the Japanese tea ceremony, *chanoyu* (see Chapters 7 and 8).

In his *Mingchuan Lu,* a short record of tea curiosa written in the 960s, the Song official Tao Gu described the latest trend in tea-drinking:

> In recent times there are those who pour hot water over tea and stir it with a spoon in such a special manner involving secret techniques so as to cause the hot water to have patterns and veins that seem like images of things: birds, beasts, bugs, fish, flowers, grasses, and the like, with the lines as skillful as those in a painting. In an instant, however, they dissipate. Such are the transformations of tea, which contemporaries call "the hundred diversions of tea."

From such amusements, a pastime known as *doucha* ("tea contests") emerged among the people of Jian prefecture. In its simplest form, *doucha* was a competition to see who could whisk the tea into the thickest, most enduring froth. The game caught on, and as the popularity of *doucha* spread across the land, it became a fashionable entertainment among scholars, poets, and officials, who evolved it into a sophisticated form of tea appreciation, something like a modern wine-tasting party. The preferred tea for *doucha* gatherings was good-quality wax tea from Jian prefecture. First, the participants competed to see who was the most skillful in preparing the tea, which included the steps of grinding, sifting, determining the temperature of the water, heating the cups and whisking the froth. Since the lidded porcelain ewers made a visual inspection of the boiling water difficult, *doucha* contestants were expected to determine the water's temperature from the sound of the boil: the temperature was right when it sounded like "wind in the pines and water in a mountain gully."

The cups had to be heated to the right temperature, because if they were too cold, the tea would not "float." The correct amount of tea was placed in the cup and mixed with a little hot water into a paste. The cup was then filled with hot water without disturbing the paste, and the contents whisked with measured movements. The perfect froth was supposed to "bite the cup," that is, stick firmly to its edge. If the froth on the surface was broken or separated from the edge, this was known as having "cloudy feet." The contestant whose tea first displayed "cloudy feet" was the loser, while the tea that "bit the cup" longer than the rest belonged to the winner.

Doucha also ushered in a new fashion in tea ware. During the Tang, the most desirable color of the infused tea had been light yellow, which was best appreciated in the pale green celadon cups from the Yue kilns and the alabaster white Xing ware – by some considered the first true porcelain – produced in Hubei province. But by the Song, the perfect cup of tea had become a froth as white and pure as possible. Then there was the need to fairly determine which cup of tea got "cloudy feet" first. This turned the eyes of *doucha* devotees toward the rustic, black-glazed ware produced in the kilns of the Jian wax tea region, as the dark backdrop set off the white-ness of the froth and also made it easier to detect the first "water-scars" between the "cloudy feet."

The most celebrated ware from the Jian kilns were the purple-black bowls with "hare's fur" streaks, a glaze effect that was created when air bubbles in the coating burst during the firing. This created tiny pits into which molten iron flowed and crystallized, leaving a pattern of yellowish brown vertical streaks embedded in the cup's inner wall. Beside its dark color and intriguing glaze, Jian ware also had other properties attractive to *doucha* fiends: the walls and base were thick, so that the cup retained heat well, and its ample size and rounded bottom provided enough space for a brisk movement of the whisk. A genuine Jian tea bowl is also recognized

Rustic bowls from the Jian kilns, with their characteristic "Hare's Fur" glaze, were de rigueur for a fashionable tea party in the Song dynasty.

by an indentation running beneath the cup's rim, and a stalactite-like glaze droplet near the foot, a result of the cup being fired in a tilted position.

Throughout the Song, tea consumption continued to expand, and by the 12th century, one third of the country's prefectures were growing tea. Given only one word to sum up the Song dynasty's tea policies, laws, and taxes, extortion comes to mind. Tea farmers first had to pay an annual tax, or "tea rent," and were forced to sell their tea to the government at a fixed, low price. Merchants, for their part, had to purchase vouchers at state monopoly bureaus, then, at one of the 13 government "mountain markets," exchange them for tea at outrageous rates, carefully listed in the *Song Administrative Digest*. "Skull bone tea" from Jian prefecture, for example, was purchased from the farmers at 90 copper coins per catty and then sold to merchants for 300. A Northern Song official, Zhang Ji, observed:

> The government has established a monopoly over the sale of output from the tea-producing areas, with the profits reverting to the public coffers. The source of the people's income to buy food and clothing has

daily been whittled away, whereas the duties of picking and manufacturing [the tea] have increased year by year. The people fail to meet their quotas, whereupon they are subjected to numerous, harsh punishments. Eventually they are forced to mortgage their fields and sell their homes to meet the stipulated quotas. Once they are destitute of property, there is nothing to save the people from death and destruction. Consequently, the districts in the tea-producing areas are destitute, and the people are unable to make a living. It is all because of this tea monopoly.

Punishment for circumventing the monopoly was severe. In the early days of the Song, anybody who traded in tea outside government markets for more than 1,500 copper coins was to be put to death. Later, the law was somewhat softened: a person caught stealing and selling more than 3,000 copper coins worth of government tea was sentenced to *qingmian*, scarification of the face with a sign or character, and then thrown in jail. Unfazed, merchants banded together to smuggle tea and salt in armed convoys. Another method was to beef up approved consignments with contraband. In 1017, for example, the merchant Tian Chang, having acquired 120,000 catties of legal tea at the Lake Tai market in Shu prefecture, was caught with an additional 70,000 catties of black-market tea in his caravan. Buddhists monks, too, peddled tea under the table. "There are impudent persons [monks] who travel to far away places under the pretext of bringing gifts, selling them in violation of the law," states the *Song Administrative Digest*.

It was also during the Song that the peculiar liaison between tea and illicit sex began in the tea houses of Kaifeng, the capital of the Northern Song, situated on the lower reaches of the Yellow river, where the "lanterns of tea shops burned all through the night." In Hangzhou, there were tea houses where one could learn how to play a musical instrument; one could go to chat and socialize in *renqing chafang* ("tea houses for human emotions"); and, in the tea houses along the Imperial Way running through the center of the city, the world of sensual pleasure among consorts known as "hot dregs" could be found. "On the main street there are several tea houses with prostitutes on the second floor," wrote Wu Zimu in his 13th-century *Mengliang Lu* ("Record of Millet Dreams"). "They are called *hua chafang*,

A POETIC TOUR DE FORCE

In 1078, a critical poem written by the great statesman and poet Su Dongpo in opposition to the government's harsh monopoly on salt, incurred the ire of the political faction headed by the powerful Song reformer Wang Anshi, who exiled him to the town of Huangzhou in present-day Zhejiang. There, Su cultivated a small garden that included tea, and composed many of his finest poems and essays. In his "Two Palindromes Occasioned by a Dream, with Preface," Su wrote: "On the 25th day of the 12th month, a heavy snow had just cleared up. I dreamed that someone boiled a small lump of tea and had a beauty offer it to me while she sang. In my dream, I composed a palindromic poem."

Flushed face jade bowl – offer slender hands,
Scattered drops remnant petals – spittle blue-green blouse;
Song chokes water clouds – congeal quiet courtyard,
Dream startled pine snow – fall empty crags.

Hands slender offer bowl – jade face flushed.
Blouse blue-green spittle petals – remnant drops scattered;
Courtyard quiet congeal clouds – water chokes song,
Crags empty fall snow – pine startled dream.

Empty flowers fall finished – beer drained vat,
Sun rises mountain melts – snow swells river;
Red roast shallow cup – new fire lively,
Dragon lump little mill – compete clear window.

Vat drained beer finished – fall flowers empty,
River swells snow melts – mountain rises sun;
Lively fire new cup – shallow roast red,
Window clear compete mill – little lump dragon.

The four stanzas above are actually only written as two in the original Chinese text; the translation above results from reading each of the stanzas first in one direction, then the other. The allusion in line 2 of the second stanza is to a story about the Han-dynasty Flying Swallow Zhao (d. 6 BC). Once when drunk, Flying Swallow drooled on the blouse of a concubine, who referred to the flecks of her spittle as flowers.

flower tea houses... are full of hubbub, and not places where a gentleman would set his foot."

In 1101, Hui Zong, the greatest tea-drinking emperor in Chinese history, ascended the throne. An accomplished artist, great patron of culture, and author of the *Grand Treatise on Tea*, Hui Zong, dubbing himself the "Daoist Prince Emperor," preferred to play *doucha* with his concubines and collect strange stones for his imperial garden in Kaifeng. He left the country's administration to his ministers Cai Jing and Dong Guan, who are customarily castigated for their greed and venality in the historical records. As a painter, Hui Zong's special forte was birds and other animals, which he observed and depicted with great expertise. According to one popular story, he once arranged a competition among the country's finest artists on the topic of the pheasant. But when the painters had handed in their work, Hui Zong declared himself sorely disappointed, as all of them had failed to notice that a pheasant always mounts a stone with its left leg first.

While the emperor and his friends nurtured their refined sensibilities, the less fastidious Tungus Jurchens were gathering strength up in Manchuria. Having driven the Turkic Khitans out into western China, the Jurchens established Yanjing (present-day Beijing) as the capital of their Jin dynasty (1115–1234), and by 1125, Jurchen forces were knocking on the gates of the Song capital Kaifeng. Despite its huge standing army, advanced weaponry, and kegs of gunpowder, the Song army and its decrepit horses were unable to withstand the onslaught of the nomads' stampeding cavalry. Hui Zong hurriedly abdicated in favor of his son, packed his brushes, and fled south. During the subsequent negotiations, a large quantity of the finest tea from Fujian was among the gifts presented to the Jurchen chieftain, who proceeded to exact an exorbitant price for peace: 5 million taels (415,000 lb; 1 tael equates to 1 *liang* or 1⅓ oz) of gold, 50 million taels (4.2 million lb) of silver, 1 million bolts of silk, and 10,000 horses and oxen for the army. The Song soon reneged on this indemnity, causing the Jurchens to turn around and lay waste to to Kaifeng. Hui Zong and his son were captured and taken to the north, where Hui Zong had had plenty of time to ponder the irony of this passage from his grand treatise:

We rule peacefully and in confidentiality, yet everything is done with utmost effortlessness. Both the gentry and the commoners are bathed in our bounties and suffused by our transformative virtue, such that everyone can participate in the elegant drinking of tea. Therefore, in recent years the excellence of picking and selecting tea, the skill of processing it, the correctness of grading it, and the wondrousness of infusing and steeping it have all attained the utmost [degree of perfection].

Harried southward, the Song court established its new capital in Hangzhou. Late in 1141, a peace treaty set the Song's annual tribute to the Jurchens at 250,000 taels of silver and 250,000 bolts of silk, and established the border of the two empires along the Huai river in the present-day provinces of Henan and Hubei, between the Yangtze and Yellow rivers.

The normalization of relations allowed the Jurchens to procure a steady supply of tea, both for the Chinese population in the lands they had conquered and for themselves, as they were fast becoming addicted to the brew. By the 13th century, tea imports had become a heavy financial burden on the Jurchen government, evident in a memorandum submitted by the Presidential Council in late 1206: "Everyone, high and low, all drink tea, especially the farmers. Tea shops at the market places are numerous; merchants and travelers frequently exchange silk and lustrings for tea. The annual expense is no less than one million *guan* [1 billion copper coins; 1 *guan* is 1,000 coins or 9¾ lb of copper]." With an annual budget of some 15 million *guan*, the Jurchens were spending almost 7 percent of their revenue on tea. Subsequently, Emperor Zhang Zong ordered that only families of officials above the seventh rank be allowed to drink, sell, give, or receive tea.

In June 1214, yet another hardy tribe from the north, the Mongols, came sweeping down through the Great Wall, invading Jurchen territory and ousting them from Beijing. Deprived of the productive Hebei province and burdened with enormous military expenses, the Jurchens were plunged into a severe fiscal crisis. Nothing, however, could come between the people and their daily cup of tea. In 1223, the Presidential Council reported that the public frequently ignored the prohibition against tea, and again, the court attempted to curtail consumption by edict: only princes, princesses, and officials above the fifth rank, Chinese and Jurchen alike, were allowed to possess tea. Persons who violated this restriction were to be punished with five years of forced labor, and informants awarded 10 million copper coins. But all these measures proved to no avail: in 1234, the Jurchens were finally swept into history's dustbin by the charging Mongols.

The Mongols took Hangzhou, the capital of the Southern Song, in 1276, apparently with little destruction, for when Marco Polo visited the city around that time, he described it as "the greatest city which may be found in the world, where so many pleasures may be found that one fancies himself to be in Paradise." Remarkably, however, Polo, who is said to have stayed 17 years in China, fails to mention tea anywhere in his famous *Description of the World,* although cities like Hangzhou were bustling with tea houses at the time. Polo's glaring omission of tea, in addition to his failure to describe the Great Wall, the Chinese writing system, bound feet, cormorant fishing, woodblock printing, and chopsticks, has been held up by scholars as evidence that he never actually visited China, but rather, with the help of his ghostwriter Rustichello da Pisa's fecund imagination, cobbled together his famous book from Persian travel guides and other accounts of China in circulation at the time. In defense of Polo, other scholars point to his explicit declaration that he had no intention of describing details that could not be appreciated or understood by fellow Europeans.

While Marco Polo did not note the presence of tea in China, Chinese writers of the period did record the absence of tea in distant countries. In his *c.* 1225 *Zhufan Zhi* ("Gazetteer of Foreign Peoples"), Zhao Rugua, the Inspector of Foreign Trade in Fujian, having culled most of his information from Chinese and Arabic traders, describes places as far away as Mosul in present-day Iraq, as well as commodities such as liquid storax (a balsam), sapan wood, and kingfisher's feathers. In his section on Annam, present-day Vietnam, where the people "bathe from three to five times daily," he wrote that they "do not cultivate tea, neither do they know how to make fermented liquors." As for Java: "No tea is raised in this country. Their wine is derived from the coconut and from the inner part of the gomuti (or sugar) palm, which tree has not been seen in China, or else by fermenting the fruits of the sago palm and of the areca palm; all of these liquors are clear and well-flavored."

In the late Southern Song, Wu Zimu could report that "the things that people cannot do without everyday are firewood, rice, oil, salt, soybean sauce, vinegar, and tea. Those who are slightly better off cannot do without appetizer and soup." By this time, the vogue for wax tea and *doucha* had already long since waned, and loose-leaf green tea, which was much cheaper to produce and easier to prepare, had become the most popular kind among ordinary people. One of the finest green teas of the time, *rizhu,* produced by monks at the Zishou Temple near the town of Shaoxing in Zhejiang province, was in such demand that it was counterfeited by "Viet people," who flavored ordinary tea with musk to imitate the aroma of *rizhu*. In the *Book of Agriculture*, published in 1313, the writer Wang Zhen listed three types of tea – loose leaf, powder, and wax tea. Of these "wax tea is most expensive," but "it only serves as tribute tea, and is seldom seen among the people." In 1391, wax tea was dealt the final death blow when it was abolished outright for "overtaxing the people's strength."

Among China's scholar-officials and poets, tea in the Song was an elaborate affair, with expensive wax teas and noisy *doucha* contests. But while the court and its courtiers idled away their days in pleasant amusements, the empire's frontiers were under constant threat from a host of restless nomadic tribes – Khitans, Jurchens, Tanguts, and Mongols. Since ancient times, the achilles heel of China's defense had been its poor horsemanship and lack of worthy horses needed to meet the nomads in open battle. With the burgeoning tea trade, however, China discovered a new weapon (for caffeine addiction is a subtle, but powerful, persistent force) in its Sisyphean attempts to appease and bridle and the nomads. This was the beginning of the fabled tea and horse trade, which turned the Tibetans into the most copious tea-guzzlers on the planet, opened up some of the world's most daunting trade routes, and remained a cornerstone of China's foreign policy until the Qing dynasty.

6

BUYING
PEACE WITH
THE CELESTIAL
BEVERAGE

THE TEA AND
HORSE TRADE

T he opposition between farmers and pastoralists, between people who cultivate the land and those who seek pasture for their animals, between sedentary security and nomadic freedom, has been one of the enduring themes of human history. For the hardy peasants of the Yellow river valley, bordering on the vast grasslands of Mongolia, Qinghai, and Central Asia, this conflict has been etched upon the collective psyche. The Great Wall, marking the border, is not only an immense defensive structure. Throughout Chinese history, it has also formed a state of mind, a way of viewing the outside world that has dictated China's foreign policy and determined the timbre of its relations with other nations.

From the 4th century BC until the age of European expansion, China's principal wars were fought against horse-borne nomads such as the Xiongnu, Xianbei, and Uyghurs, attacking from the north and northwest.

In addition to the Great Wall, the "Central Kingdom" maintained a huge standing army, equipped with advanced weaponry which by the Song included incendiary projectiles fired with gunpowder. But its neighboring adversaries possessed an even more lethal weapon – swift, splendid Central Asian horses, and sturdy, agile Mongolian ponies. By contrast, the horses of China were often too scrawny to pull a plow, or carry an armored mount in battle. Between 121 and 118 BC, for example, the Chinese lost 100,000 horses in battles against the Xiongnu nomads. So throughout its history, attempts to procure strong, healthy horses to counter the nomads formed a cornerstone of China's defense strategy.

"Horses are the foundation of military strength, the state's great resource," wrote the Han-dynasty general Ma Yuan (14 BC–AD 49). The most sought-after were the "blood-sweating" horses of the Ferghana valley in present-day Uzbekistan, which could carry heavily armed men and supposedly cover 1,000 *li* (*c.* 330 miles) per day. The Chinese traded gold, silver, and silk for these horses, until one time, in 106 BC, the king of Ferghana refused to do business, hid the horses, and killed the envoy. The emperor's first punitive campaign, conducted by a ragtag army of thieves and vagrants, ended in unmitigated disaster. Subsequently, in 103 BC, a second expedition of 60,000 soldiers under the command of General Li Guangli was dispatched, laying siege to the Ferghana capital Ershi for 40 days, before the town elders murdered their obstinate king, sent his head to Li Guangli, and exchanged a few scores of first-rate horses, and 3,000 mares and stallions of the second and third grades, for Li's agreement to withdraw his forces.

During the Han dynasty some 300,000 horses were reared in pastures on the northern and northwestern frontiers of the country, but when the Eastern Han fell in AD 220, northern China was overrun by the Tabgatch and other nomadic federations. The Tang, starting with only 5,000 horses, quickly built up a herd of 760,000. In 643, the emperor Tai Zong (r. 626–49) granted the request for a royal princess from a Turkish khan who sent 50,000 "grizzled black-maned horses" as a gift to the imperial court. Tai Zong also received splendid Afghan horses as a present from the king of Kapisa, a kingdom north of Kabul, and had his six favorite steeds carved in

Led by a Central Asian groom, this is the first of five horses painted on a scroll by the Song period artist, Li Gonglin (1049–1106). The inscription, written by the famous poet and calligrapher Huang Tingjian (1045–1105), reads: "The horse to the right was received by the Mounts Service [a unit of the Court of the Imperial Stud] from the kingdom of Khotan on 22 January, 1087. It is a greenish-white piebald with the name 'Phoenix Head.' The horse is eight years old and its height is 5 feet 4 inches."

stone to accompany him at the site of his tomb. These magnificent reliefs still exist and may be seen in the Pennsylvania Museum (two) and in the Shaanxi Provincial Museum (four). In times of strength, China received horses as tribute from its nomad neighbors. In times of weakness, it purchased them with immense quantities of silver and silk, until a new commodity emerged that the nomads coveted and needed even more – tea.

"In the past, the Hui Gu [Uyghurs] came to the court with many horses and traded them for tea," states *A Record of Things Seen and Heard by Mr. Feng*, compiled around the beginning of the 9th century. When the Tang dynasty collapsed in 907, northern China was once again invaded by a horse-borne nomadic people, the pre-Mongolic Khitans, who set up the Liao dynasty (907–1125) with its capital in Shenyang, 400 miles northeast of Beijing. In the south, following the turmoil of the Five Dynasties, the

Song succeeded in re-establishing a central government in 960. One of its first priorities was to retake the Sixteen Prefectures of northern China from the Khitans, and in 979, a great army under the personal command of the emperor Tai Zong (r. 976–97) marched north to do battle. In July that year, the Song infantry launched an attack against the Liao's southern capital at present-day Beijing, but was utterly demolished by the Khitan cavalry. In 986, the Khitans dealt the Song army another devastating blow at the Qigou Pass, and later imposed an annual tribute of 200,000 bolts of silk and 150,000 taels (12,500 lb) of silver. Further to the west, the Song was also bullied by the Tangut Xixia, which in 1006 forced the Song to make an annual payment of 20,000 taels (1,650 lb) of silver, 10,000 bolts of silk, and 20,000 catties (26,500 lb) of tea.

The string of severe defeats caused the government official Song Qi, Director of Herds and Pastures, to lament: "The northern Liao and western Xixia are able to oppose China only because they have numerous horses and practice riding. China has few horses, and its men do not practice riding. This is China's weakness. Whenever the enemy transgresses against us, the court confronts strength with weakness. Thus in ten battles there are ten defeats, and the principle of victory is rare." While the Khitans possessed as many as 1.8 million battle-ready mounts, the Song had no more than 200,000 horses. An attempt to rear horses in pasturages near the capital Kaifeng on the Yellow river's middle reaches failed miserably. In this desperate situation, the Song's sole major ally and source of horses were the Tibetans, who shared a common enemy in the Tangut Xixia. In 1055, the Song spent 100,000 taels (8,300 lb) of silver, half of its annual production, procuring horses from the Tibetans.

Faced with the constant threat of military invasion and financial crisis, drastic measures were required. Up to this point, the Sichuan tea industry had been exempt from the harsh monopoly imposed by the Song government on the rest of southern China, while in return, Sichuan farmers and merchants were only allowed to sell their tea within the province, or to the neighboring Tibetans. But, in 1074, the Song government established the Tea and Horse Agency with the specific aim of using Sichuan tea to purchase

Tibetan war horses. Sichuan's tea farmers and merchants were given short notice to clear out all their old stocks, and then forced to sell their new spring tea to the government at a poor price. Early in 1077, 300 tea households in the Sichuan town of Pengzhen demonstrated against the monopoly, presenting their petitions to the local government officials. The Attendant Censor Liu Zhi summed up the situation in an official memorandum:

> The damage done by the Sichuan tea monopoly is such that the owners of the tea gardens either flee or commit suicide to escape it, with the damage extending to their neighbors. If one wishes to cut back tea production, there is a prohibition against it, and if one wishes to build up production, there's an increase of [government] markets [to buy the tea at low prices]. Consequently, the people say, "The land is not for growing tea, it's for growing misery."

The commandeered tea was carried from Sichuan over treacherous terrain several hundred miles to the west by convoys of coolies, each one hauling a wheelbarrow loaded with some 520 lb of tea. "If mud or slippery stretches are encountered, a man's strength is exhausted; and the porters run off and seek relief in death. Alas, anger fills the roads. Last year, in the 8th and 9th months, all the men of the Jianyang Depot fled. The tea depots along the way are called 'death traps'," the official Su Che wrote in his 1086 *A Discussion of Five Circumstances that Hurt Shu [Sichuan] Tea*. The coolies were also accused of adulterating the tea with the leaves from trees along the way, and selling the finest tea to line their own pockets. "When the time comes to trade for horses," an observer reported, "the Tibetans recoil in horror."

The Tibetans pastured their horses over the summer in the cool, high-lying grasslands of Qinghai, northeast of present-day Tibet, before bringing them to one of the six main northwestern tea and horse markets, where Chinese officials feted the Tibetan merchants "to make far-away people happy to sell horses in the frontier markets." In the subsequent bargaining, either native Tibetans living on Song territory (known as "cooked households") or Uyghur merchants were employed as interpreters and middlemen. The Song officials, for their part, had a reputation for gross

Class and Size of Horse (in hands)	Price in Mingshan Tea (in catties)
"Fine Horses"	
14¼ and up (superior)	250
14¼ and up (inferior)	220
"Convoy Horses"	
14¼	176
14	169
13½	164
13¼	154
13	149
12¾	132

Tea-horse exchange rates in Minzhou, 1105. The Chinese government monitored the strategic exchange rate carefully, but its attempts to control the market proved futile.

incompetence as horse buyers, often "mistaking sick horses for strong, small for large, and old for young."

In 1078, one Tibetan horse cost 100 catties of Sichuan tea, or 25,000–30,000 copper coins, and that year the Song acquired a total of 15,000 mounts at the six Shaanxi markets. In 1085, Sichuan produced 29 million catties of tea, and by the reign of the emperor Hui Zong (1101–25), over-production had pushed the price for a Tibetan pony up to 174 catties, with 22,834 horses purchased in 1121.

But in numbers of horses the Song still lagged far behind the Xixia, Liao, and Jurchens, and with the fall of northern China to the Jurchens in 1126, it was also deprived of the strategic northwestern horse markets. The price of tea plummeted further, and by 1164, the price for a 13¼-hand horse had rocketed to 700 catties. Six years later, only 5,900 horses were acquired at the markets that remained, and many of these were too weak to make the long journey to their patrol posts along the northern frontiers.

As hyperinflation continued to undermine the tea and horse trade, and the Southern Song struggled to fend off the Jurchens, yet another nomadic tribe, the Mongols, were beginning to stir in their homeland southeast of Lake Baikal. By 1206, the khan Temüjin had united the Mongol tribes, set up his headquarters at Karakorum in the Orkhon river valley, and taken the name Chinggis – "Perfect Warrior." Having subdued the Nestorian Christian Naiman empire on the Altai Plateau in the northwest corner of present-day Mongolia, he turned his horses first on the Xixia, then on the Jurchens, and finally on the Song. Until then, no nomadic tribe had been able to cross the Yangtze river and fight the Chinese among the rice paddies of the southern empire. But the Mongols, having captured the strategic Song strongholds of Xiangyang and Fancheng after a five-year siege, would not be stopped by this formidable barrier. In March, 1275, the Mongol general Bayan attacked the Song by the Yangtze in Anhui province with cavalry backed up by catapults, forcing the Song army to flee in disorder, and in 1276, the last emperor of the Southern Song surrendered to Bayan in the capital of Hangzhou.

During the short-lived Yuan dynasty (1280–1368) which followed, the Mongol rulers continued the tea monopoly, though of course not for the purpose of procuring horses. Already with the death of Chinggis Khan's grandson Khubilai Khan in 1294, their vast empire began to fall apart as the four branches of the Chinggis Khan clan took independent control of their respective dominions. In China, seven Mongol emperors came and

Chinggis Khan, founder of the Mongol empire. While the Tibetans took to tea with an immediate passion, the conversion of the Mongols to a nation of tea-drinkers was a more protracted process.

went in rapid, often bloody, succession, and among the rebel groups that rose up in opposition to Mongol rule, the ragtag peasant army led by the Buddhist monk Zhu Yuanzhang emerged victorious. In 1356, Zhu and his men captured Nanjing on the Yangtze river, and then, having gained control of the Yellow river valley basin, marched into Beijing in 1368, sending the last Mongol emperor galloping off to the grasslands of Mongolia with his entourage.

Founding the Ming dynasty (1368–1644) under the imperial title Hongwu (r. 1368–99), Zhu Yuanzhang restored China to rule by the native Han Chinese, unified the empire, improved agriculture, and revived the tea and horse trade with the Tibetans as a major part of his defense strategy. "All the barbarians need tea to survive. If they cannot get tea, they become ill and die," as one Ming official hyperbolically described the Tibetans' subconscious caffeine addiction fueling the trade and shaping political reality. The Ming court appropriated 1 million catties of Sichuan tea per year, and ordered soldiers to cultivate tea on idle land. Peasants who avoided government impositions by selling tea to private merchants were given 20 lashes for the first offence, and Hongwu even had his own relative Ouyang Lun executed for smuggling tea to nomads outside China. By only doing business with the Tibetans, Hongwu hoped to draw them close and prevent an alliance between the Tibetans and Mongols, who, according to the same strategy, were deprived of any opportunity to purchase tea through official channels.

In 1375, Hongwu dispatched the eunuch Zhao Cheng with a convoy of silk, tea, and other precious items to trade for horses at the Hezhou market in Gansu province. The price for a superior horse was set at 120 catties of tea, 70 catties for an ordinary horse, and 50 catties for a substandard mount. But in 1392, another imperial eunuch emissary purchased 10,000 horses at the Hezhou market for a mere 300,000 catties of tea – 30 catties of tea per horse. In order to strengthen state control over the tea and horse trade and prevent smuggling, Hongwu also established a contract system in which 41 gold tablet tallies – a tablet of gold divided into two pieces with a unique fit – were distributed to chosen Tibetan merchants, who by the possession of such a tally were conferred exclusive rights to trade horses for tea with the Chinese. Every three years, Chinese government officials called on these merchants, checked to see if their gold tablet tallies matched, and when the authenticity had been verified, proceeded to trade tea for horses. In this manner, Chinese and Tibetan merchants who did not possess such tallies were excluded from trade on pain of stiff punishment, with the privileged Tibetan merchants policing the far-flung Qinghai grasslands to protect their trade monopoly.

Hongwu's successor Yongle (r. 1403–24), who moved the Ming capital to Beijing, adopted a less miserly, more magnanimous approach in his relations with the northwestern nomads, allowing private trade and raising the remuneration to the Tibetans for their horses, once paying 80,000 catties of tea for 70 horses (1,140 per horse). But the loosened reins encouraged corruption and smuggling, and to procure the horses necessary for his punitive campaigns against the Mongols, Yongle was soon forced to reassert state control over the tea and horse trade. Tea smugglers were threatened with execution, and during the trading season between March and September, special officials were dispatched four times a month to prevent unsanctioned trade in tea. His measures succeeded in improving horse procurement, and in 1421, the gold tablet tally system was temporarily suspended, only to be reinstated in 1435.

Under their ambitious chief Esen, the western Mongols, known as the Oirat, began expanding eastward. By the 1440s, the Oirat controlled most of Mongolia, and in 1449, Esen raided the Chinese northwestern frontier, captured the Ming emperor Ying Zong (1436–49, 1457–64), devastated his army of 50,000 men, and wreaked havoc on the tea and horse trade. The Tibetan merchants were forced to seek refuge in China, soldiers engaged in tea transportation were ordered to the battlefront, and the gold tablet tallies that had governed the exchange of tea for horses were dispersed or destroyed.

The next Chinese emperor, Chenghua (r. 1465–87), first changed the tea tax so that growers had to pay in silver, which he used to purchase horses, but soon realized the disastrous effects that this would have on the state coffers, and instead tried to re-establish the tea and horse trade as it had been before the invasions of Esen. Private tea trade with the nomadic tribes was prohibited, and anybody caught smuggling more than 500 catties was drafted into the army. Chenghua also discontinued the old custom of allowing tribute-bearing Muslims and Buddhist abbots to purchase tea when returning to their home countries. To reduce the enormous cost and burden of transporting the necessary tea all the way from Sichuan, he greatly expanded tea cultivation in Shaanxi's Hanzhong region, which lay much closer to the tea and horse markets. Finally, to alleviate the perennial famine in Shaanxi, he instituted the Tea Exchange system, in which merchants were ordered to transport grain to Shaanxi, and paid with tea from the Tea and Horse Agency.

In the Taklamakan Desert's northeastern corner, the state of Turfan had risen to become a great Muslim power, and in 1469 its leader Sultan Ali requested a precious four-clawed dragon robe from the Ming court in recognition of his might. When the Board of Rites brushed aside this demand as presumptuous, the insulted sultan responded by invading Hami and cutting off the Silk Road route between China and Central Asia. The ensuing clashes between Turfan and China further exacerbated the Ming court's need for cavalry horses. In 1494, Shaanxi was struck with famine once again, forcing the Hongzhi Emperor (r. 1488–1505) to release 2 million catties of government tea to merchants who transported grain to the region. The following year, the tea and horse trade was suspended, and 4 more million catties of tea exchanged for grain to head off the looming starvation in Shaanxi.

In a memorandum from 1505, Shaanxi's vice-censor-in-chief, Yang Yiqing, formulated his plan to reform China's horse procurement policy. First, he presented a short history of China's relations with the nomadic federations on its frontiers, and pointed out the pivotal role of tea in regulating these relations. Acquiescence was rewarded with ample supplies of tea, recalcitrance punished by cutting off tea supplies, and without tea, the nomads would fall ill and die. After the collapse of the gold tablet tally system, however, the nomads had been able to purchase tea from private merchants, depriving the Chinese government of their horses. With abundant supplies of tea, the nomads became bolder, attacked China and looted the towns and villages on its frontiers. Yang proposed punishing one or two tribes to set an example, and advocated the reestablishment of the gold tablet tally system. To solve the problem of transporting the tea from Sichuan to the frontier, he commanded wealthy Shaanxi to buy some 500,000 catties of tea each year and transport it to the frontier, where they would be allowed to sell one third of their tea privately at 50 silver taels per 1,000 catties of tea, while the remaining two thirds would be used by the government for the tea and horse trade. Understandably, the merchants balked at these harsh conditions, and the plan was amended to allow the merchants to sell 50 percent of their tea privately. In its first four years, Yang's scheme managed to procure 19,077 horses for the Ming court, but the plan soon faltered, as the merchants kept the best half of the tea for their private business, leaving the government with only low-quality tea to barter for horses.

The staple tea of the tea and horse trade was Mingshanxian tea from Yazhou, east of Chengdu in Sichuan. Tibetans were said to prefer "aged" teas, a taste they may well have acquired due to the fact that by the time any tea reached Tibet – having traveled many months and more than 1,000 miles in wheelbarrows, oxcarts, and sewn up in hides on yak backs – the originally greenish cakes had, through a process known as post-fermentation, turned a dark, reddish brown. Either by necessity or accident, the pungent infusion of this tea suited the Tibetans and other nomads, who mixed it with nourishing ingredients such as butter and barley meal, and who prized its ability to aid the digestion of yak meat and other heavy foods.

In the early 16th century, this accidental production process was rationalized by the tea-makers of Anhua county in Hunan province. After the tea leaves had been steamed and rolled in the same manner as for green tea, they were "piled" together in a hot and humid room for a period of time, which facilitated the growth of various benevolent microorganisms, until the leaves had assumed the characteristic dark brown hue and musty aroma of post-fermented tea. After this, the leaves were rolled again, pressed into cakes, and dried. Production of this Hunan tea expanded rapidly, as tea merchants, attracted by its low price, began purchasing and selling it to the nomadic tribes. In 1595, the censor Li Nan criticized Hunan tea, which he said was bitter, harmful to health, and often not even real tea at all. But the government needed all the tea it could get to barter for horses. The Censor Xu Qiao, defending the government's decision to permit the trade in Hunan tea, agreed that it was bitter, but said that at least it did not cause sickness if mixed with fermented mare's milk.

At this time, according to the official Ming history, regardless of all efforts to the contrary, "the tea laws, the horse administration, and the border defenses were all ruined" as the empire was invaded and fell apart. Matteo Ricci, the famous 16th-century Jesuit missionary, summed up China's centuries of hapless attempts to befriend the horse, writing: "The Chinese know little about the taming or training of horses. Those which they make use of in daily life are all geldings and consequently quiet and good tempered. They have countless horses in the service of the army, but these are so degenerate and lacking in martial spirit that they are put to rout even by the neighing of the Tartars' steeds and so they are practically useless in battle."

In Manchuria, the horse-borne Tungus Jurchens, who had been licking their wounds since the fall of their Jin dynasty (1115–1234), were once again beginning to stir. As peasant rebellions wreaked havoc on Ming rule in the south, the Jurchens, from 1635 known as the Manchus, readied themselves for an invasion of China from the north. The opportunity came in 1644, after peasant rebels led by Li Zicheng entered Beijing and drove the Ming emperor to hang himself on a hill overlooking the Forbidden City. When Wu Sangui, the Ming general guarding the strategic Great Wall gate at Shanhaiguan, learned that his favorite concubine Chen Yuanyuan had been taken prisoner in Li Zicheng's harem, he threw a famous apoplectic fit that stood his hair on end. In a moment worthy of Greek myth, the Great Wall – the world's mightiest defense structure, mortared with countless centuries of blood, sweat, and tears, traversing deserts, scaling impossible cliffs — was breached through the jealousy of the heart-broken commander. The Shanhaiguan gate was opened to the Manchus, who flooded through it with their cavalry, crushing Li Zicheng's peasant foot-army and establishing the Qing dynasty. Once again, China was overrun by horse-borne nomads, and neither tea nor the Great Wall had been able to keep them at bay.

The tea and horse trade worked for a while, but in the end it was doomed to failure, as the nomads' craving for tea proved stronger than the emperor's ability to maintain and police his monopoly. In the Chinese heartland, whisked tea was succeeded during the Ming by loose-leaf tea infused in proper teapots (see Chapter 9). In Japan, however, where tea had lain dormant since its first introduction by Kūkai and Saichō in the 9th century, and interest in the beverage only reawakened in the 12th century, it was the Song fashion for whisked tea that became the enshrined method of preparation. The Chinese often lament the Japanese propensity to adopt their ideas and culture, and refine and improve them beyond recognition. Nowhere does this appear truer than for the Japanese tea ceremony that evolved during the 14th and 15th centuries.

7

THE TASTE OF ZEN IS TEA

JAPAN IN THE 12TH TO 15TH CENTURIES

Furu ike ya!	The old pond, ah!
Kawazu tobikomu:	A frog jumps in:
Mizo no oto!	The water's sound!

In the last decades of the 12th century the apocalypse seemed near in Japan. As the Taira and Minamoto clans struggled for political power, the capital Kyoto was afflicted by a series of natural disasters. In 1177, the city caught fire in the midst of typhoon, and one third of its houses, including the Imperial Palace, were burnt to the ground. Three years later, a tornado flattened the city. With "drought in spring and summer" or "storms and flood in autumn and winter," famine followed, and beggars, unshod and shod, thronged the roads. "But that nothing might be left to complete our misfortunes," wrote the famous hermit artist Kamo no

Chōmei in his 1212 *Hojoki* ("Visions of a Torn World"), "a pestilence broke out and continued without ceasing. Everybody was dying of hunger, and as time went on, our state became as that of the fish in the small pool of the story: the numbers of those who died in central Kyoto during the 4th and 5th months alone were 42,300."

Anthropologists speak of an "incubation period" between the initial arrival of a cultural borrowing and the time of its actual popularization, during which it either "sleeps," or diffuses at a snail's pace. It is an idea that fits well with the transfer of tea to Japan, for in the centuries following its first introduction by Kūkai and Saichō, the use of tea did not become widespread among the Japanese, and by the time of the Kyoto disasters, amidst the strife that was the rending the country at its seams, tea had been all but forgotten. It was not until 1191, when the Buddhist monk Myōan Eisai (1141–1215), having returned from studies in China, began to propagate Zen as a teaching that could save Japan, and tea as a medicine that could restore the Japanese people to health, that Japanese tea culture began to develop in earnest.

Eisai planted tea at the Senkōji Temple on Hirado, a small island near Nagasaki, and at Tendaijiin in the Seburi Mountains on Kyushu, the southernmost of Japan's main islands – tea gardens that remain to this day. He also sent some tea seeds to Myōe, the abbot of the Kōzanji Temple in Kyoto, in a tea jar named *Kogaki* ("Little Persimmon") which is still one of the temple's most treasured possessions. Abbot Myōe planted the seeds in the mountains of Toganoo near Kyoto, and later in Uji, south of the city, where

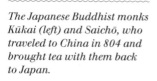

The Japanese Buddhist monks Kūkai (left) and Saichō, who traveled to China in 804 and brought tea with them back to Japan.

according to tradition the seeds were first sown in the hoofprints of a horse in a garden subsequently dubbed *Koma-no-Ashikage* ("Colt's Hoofprint"). The soil in Uji proved ideal for the *Camellia sinensis* plant, and the excellent tea produced there became known as *honcha* ("real tea"), against which teas from other parts of Japan, called *hicha* ("non-tea") were measured.

In the second month of 1214, tea received an endorsement from the highest echelons of political power, when the Shogun Sanetomo, having drunk too much sake (rice wine), was sobered up with a bowl of tea prepared by Eisai, who also presented the shogun with a scroll of the *Kissa Yōjōki,* a treatise on the miraculous medicinal properties of tea and mulberry. In its first section, "The Harmonizing of the Five Organs," Eisai quotes an esoteric scripture entitled *The Secret Treatise on the Formula for the Conquest of Hell*, which propounds a theory according to which the liver prefers acid taste, the lungs pungent, the spleen sweet, the kidney salty and the heart bitter. While Japanese food contains ample sour, pungent, sweet and salty tastes, it is deficient in the bitter. Eisai, who died in 1215, and who every year is commemorated on the anniversary of his death at the temple he founded, Kennin-ji, with a tea ritual known as *Yotsugashira* ("Four Pillars"), wrote:

> I wonder why the Japanese do not care for bitter things. In the great country of China they drink tea, as a result of which there is no heart trouble and people live long lives. Our country is full of sickly-looking, skinny people, and this is simply because we do not drink tea. Whenever one is in poor spirits, one should drink tea. This will put the heart in good order and dispel all illness.

Unable to bear life in this "polluted and wicked world," the monk Chōmei built a 10-foot-square hut in the mountains southeast of Kyoto, where he wrote *Tales of Aspiration for Enlightenment*, a compilation of Buddhist-inspired biographical stories. In this work, he discusses *suki*, or "devotion to art," a key concept in Japanese culture according to which the practice of arts such as *go* chess, swordsmanship, flower arranging, horseback riding, archery, poetry, calligraphy, and music can lead to self-transcendence, religious awakening, and attainment of the Buddha mind. Through the total immersion in one of these arts, the disciple can liberate himself from the enslavement to the palette of fickle emotions that seize, steer, and goad one through life, and attain the acute sensitivity and aliveness of mind that form the precipice for the final plunge to enlightenment. As the popularity of tea spread in Japan, it was incorporated into this religious-esthetic way of life, and, precisely situated at the junction of nature, art, and human relations, later evolved into its foremost expression – the Japanese tea ceremony, known as *chanoyu* (literally, "boiled water for tea"). This quasi-religious ritual reached its apogee in the 16th century (see Chapter 8); some scholars believe it may even have incorporated elements from the Christian liturgy transmitted to Japan by Portuguese Jesuits.

Zen Buddhism, with its insistence that enlightenment can be achieved in a flash sparked by meditation or direct transmission from mind to mind, greatly appealed to the warring samurai, who lived by the sword and always had to be prepared to die in an instant. The samurai, members of the hereditary warrior class, were also attracted by the military discipline, tight regimentation, and strict hierarchy of the Zen monasteries. From the moment he awoke till the moment he went to bed, the Zen monk's every action was prescribed by rules known as *shingi*. The oldest *shingi*, *Rules of Purity for Chan [Zen] Monasteries*, were compiled in China in 1103, and established the minute precepts, code of conduct, and etiquette for a Zen Buddhist temple. Based on this work, the Japanese Zen monk Dōgen (1200–53), wrote his *Eihei Shingi* ("Dōgen's Rules for Purity"), which includes instructions, known as *sarei* ("tea etiquette"), on the complex ritual of serving tea. For the New Year's celebration, for example, the leader of the ceremony should "sound the gong two times before the hall, and the lay brothers will offer bowls of tea, first to the head priest, then to any special guests, and finally to the general assembly." And in his essay "Everyday Activity," Dōgen stated: "In the domain of Buddha ancestors, drinking tea and eating rice are everyday activities. Having tea and rice has been transmitted over many years and is present right now. In this way the ancestors' vital activity of having tea and rice comes to us."

In 1223, the potter Katō Shirōzaemon, accompanied by Dōgen, traveled to China to study the manufacture of Song ceramics. Upon his return six years later, Katō set up his workshop at Seto in Owari province, where he produced tea caddies, known as Tōshiro-yaki, that are still highly valued among tea ceremony devotees. Another seminal event in the evolution of the Japanese tea ceremony occurred in 1267 when, according to tradition, Nampo Jōmyō, brought the first *daisu* ("tea shelf," used for holding the tea and all the implements necessary for the ceremony), to Japan from Jingshasi in China. This shelf was later moved to Kyoto's Daitokuji Temple, where Zen monk Musō Kokushi (1275–1351) incorporated it in the first model for the formal Japanese tea ceremony.

In the late 13th century, the age of European maritime exploration still lay some 200 years ahead, and the Mongols ruled the Eurasian continent from Persia to Korea, the eastern end of their vast empire. Standing on the tip of that peninsula, the still unslaked conquerors cast covetous eyes across the straits, transported their bow legs from the saddle to a hastily assembled armada, and in November, 1274, set off to conquer the islands of Japan. Having inflicted terrible damage on the defenders, the Mongols and their Korean cohorts were eventually beaten back and forced to withdraw. But Khubilai Khan, flush with his defeat of Song China, would not let the matter rest, and in 1281, a second, even more powerful Mongol fleet, carrying some 140,000 men, was dispatched to subdue the recalcitrant islanders. After seven weeks of intense battles, on 14 August that year, Mother Nature finally intervened in favor of the Japanese. A violent typhoon struck the bay that was sheltering the Mongol armada, and when the ships attempted to escape storm, they jammed the mouth of the harbor, till "the bodies of men and broken timbers of the vessels were heaped together in a solid mass so that a person could walk across from one point of land to another on the mass of wreckage causing complete ruin to the fleet." Every year since then, a mass tea ceremony known as the Ōchamori ritual is held at the Saidaiji Temple to commemorate Japan's miraculous deliverance from the Mongol barbarians.

Returning home as heroes, the samurai who had rescued the country passed their idle days playing the popular traditional game of *monoawase*, comparison contests, be it between paintings, cocks, insects, flowers, fans, seashells, incense, or armor, that were often accompanied by heavy gambling. Another fashionable type of entertainment was *renga* ("linked-verse") meetings, where a small group of people gathered in a specially furnished room to compose *renga* poetry. Taking turns, each participant proposed a line of poetry linked to the previous line and alternating between two different meters, thereby creating a collective poem. The composition of the poem was governed by the previous content and by intricate rules that restricted or demanded changes in subject and diction.

In the early Muromachi period (1336–1573), drawing on these entertainments as well as the whisked tea contests of Song China, the Japanese developed their own kind of tea competition, *tōcha*, where the object of the game was to be able to distinguish *honcha* from *hicha*. Modeled on an incense-testing competition, the most common form of this game involved tasting four types of tea in ten cups: three cups each of three types of tea, and one cup of the fourth type, called "guest tea," as the contestants were

A screen depicting the theater and music performances, family picnics, children swimming, and tea preparation at Shijogawa, Kyoto, in the Muromachi period.

given only one chance to identify it. The person who could identify the most of the ten cups correctly was declared the winner.

So great was the fashion for tea during this period that a military commander is said to have ordered the nine horizontal rings (made of *shakudo* – an amalgam of copper and gold) decorating the pinnacle of the Ten-no-ji Pagoda to be taken down and used to cast tea urns. In 1336, Sasaki Dōyo, known in Japanese as a *basara*, a person with a taste for extravagance and vulgarity, threw a big tea contest in Ōhara, which involved 100 different types of tea. Delicacies of all kinds were served, and fine incense, expensive silks and brocades, gold dust, armor and swords were wagered on the connoisseurship of the contestants, with the winner most often bestowing his prize to a favorite dancing girl or *dengaku* (ritual music and dance performed in shrines and temples) player. The wanton atmosphere of such contests prompted the newly established Ashikaga shogunate to bemoan: "People are addicted to the pleasures of loose women, they fall into gambling, and in addition at the tea contest gatherings and the *renga* assemblies they make enormous wagers whose size can hardly be measured."

Shōtetsu (1381–1459), a Zen monk and *waka* poet, described three typical tea-drinkers of the times:

> First is the "tea enthusiast"; this is one who, keeping his utensils in immaculate order, owns and savors to his heart's content a variety of pieces [of tea-making paraphernalia] – Kensan tea bowls, Temmoku tea bowls, tea kettles, fresh water jars, and so on.... Next is the "tea drinker." He has nothing in particular to say about utensils and from any will drink the ten bowls [in tea-identifying contests]. If it is tea from Uji he will drink it and declare, "It is from the third picking," "In season it is from after the first of the third month." ...Finally there is the "tea guzzler." Be it a mean grade of tea or a lofty one, if only it is called "tea" this man will drink it from a large bowl, consuming quantities without the slightest idea of whether it is good or bad.

In the second half of the 15th century, when the Ōnin and Bummei Wars (1467–80) ravaged the country and once again laid waste to Kyoto, the vogue for tea contests petered out. In 1474, the Ashikaga Shogun Yoshimasa abdicated in favor of his nine-year-old son and withdrew to the famous Higashiyama retreat on the outskirts of the city, where "he spent his days and nights throughout the four seasons in pleasurable diversions." In a simple, small building on the grounds named the Tōgudō, there was a Buddhist altar dedicated to the Bodhisattva of Compassion, as well as a small room of four-and-a-half tatami mats (made of thick, woven straw, about 3 by 6 feet each) known as the Dōjinsai – the country's first tearoom in the *shoin* ("reception room") *chanoyu* style. Other than the mats on the floor, all this modest room contained was an inset asymmetrical shelf called a *chigaidana*, and a low built-in *shoin* desk, both used to display Yoshimasa's beloved *karamano* ("things Chinese"): antiques, ceramics, paintings, and calligraphy.

In this room, out of a fusion between the austere monastic tea rituals, the profligate tea gatherings, and an inordinate passion for *karamano*, the *shoin chanoyu* was further developed by Yoshimasa's artistic and cultural advisors, known as *dōbōshū*. This Japanese passion for things Chinese is known as *karamano suki*, and a tea ceremony held in a simple, elegant room was the perfect opportunity to show one's most treasured possessions,

The host of chanoyu *gathering prepares bowls of tea for his four guests. The ceremony itself became ever more elaborate.*

culled from centuries of pilgrimages and trading ventures to China. The rules for decorating a room with *karamano* were laid down in the *Kundai-kan Sōchō ki* ("A Manner Book for the Assembly Hall"). The first part of this work lists and ranks the most famous Chinese painters of the Yuan and Song dynasties. The second part deals with the decoration of the *shoin* room, and its alcove, desk, and shelves, while the third part contains drawings of and explanations for pottery pieces, ceramics, and lacquerware. The book also discusses how to display flowers on or below the asymmetrical *chigaidana* shelves, and in vases hanging from pillars.

According to Japanese tea lore, Yoshimasa's tea master was Murata Shukō (1422–1502), who is credited with having returned tea to its humble roots and putting *chanoyu* on the path to its consummation. "It appears that from the innate flavor or taste of tea arose a sensitivity which pointed in the direction of the simple, the frugal, and the 'cool' as the most appropriate setting for drinking tea and, by extension, as the most fitting mode of life for the tea drinker," writes Theodore Ludwig, a modern American scholar of Japanese religious history, on Shukō's contribution to *chanoyu*. As a young student of Buddhism, Shukō was expelled from his temple in Nara for "conduct unbecoming a monk." At about the age of 30, he became a Zen priest at the Daitokuji Temple in Kyoto, but his restlessness, inability to follow orders, and tendency to fall asleep when meditating or reading the Buddhist scriptures continued to plague him. To find a remedy, he consulted a famous physician, pleading with him: "If you in the pharmacopoeias of Japan or China can find a medicine that cures sleepiness, please give it to me." The doctor lectured him on the theory of the five organs, told him that he had a weak heart and prescribed tea, which Shukō ordered from Toganoo. Thus cured, Shukō became a fervent tea devotee, read all the Chinese tea classics, and embarked on his study of *chanoyu*.

At Daitokuji, Shukō became a disciple of Ikkyū Sōjun, a rebel Zen master who attended important religious ceremonies wearing peasant clothes and straw sandals, attacked the powerful abbots as prostitutes for fame and fortune, wrote erotic poetry, and refused to accept or bestow *inka* – the formal certification of Zen enlightenment. Under the influence of Ikkyū, Shukō began to practice *chanoyu* in a simpler manner known as the *sōan* ("grass hut") style, juxtaposing precious Chinese objects with rustic Japanese wares and using a less elaborate form of service. Instead of boiling the water with a bronze brazier on a shelf of the *daisu*, he cut a square hearth in the floor, and instead of the traditional paintings with motifs from nature, he displayed a calligraphy scroll that Ikkyū had bestowed on him in lieu of a formal certificate of enlightenment.

According to a popular story, Ikkyū once made tea for Shukō, but when the disciple took the bowl to his mouth, Ikkyū knocked it out of Shukō's hand with his iron scepter. This upset Shukō, who sprang up from his seat. "Drink it up!" Ikkyū shouted. Realizing his master's intention, Shukō then replied: "Willows are green and flowers red." "Good," said Ikkyū, pleased at this enlightened response of his pupil, who had realized that the nature of reality cannot be changed any more than spilt tea can be drunk.

In his "Letter of the Heart," addressed to one of his disciples, Shukō emphasized the importance of dissolving the boundary line between Chinese and Japanese utensils. His esthetic, encapsulated by his aphorisms "the moon is not pleasing unless partly obscured by a cloud," and "a splendid horse looks good tied to a thatched hut," marked the beginning of a new trend towards things Japanese, *wamano*, the crude and imperfect. One of Shukō's disciples, the recluse Jūshiya Sōgo, took his master's esthetic one step further and developed an extreme simplicity and poverty that discarded all famous, refined tea utensils. And following in the footsteps of Sōgo was his disciple Takeno Jōō (1502–55), the son of a leather merchant in the bustling port town of Sakai who at an early age went to Kyoto, where he studied *renga* poetry under Sanetaka, Zen under Dairin Sōtō, and tea with Sōgo. Jōō's great contribution to the evolution of *chanoyu* lies in his introduction and formulation of two of its key esthetic precepts – *wabi* and *ichigō ichie*. Doctoral dissertations have been written on the idea of *wabi*, the original meaning of which was the feeling of despair and loneliness as experienced by an abandoned lover or an official exiled far from home. Gradually, however, the word *wabi*, turning on itself, was transformed into an esthetic affirmation of insufficiency that placed itself at the core of *chanoyu* and, some say, the spiritual identity of the Japanese people, a positive ideal beautifully captured in a poem by Teika that Jōō loved very much:

> As far as the eye can see,
> There are neither cherry blossoms
> Nor tinted maple leaves;
> Nothing but the thatched hut on the coast
> In the dusk of the autumn evening.

It is when the tea ceremony disciple has absorbed the spirit of *wabi* that he or she may begin to grasp Jōō's second key concept, *ichigō ichie*, which means "one time, one meeting." As a master of the collective art form of linked-verse *renga* poetry, Jōō stressed the creation of fellowship in the tea ceremony, and viewed every human encounter as a unique event that closes the chasm between life and art. Each gathering creates an ambience and feeling that has never existed before, and will vanish forever with the ceremony's conclusion, impossible to recall (except, perhaps, with the help of Proust's madeleine; see Chapter 18). The depth and art of this ambience is determined by the experience, philosophy, and wit of the gathering's host and guests, who at every turn must apply the whole of their humanity and tacitly commune to create this artwork of "one time, one meeting," rendered literally priceless by its impermanence.

With the foundation for the *chanoyu* ceremony laid by Murata Shukō and Takeno Jōō, its consummation was left to the Sakai merchant Sen Rikyū. As the tea master and close confidante of Toyotomi Hideyoshi, the unifier of Japan, Sen Rikyū was elevated to the highest echelons of political power, and every word he uttered on the way of tea became worth its weight in gold. Under Rikyū's creative auspices, *chanoyu* was perfected as an art form that fuses nature, the crafts, philosophy, and religion, lending poignant expression to the Japanese spirit. Yet the same hand that lifted Sen Rikyū to renown also cast him into the abyss, and never did the inscrutable master of tea evince more greatness than in his final moment.

8

SEN RIKYŪ
THE TEA MASTER

THE PERFECTION OF THE
JAPANESE TEA CEREMONY

Tea is nought but this,
First you make the water boil,
Then prepare the tea.
Then you drink it properly.
That is all you need to know.
Sen Rikyū

The 16th century was another momentous, tumultuous period in the history of Japan. On the battlefield, its political identity was being forged by the *daimyō* warlords of the main islands' numerous, virtually independent fiefs, who lay siege to each others' castles, torched each others' towns, and made off with each others' treasured tea utensils. It was a war for brute power; a labyrinthine conflict that left the defeated curled up in the cold mud, and the victorious to drown the dark memories of bloodshed with the beauty of their *meibutsu*, "famous, treasured objects."

In the midst of this intractable warfare, Sakai, just south of present-day Osaka, beamed like a lonely lighthouse of peace and prosperity. Ruled by a council of elders known as the *egōshū*, the town was able to hold the local *daimyō* at bay, and prohibited fighting within its limits, even as it grew richer by manufacturing arms and selling them to the warring parties. Monks, actors, and poets were drawn to this rare, orderly environment, where the arts and religion were allowed to flourish. As war raged all around them, the Sakai merchants patronized the Zen temples, accumulated splendid collections of Chinese antiques, and entertained each other with the new fashion for *chanoyu*, creating a room and ritual that could give full resonance to the remarkable idiosyncrasies of the Japanese mind.

Sen Rikyū (1522–91), the son of a Sakai fish merchant, was introduced to the town's thriving cultural life at a young age. His first teacher was the Sakai tea man Kitamuki Dochin, who instructed Rikyū in the elegant *shoin* style of tea, and who later commended Rikyū to Takeno Jōō with the words: "His tea does not look bad, and his conversation is

provocative." According to Japanese tea tradition, Rikyū arrived at his first tea gathering with Jōō dressed as a monk with a shaved head to show his devotion. Under Jōō's tutelage, Rikyū soon acquired a deep understanding of the "chilled and withered" *wabi* esthetic, as illustrated by this

Sen Rikyū, the greatest master of the Japanese tea ceremony.

popular anecdote: one day, Jōō asked Rikyū to sweep the *roji* – the garden around the tea hut. The *roji* had already been swept by Jōō, and when Rikyū came out, he found the yard the picture of perfection. Intuitively realizing the intention of his master, Rikyū shook one of the trees gently, causing a few leaves to fall to the ground. This, it is said, pleased Jōō greatly.

In 1544, Rikyū held his first recorded tea gathering for Matsuya Hisamasa, a Nara tea man, and Ejunbō, head priest of the Shōmoji Temple in Nara. As was the custom for all such tea parties, the utensils were carefully recorded: For this gathering, Rikyū used a simple *karamano* tea bowl of celadon porcelain, and a Segai incense burner. Ten years later, at a tea gathering held by Rikyū for Takeno Jōō seven month's before the master's death, the careful records kept in the diaries of the partici-pants reveal that Rikyū used a Korean tea bowl, a kettle with a pattern of clouds and dragons, a Hotei incense container, a Kinrinji tea caddy, and a water jug of Shigaraki earthenware, while in the alcove, he had hung a painting by Muqi (Mu-Ch'i), one of the greatest Zen monk-painters, with his own inscription.

The tea used by Rikyū and other tea men in their *chanoyu* gatherings came from the renowned gardens of Uji, just south of Kyoto, described by the Jesuit monk João Rodrigues in his *This Island of Japan*, an account of the country in the 16th century. There, from February until the new leaves began to bud at the end of March, the tea bushes were protected from frost with mats of rice straw or thatch. After the new leaves had been picked, they were steamed in a solution of water, wine, and other ingredients until soft, then roasted on cane grills overlaid with a special thick paper above boxes containing ash-covered charcoal that produced a slow, gentle fire. Using their bare hands, three people on each side of the stove moved the leaves to roast them evenly, until they became curled up like a hawk's claw. The finished tea was then graded into five qualities. The finest tea did not even have a name, but was simply called *shirabukuro* after the small white paper bags in which it was packed. Following this grade was *goku*, which cost six silver taels per catty; *betsugi*, four silver taels; *goku sosori*, two taels; and, *betsugi sosori*, one tael.

According to Rodrigues' information, in the 16th century Uji produced some 40,000 lb of first-class tea per year, and this was sold to nobles, wealthy merchants, and tea men from all over Japan, who every year sent their own caddies to the town to be filled with "the new season's tea." This tea was not, however, consumed directly, but instead transported in the protective caddies to monasteries high up in mountains famous for their coolness, and kept by the monks "so that the *cha* may be safely preserved there from all harm during the hottest days of the summer and not lose its green color." Then in the 10th month, the owners sent for their caddies and held a special tea ceremony called *kuchi-kiri* ("firstlings") on the day the caddy was first opened.

On 1 March, 1565, Sen Rikyū made his entry into the highest echelons of Japanese society, when the warlord Matsunaga Hisahide, master of the Tamonzan Castle in Nara, invited him to a prestigious tea gathering, with tea from Uji's famous Mori fields and water from the equally renowned area of the Uji Bridge. Hisahide even displayed his prized caddy, the eggplant-shaped *Tsukumonasu*, one of the most legendary utensils in Japanese tea history. The fame of the *Tsukumonasu* was so great that three years later, when Hisahide submitted to Oda Nobunaga, the rising warlord of Owari province, Nobunaga confiscated the beloved caddy. In the same campaign, Nobunaga also imposed a heavy war tax of 20,000 *kan* on the town of Sakai and forced it to surrender a number of its most precious *meibutsu* pieces. João Rodrigues remarked on the extraordinary Japanese passion for these tea utensils:

> In keeping with their naturally melancholy disposition and character and also with the purpose for which they collect these things, the Japanese find such mysteries in these *cha* utensils that they attribute to them, as well as to their ancient swords and daggers, the value and esteem which other people place in precious stones, pearls and old medallions.... Thus there are utensils, albeit of earthenware, which come to be worth ten, twenty or thirty thousand *cruzados* or even more – something which will appear as madness and barbarity to other nations that come to hear of it.

The first undisputed *chanoyu* meeting between Rikyū and Nobunaga took place in the third month of 1574. Rikyū soon became drawn into the country's political and military affairs (on the side of Nobunaga), and in the fall of 1575, Nobunaga sent a note thanking him for a gift of 1,000 musket balls. Surrounding himself with tea masters such as Rikyū, Nobunaga skillfully used *chanoyu seidō* ("tea ceremony politics") to make alliances, establish his claim to power, and celebrate military victories, expressly prohibiting all except his most loyal vassals from practicing the ceremony.

Chanoyu and Flowers, an 18th-century painting by Torii Kiyohiro.

But while Rikyū supported Nobunaga and served tea at his large, sumptuous tea gatherings, the style of Rikyū's tea in more intimate, private settings was growing increasingly *wabi*. The *Nampōroku*, a compendium of Rikyū's tea philosophy recorded by his disciple Nambō Sōkei, explains:

> *Chanoyu* of the small room is above all a matter of performing practice and attaining realization in accord with the Buddhist path. To delight in the refined splendor of a dwelling or taste the delicacies belongs to the worldly life. There is shelter enough when the roof does not leak, food enough when it staves off hunger. This is the Buddhist teaching and the fundamental meaning of *chanoyu*. We draw water, gather firewood, boil the water, and make tea. We then offer it to the Buddha, serve it to others, and drink ourselves. We arrange flowers and burn incense. In all of this, we model ourselves after the acts of the Buddha and the past masters. Beyond this, you must come to your own understanding.

By 1582, Nobunaga had conquered the main Japanese island of Honshu, broken the powerful legionnaire armies of the Buddhist temples, and stood on the cusp of unifying Japan. Having subdued the recalcitrant Takano clan, he returned to the Honnōji Temple in Kyoto, and was entertaining court nobles there when, on the morning of 10 July, he awoke to find the temple grounds surrounded by the troops of Akechi Mitsuhide, a disgruntled general who in the ensuing fight promptly ended Nobunaga's life. A few days later, Mitsuhide was in turn killed in the battle of Yamazaki by Toyotomi Hideyoshi, the son of a peasant who had started out as Nobunaga's sandal-bearer, risen through the ranks to become his most powerful general, been granted the right to serve tea after his conquest of the Bessho clan in 1578, and who now succeeded the slain leader.

"Impossible to forget in this life or the next is the permission to practice the tea ceremony," wrote Hideyoshi, who inherited Nobunaga's fabulous collection of *meibutsu,* and adopted his use of lavish, ostentatious *chanoyu* gatherings as an important political tool. At the same time, his rustic origins drew him to the "chill and withered" *wabi* ceremony evolved by Rikyū, who became Hideyoshi's tea master, retained with a salary of 3,000 *koku* (bushels) of rice. Rikyū accompanied Hideyoshi on his military campaigns, conducted tea gatherings in the lull between battles, gave advice on military affairs, and became privy to top-secret information. At Yamazaki, Rikyū designed a famous two-mat Taian *wabi* tea hut overlooking the Yodo river, which was one of Hideyoshi's favorite tearooms and is now a national treasure. It was during these years under Hideyoshi's patronage that Rikyū, living between the conflicting forces and demands of the political tea gatherings that paid his salary and his personal preference for quiet, contemplative tea, consummated his *chanoyu* art, profoundly influencing the future direction of Japanese culture.

In the *chanoyu* established by Rikyū and practiced with variations to this day, there is a difference between the winter ceremony, known as *Rō,* in which a hearth (*rō*) is positioned in a space cut out in the middle of the room, and the summer ceremony, called *Furō,* where a portable brazier (*furō*) is positioned in a corner of the room to reduce any discomfort from the heat, and placed on a tray, board, or special type of square tile to protect the straw mat. "In summer, impart a sense of deep coolness, in winter, a feeling of warmth; lay the charcoal so that it heats the water, prepare the tea so that it is pleasing – these are all the secrets," Rikyū instructed his disciples.

The ceremony is always given in honor of a *first guest*, who, in a four-and-a-half mat room, may be accompanied by at most three other guests, of which the *last guest* also plays an important role and must be well-versed in the etiquette of *chanoyu*. After the invitations have been issued and accepted, the guests gather at the designated time in a pavilion outside the tearoom's *roji*, and when all are present they inform the host by rapping on a board. Before greeting his guests, the host fills the water-basin and sprinkles some water onto the bushes and plants in the *roji*, then welcomes his guests with deep bows but no words.

After this, he returns to the tearoom, while the guests, treading the carefully chosen and positioned stepping-stones, proceed to the water-basin, clean themselves, remove their swords and sandals, and then enter the tearoom by crawling through the *nijiriguchi* entranceway, the small opening that, by forcing the guests to literally crawl on hands and knees, forms a ritual passage from the mundane world to the utopian realm of the *chanoyu*. According to the *Chadō Shisō Denshō* ("Transmission of the Thought of the Way of Tea" – a modern book), Rikyū got the idea for the *nijiriguchi* from watching fishermen in Osaka crawl in and out of their boat cabins, but he may also have been inspired by the minuscule doors to traditional Japanese theaters, mere apertures known as "mouse wickets," which separated the ordinary from the extraordinary in the manner of the rabbit's hole in *Alice in Wonderland*. But other scholars contend that Rikyū simply moved the *nijiriguchi* entrance from the gate to the *roji* (where it had been in evidence as early as 1462), to the tearoom itself.

The first obligation of the *first guest* is to view and contemplate the carefully chosen calligraphy scroll, considered by Rikyū as the room's most important object, which has been hung in the *tokonoma* ("alcove"). Having entered the room, the *last guest* must shut the *nijiriguchi's* sliding door with a concise thud that symbolically shuts out the world and encloses the gathering. A polite conversation ensues, and is ended by the host with the words: "The fire is going out. I shall get some charcoal to relight it." After a

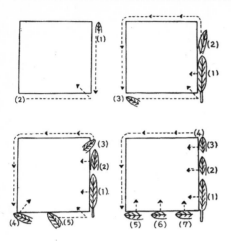

The Japanese tea ceremony is governed by some 1,000 variations of temae ("rules of body movement"), including the intricate ways in which the hearth can be brushed.

charcoal and incense ceremony, the *shozumi*, the host serves a meal, *kaiseki*, consisting of a soup and two or three dishes, served with sake and concluded with a mixed dish of the leftovers from the preparation, to express the gathering's spirit of frugality. Before returning the bowls and dishes to the host, the guests must clean them with a soft piece of paper they have brought, and place fish bones and other remains in a small box that they hide in a pocket in their long sleeves.

Then there is a pause in the ceremony, during which the guests are free to enjoy the *roji*, make use of the real toilet, *kafuku setchin*, and inspect its ornamental counterpart, the *kazari setchin*, while the host prepares the most important part of the *chanoyu*, the *koicha* ("thick tea"), and exchanges the calligraphy in the alcove for an arrangement of one or two flowers in a vase. (In evening ceremonies, however, the order of scroll followed by flower arrangement is reversed, as Rikyū did not like to use flowers at night, finding their colors hard to discern and their shadows ominous.) "When the water in the kettle produces the sound of wind rustling in the pines, the gong is struck. To be at variance with the proper conditions of the boiling water and the burning charcoal is a consequential failing," is how Rikyū explained the correct moment to summon the guests to *koicha*.

The artless earthenware raku *bowl embodies the philosophical and esthetic concept of* wabi – *chill and withered – which lies at the heart of* chanoyu.

A skilled practitioner of *chanoyu* listens carefully to the gong, for by the manner in which it is beaten, he can know along which path through the garden the host wishes them to return.

"When you handle any utensil take it up lightly but put it down heavily," said Rikyū. Having cleaned and arranged the *raku* teacup, whisk, teaspoon, tea caddy and water-ladle, the host opens the tea caddy and uses the tea-spoon to place the prescribed amount of tea powder into the *raku* bowl. Before Rikyū, the most popular tea bowls in the *chanoyu* had been Chinese *Tenmoku* ("Heaven's Eye," including the so-called "hare's fur" cups, see pp. 63–64) bowls, and celadon bowls. But Rikyū preferred rustic Korean ware, and rough, indigenous *raku* bowls, made by the potter Chōjirō, which have wide bottoms that allow ample room for tea whisks, hold heat well with their thick walls, and are pleasing to the touch. "This sense of touch is highly developed among devotees of *Chanoyu*, and they obtain very great satisfaction from the mere feel of the Tea-utensils. ... Then also the taste of tea from Raku bowls far surpasses that of the same liquor drunk from the celadons of China and Korea. And when connoisseurs wished to judge of the quality of water for making tea, it was the Raku Cha-wan they used to taste it," wrote Arthur Sadler in his 1934 book *Cha-No-Yu*.

The host then takes the ladle and pours some boiling water from the kettle into the cup, whisks the tea, pours in more boiling water, then whisks the tea into a froth and places the cup to the right of the hearth. The *first guest* crawls over to retrieve the cup, returns to his position, raises the cup to his forehead in thanks and then swallows a mouthful of tea.

"Is the tea to your taste? Don't you find it too strong or too weak?" the host asks the *first guest,* who replies:

"It is just right. You know how to blend tea and water well."

The *first guest* drinks another two-and-a-half mouthfuls, wipes the cup and hands it to the *second guest* to repeat the process. After the *last guest* has finished the tea, the cup and its dregs are inspected in turn by the guests, who are also allowed to appreciate the "three treasures": the tea caddy, its silk-brocade bag and the teaspoon. When the *chanoyu* is concluded with *koicha*, it is known as a formal tea ceremony. But if *koicha* is followed by a second incense and charcoal ceremony, the *gosumi*, and the serving of thin tea, *usucha,* it is called an informal *chanoyu*. In modern practice, *koicha* is almost always followed by *usucha; gosumi* may be omitted (in what is called *tsuzukiusu*). In the *gosumi*, two balls of incense and a large lump of cherry-tree charcoal are placed in the fire. As the guests admire the incense box, fresh water is poured into the kettle. "The water is beginning to boil. Before I made thick tea for you, now I would like to make thin tea," says the host, and commences the final *usucha* tea ceremony. In this ceremony, two or more cups may be used. When the tea has been prepared and drunk, and the cups returned to the host, the *first guest* says:

"Please finish now."

"Would you like some warm water," asks the host.

"No thank you."

"Yes, let us finish then," says the host, carries out all the utensils, fills the *mizusashi* water jar with cold water, and closes the door behind him.

The distinction between the formal and the informal ceremony is a fine matter, which even expert tea masters struggle to grasp. "In the making of *koicha* there is an element of the especially informal, in the making of *usucha* there is an element of the extremely formal. Be well aware of these distinctions. There is variation according to time and place. This may seem a simple matter, but is a critical secret of *chanoyu*," said Rikyū, good advice that he apparently forgot to transmit to his disciple Yamanoue Sōji, who according to tea lore had his nose cut off and was exiled by Hideyoshi for failing to understand the difference between the formal and informal tea ceremony.

At the beginning of December, 1585, Hideyoshi hosted a tea ceremony for the Ōgimachi emperor, who wielded little influence outside the palace walls, in order to strengthen relations between the court and his own regime (the house of Paulownia), thank the emperor for his accession to *kampuku* ("regent"), and to curry the conferral of the surname Toyotomi. After Hideyoshi had prepared and served tea to the emperor, who had never before attended a formal *chanoyu*, Sen Rikyū, in the capacity of Hideyoshi's tea master, prepared tea in a corner of the room for the imperial courtiers. The occasion firmly established Sen Rikyū's position as the greatest master of tea in Japan, as well as his role as Hideyoshi's closest advisor and confidant. Then, in March the following year, Hideyoshi took the bold step of constructing a three-mat tearoom entirely of gold and transporting it from Osaka Castle to the imperial palace, where this *ōgon chashitsu* ("golden tearoom"), was used by Hideyoshi to serve the emperor tea a second time. Although the records of this historic gathering make no mention of Rikyū, as Hideyoshi's tea master he undoubtedly played a key role in planning the golden tearoom – the absolute counterpoint to the "chill and withered" *wabi* tea hut that was his greatest artistic achievement.

On 12 June, 1587, Hideyoshi launched his final, successful campaign to subjugate the southern island of Kyushu, and in the fall that year, convened the great Kitano tea gathering in Kyoto to celebrate his victory. As the gathering's main attraction, Hideyoshi announced that all of his famous *meibutsu* tea utensils would be put on display, and that the meeting was to take place for a period of ten days in order to allow people from distant parts of the country to view the treasures. On the day of the great gathering, 550 tea masters from all over Japan presented their art, and Hideyoshi himself served tea to his special guests. After this, he went for a walk to inspect the gathering, and came to a place where an eccentric tea master by the name of Sakamotoya Hechigan had set up a great red umbrella 9 feet across mounted on a 7-foot stick. Around this stick, he had placed a reed mat in such a way that made it reflect and diffuse the color of the umbrella all around, and it is said that Hechigan's contraption so pleased Hideyoshi that he remitted the master's taxes in reward.

In 1590, Hideyoshi set forth to finish his mission of unifying Japan by attacking the last bastion of resistance to his rule, the Hōjō clan of Odawara on Sagami Bay, 50 miles southwest of present-day Tokyo. During Hideyoshi's siege of the Hōjō's castle, his camp served as a pleasure ground for tea masters, artists, and courtesans, who composed *renga* poetry, played games of *monoawase*, and held *chanoyu* gatherings. According to tea lore, it was here that Rikyū made three famous *meibutsu* bamboo vases. As the story goes, Hōjō sent Hideyoshi a present of three pieces of bamboo in return for the three bales of rice which Hideyoshi had sent to Hōjō's castle as a joke. Of these three pieces, Rikyū fashioned a single vase, a two-storied vase, and a flute-shaped vase. The first and most famous was named Enjōji, since, like the bell of that temple, it had a crack. The third, flute-shaped vase, named Shakuhachi after the instrument, was handed down from generation to generation and then sold at an auction in 1918 for £8,600, the equivalent of £287,885 in today's money (rather missing the point of the concept of *wabi*).

Already in January, 1590, a wooden statue of Rikyū had been erected on top of

Sen Rikyū's way of tea was challenged by the monk Baisaō, above, who introduced sencha *to Japan (see box overleaf).*

the gate of the Daitokuji Temple in Kyoto in gratitude for a contribution by him, which must have angered Hideyoshi, as he was forced to walk under the statue every time he entered the prominent temple. Then, in February, 1591, Hideyoshi suddenly issued a sentence condemning Rikyū to death by crucifixion. Several inconclusive theories for the capital punishment have been put forth, such as a power struggle in Hideyoshi's court, that Rikyū had created confusion in the ceramics market by calling "new pieces old and old pieces new," that he had converted to Christianity, irreconcilable differences between Hideyoshi and Rikyū on *chanoyu*, that Rikyū had refused to allow his widowed daughter to become Hideyoshi's concubine, or the simple caprice of a dictator. In all events, what matters for the purposes of history is the courageous poise Rikyū demonstrated in meeting his end.

On 25 February a violent thunderstorm struck Kyoto and pummeled the capital with half-inch hailstones. Outside Rikyū's villa, 3,000 soldiers stood guard, as the master of the house, his crucifixion commuted by Hideyoshi to the more honorable *seppuku*, suicide by disembowelment, prepared to slice out his own entrails. After arranging flowers and holding a final tea ceremony for his disciples, Rikyu gave some of his tea utensils away to his pupils, and then composed two death poems, the first in Chinese:

> Seventy years of life —
> Ha ha! and what a fuss!
> With this sacred sword of mine,
> Both Buddhas and Patriarchs I kill!

and the second in Japanese:

> Now my girded sword,
> That upon my armed side
> Hitherto I've worn
> Draw I forth, and brandishing
> Fling it in the face of heaven

THE OTHER JAPANESE TEA CEREMONY

First imported into Japan in the late 16th century, *sencha* ("boiled tea") evolved as an alternative tradition to the increasingly fragmented and constricted *chanoyu* ceremony. The first *sencha* master was the "Old Tea Peddler," Baisaō (1675–1763), an eccentric Zen monk who, in around 1735, began serving *sencha* in Kyoto. Moving his utensils between the city's many famous scenic spots in a bamboo basket named *senka* ("den of the sages"), Baisaō espoused a new, free and easy way of tea, which he prepared simply by throwing a handful of leaves into a teapot with boiling water, and which was renowned for its exquisite aroma and sweetness. Impoverished yet content, clad in his trademark Daoist garb, Baisaō never charged a fixed fee for his tea, but merely asked his customers to drop whatever coins they could spare into a special bamboo tube. As his renown spread, he came to symbolize the possibility of freedom and individuality in a society evermore obsessed with hierarchical distinction and material possession. Shortly before his death in 1763, Baisaō, in defiance of the *chanoyu* tradition, threw his own tea utensils into a fire to avert the creation of another stultifying cult.

Baisaō and other devotees of *sencha* drew their inspiration from the ancient Chinese sages, who, caring little for the rewards and comforts of social intercourse, withdrew to their mountain hermitages in order to focus on the true pleasures of life: the simple contemplation of nature; the company of a few close friends; painting, calligraphy, and music; and making tea with sparkling fresh spring water. If *wabi* lies at the heart of *chanoyu*, the pivotal concept of *sencha* is *fūryū*, a term derived from the Chinese *fengliu*, which literally means "wind current," and embodies a sense of perfect existential freedom and nobility of spirit.

It was not long after Baisaō's death, however, that the deep-seated Japanese yearning for lineage, codified rituals, and a virtually religious veneration of objects went to work on *sencha*, as his disciple Kimura Kenkadō produced a detailed, illustrated record of the master's utensils, thereby laying the foundation for a *sencha* cult that has persisted to this day, replete with its own etiquette, rules, esthetic, and pantheon of treasured utensils, such as the 17th-century Ming stoneware teapot known as *Gikōkan*. But in contrast to *chanoyu*, which is often said to be about everything except the tea itself, the focus of the *sencha* cult lies more squarely on the tea – its cultivation and processing, the selection of water, and the manner of its preparation.

Indeed, the emerging *sencha* tradition greatly spurred the development of Japan's indigenous tea industry. In the middle of the 19th century, Yamamoto Tokujun, the 6th generation head of the famous Yamamotoyama tea shop (founded in 1690), asked the *sencha* tea growers of Uji to, in the same manner as for *matcha*, shade their tea plants during the last couple of months before picking to protect them against both frost and excessive sunlight, which reduced the finished tea's tannin while increasing its caffeine content. He also pioneered a new way of drying the steamed leaves in order to preserve their bright green color and increase their sweetness. Tokojun's new tea became known as *gyokuro* ("jade dew") and to this day, it remains one of the world's finest and most expensive teas.

Ueda Akinari, a prominent writer and poet in 18th-century Japan, brews sencha *in this portrait by Matsumura Goshun.*

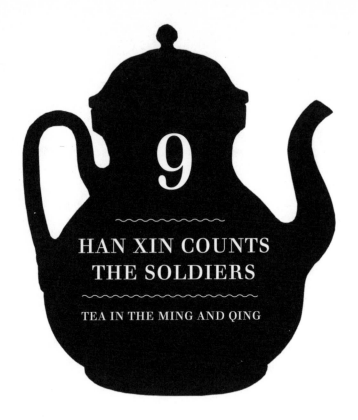

9

HAN XIN COUNTS THE SOLDIERS

TEA IN THE MING AND QING

Just as *chanoyu* harks back to the Song custom of whisking tea, *sencha* traces it roots to China and the early Ming, when the Hongwu emperor issued his prohibition of milled wax tea. By that time, loose-leaf green tea had become the common type in the empire. This, in turn, spurred a new method of firing – the heating of the freshly picked leaves and buds to a high temperature to stop all enzymatic processes and preserve the tea's freshness, stimulating properties, and taste. Instead of the age-old custom of steaming the leaves, the monks on Songluo Mountain in Anhui province discovered that stir-roasting them in a dry hot wok improved the color, fragrance, and flavor of the finished tea. "This is the Songluo [Singlo] method. When roasting the leaves, one person must stand on the side and fan them to dispel the hot air. Otherwise, according to my personal experience, they will become yellow, and the fragrance and flavor will both be diminished. Leaves that are fanned become green. Those that are not fanned become yellow," wrote Wen Long in his *Tea Commentary* from around 1630.

The new trend of infusing loose-leaf tea also gave rise to the utensil that has come to embody the human cult of the *Camellia sinensis* plant – the teapot. Ever since the Ming, the most famous Chinese teapots have been made with a porous clay known as *zisha*, purple sand, found in Yixing just west of Lake Tai. Yixing teapots are prized for their ability to retain heat, store the aroma from every infusion, and maintain the freshness of the tea leaves during lengthy tea parties. Lovingly nursed by connoisseurs,

In 1391, the Hongwu emperor of the Ming prohibited the production of wax tea for "overtaxing the people's strength."

they grow more lustrous and beautiful with age. The most renowned Yixing teapotter was Gong Chun, a scholar's servant during the mid-16th century who in his spare time liked to help the monks of Yixing's Golden Sand Temple turn teapots. According to legend, Gong Chun once fashioned a teapot – in imitation of a gnarly tree on the temple grounds – so enticing that the old monks decided to transmit all their secrets and do everything to help him become a master teapot turner. Today, the National History Museum in Beijing holds the last remaining Yixing teapot attributed to Gong Chun, a "tree goiter" pot with a missing lid, although the pot's authenticity has been called into question.

From these pots, the tea was poured into the cups of the famous blue and white porcelain from the imperial Jingdezhen kilns in Jiangxi province. After the celadon ware from the Yue kilns of Zhejiang province, the alabaster white ware of the Xing kilns in Hebei, and the black ware from the Fujianese Jian kilns, the Jingdezhen kilns had emerged during the Yuan dynasty as China's foremost producer of ceramics. Many historians of the craft consider the wares produced in Jingdezhen during this period to be the first true porcelain. One of the secrets to the beauty of Jingdezhen porcelain lay in the fine white clay found in the nearby village of Gaoling, after which the clay was named kaolin. During the Yuan dynasty, the potters of Jingdezhen managed to raise the temperature of their kilns to about 1,285 °C (2,350 °F), which allowed the binding agent petuntse, a crystalline material, to melt and completely fuse with the heat-resistant kaolin clay. They also began using a cobalt blue pigment from Persia, which was able to withstand the high temperatures required. After the ware had been potted, it was decorated with the cobalt pigment, painted with the glaze, and fired. The process was perfected during the imperial reigns of Yongle (r. 1403–24) and Xuande (1426–35), when Jingdezhen's potters produced a blue and white porcelain possessing a delicate, translucent body and a velvet sheen that many experts consider unsurpassed.

It was during this period that the eunuch Muslim admiral Zheng He undertook seven maritime expeditions westward, venturing as far as the coast of East Africa. From these voyages, he returned with countless treasures and novelties, and a cobalt pigment known as *sulimānī*, which yielded an exquisite, flowing blue color reminiscent of Chinese ink. The translator Ma Huan, who accompanied Zheng He on three of the voyages, recorded his observations in the work *Overall Survey of the Ocean's Shores*. Describing Bang-ge-la, or Bengal, Ma wrote that "the rice and grain ripen twice in a year. The husked and unhusked rice is slender and long.... For wines, they have three or four varieties.... Tea is not sold in the market, and men use areca [betel] nut for entertaining people." Then, in 1433, just as Zheng He was on the cusp of rounding Cape Horn, the conservative Confucians in the Ming court, petrified lest any newfangled foreign ideas pull aside the curtain of their obsolete, rote learning, succeeded in persuading the emperor to halt any further expeditions. Zheng He's "treasure fleet" was destroyed, China's maritime exploration brought to an end, and the country's gates closed shut. As one consequence of this, the supply of *sulimānī* dried up, leaving the Jingdezhen potters to make do with an inferior domestic pigment known as "even blue."

As for the production of tea, with the demise of the Northern Park's wax tea, the center of Fujian's tea industry was shifted further to the west, to the fabled Wuyi Mountains in the province's northwestern corner. "Of all the mountains of Fujian, those of Wuyi are the finest, and its water the best. They are awfully high and rugged, surrounded by water, and seem as if excavated by spirits; nothing more wonderful can be seen," states a description in one of the Chinese annals. In the 16th century, the monks from Songluo were brought to Wuyi to teach their new method of processing the tea leaves. Some were still not satisfied: according to the Ming scholar Zhang Dafu, Songluo tea had "character but no taste." But in the yearly harvesting and making of tea, through decades of observations, accidents, trials, and errors, the tea-making monks of the Wuyi Mountains learned that if the tea leaves were allowed to wither in the sun for some time, and then slightly bruised through pressing, rubbing, tossing, and tumbling, they turned rust-brown along the edges and began to emit a wonderful fragrance that could be preserved by firing the leaves at the most propitious moment. This was the origin of the semi-oxidized Oolong ("black dragon") tea, the precursor to the more robust Black tea, in which the process of enzymatic oxidation is allowed to run its full course.

The most famous Oolong teas from Wuyi, known as "rock teas," were Dahongpao ("Big Red Robe"), Tieluohan ("Iron Arhat"), Baijiguan ("White Cockscomb"), and Shuijingui ("Water Gold Turtle"), each made from a few special tea bushes that grew hidden in crevices and ravines among the mountains. According to one legend, Dahongpao was prepared from three bushes that grew in the "Nine Dragon Nest" near the "Heaven's Heart Cliff," which was so inaccessible that monkeys were employed to harvest the leaves. "After the tea is picked, it is spread out and tossed. When the fragrance is emitted, it is roasted. This must be done neither too early nor too late. Upon roasting and curing, the tea is sorted again, and old leaves, twigs, and stems removed, making the tea uniform. Then it is cured to enhance its

Tea processing in the Ming: (a) slanted rack for withering freshly picked leaves on bamboo trays in the sun; (b) rattan implement for moving trays; (c) rack used to wither the leaves after they have been removed from the sun; (d) firing pans; (e) leaf-rolling technique; (f) the final drying basket.

flavor," the Qing scholar Wang Caotang wrote in his *Tea Talk*, providing the first description of the Oolong tea-making process.

While the best green tea is made with young, tender leaves, the leaves used for Oolong tea should be relatively mature, as these contain larger amounts of the compounds – catechins, carotenoids, chlorophyll, starch, sugar, and pectin – that form the raw material of Oolong tea's rich aromatic substances. When freshly picked leaves are laid out to wither in the sun, their moisture begins to evaporate and the permeability of the cell membranes within the leaves increases, allowing previously separated compounds to come into contact with each other and initiate the oxidation of the catechins and other chemical reactions crucial to making Oolong tea. The leaves are considered properly withered when they have lost their luster, feel soft to the touch, and their surface is crinkled. At this point, they are taken indoors, spread out on large, round bamboo trays, and left to "cool wither."

Now begins the key process in making Oolong tea. The trays are moved into a warm, humid, enclosed room that, in the modern age, is equipped with a "tumbler," a large, cylindrical contraption used to gently bruise the leaves and abet the various chemical processes. Dahongpao, for example, still made today, is tumbled seven times, with a fixed number of rotations each time. Between these tumblings, the leaves are piled onto bamboo trays which are placed on racks in the room and left to gently oxidize. Now and then, the tea-maker will plunge his nose into the pile of leaves to determine if they are ready to be tumbled again. After the final tumbling, known as the "big wave," the leaves are heaped thickly on the bamboo trays and left for a few hours, until the optimal aroma has been conjured forth. At this time, the leaves are promptly fired in pans, first at a high temperature, then at a lower one, until the tea's "grassy odor" has been completely dispelled and its fragrance fully expressed. Then the leaves are rolled, cured, packed, and then shipped as *maocha* ("raw tea") to the tea merchants, who then cure the tea again according to their own requirements and secret recipes to produce the finished tea.

With Oolong tea, a special tea ceremony known as *gongfu cha* ("labor/skill tea") evolved in the city of Chaozhou in northern Guangdong province. "The cups are small as walnuts, the pot as small as a fragrant lemon. No more than one *liang* (ounce) is poured at a time. Holding the cup to the mouth, you must not swallow in haste, but first smell its fragrance, and then taste and contemplate it. The delicate aroma strikes the nose, and there is a sweetness that lingers on the tongue. After one cup, you drink a second, and a third. It frees people from restlessness and pacifies arrogance," is how the Qing literatus Yuan Mei described the partaking of the complex *gongfu cha*. For genuine *gongfu cha,* the water must be taken from mountain streams, and olive pits used as fuel for the fire. The tea tray, pot, and cups are all doused with hot water in the manner of a libation, and the tea leaves separated according to their size, with the broken leaves placed at the bottom of the teapot, followed by the whole leaves, in order to prevent the smaller pieces from clogging the spout. When the water has been brought to a boil, it is carefully poured into the pot along the rim of the opening to wash the leaves, and immediately poured out. The pot is filled again, its lid put in place, and the pot doused with hot water until the water in the tea tray has risen to immerse half of the pot. Having placed the small cups on the tray touching each other, the tea is poured into the cups with an anti-clockwise, circular motion called *Gongguan xun cheng* ("Gongguan walks around the city wall," a reference to the famous Han-dynasty general Guan Di, who, with a face as red as a Yixing teapot, used personally to patrol the wall of the city he was defending). And when making sure that every last drop has been extracted, the learned tea master may also say *Hanxin dian bing* ("Han Xin counts the soldiers") while gently shaking the pot, in memory of the military strategist Han Xin, who invented an ingenious way of counting the number of soldiers in any given formation.

When European merchants arrived in the Chinese ports of Canton and Amoy in the first half of the 17th century (see Chapter 13), they were offered green tea from Songluo, and tea from Wuyi, which (in accordance with the Fujianese pronunciation of the two Chinese characters used to write the name Wuyi) became known in English as Bohea, and which may have been semi-oxidized Oolong, or fully oxidized black tea. Initially, Bohea was used by the British as a generic term for all dark, oxidized teas, but later it became the name for low grade black tea. Samuel Ball, the English East India Company's tea inspector, described this tea in his *An Account of the Cultivation and Manufacture of Tea in China*:

> It was formerly brought from the Bohea country in baskets, in an unma-nipulated state, to be roasted and packed at Canton. On its arrival, some had a heated sour smell; some a musty, and others a saponaceous smell: so that all this had, I imagine, undergone a partial, if not complete, fer-mentation [oxidation].

At all events, as tea caught on in the West, the European palate gradually settled for the fuller, more robust taste of black tea, thereby pushing the Chinese tea-makers toward letting the oxidation run its full course, until the whole leaf had turned rust-brown. This, according to one theory at least, is how Congou (*gongfu*), and Souchong (*xiaozhong* ("small category")), originally simply the names of teas from Wuyi, were transformed into the two most common types of black tea sold in Europe. Meanwhile, the finest black tea imported to England was given the name Pekoe, from the Chinese *bai hao* ("white hair") which merely denotes the white down found on the youngest, finest buds and leaves of the tea bush, and has nothing to do with the manufacturing process. Later, in the tea industries of India and Ceylon, Pekoe became the basic term in an elaborate grading system for black tea.

With their precise origins lost in unrecorded darkness, a number of rare teas other than Oolong became more widely known during the Ming and Qing. White tea was produced simply by drying the most tender, downy white buds and leaves in the sun. The Song emperor Hui Zong stated that genuine white tea could only be picked in the wild, and considered it to be the finest, a sentiment echoed by the Ming tsiologist Tian Yiheng, who wrote: "Tea processed over a fire is inferior, that dried in the sun superior. It is closer to nature, and separated from the vapors of fire and smoke." White teas are produced in Fujian province, where the three most famous types are *yinzhen baihao* ("silver needle white hair"), first produced in Fuding county

During the Ming dynasty, desiccating the tea in a hot wok became the preferred method of firing, as it improved the tea's fragrance, color, and shelf-life.

and exported to Europe in the 19th century as "Silver Tip Pekoe," *bai mudan* ("white peony"), and *gongmei* ("tribute eyebrow"). To make *yinzhen baihao*, only the downy buds of the first flush are used. The buds are spread out in single layers on bamboo trays and left to dry in the sun, with great care taken not to bruise the buds and thereby initiate any unwanted oxidation. When they have lost 80–90 percent of their water content, they are further dried over a fire with the heat precisely regulated at 30–40 degrees Celsius, for if the fire is too hot and the buds are spread too thickly, they will have a burnt red hue, and if the fire is too slow, the tea may easily turn black.

The accidental discovery of yellow tea was described by another tea master of the Ming, Xu Cishu, who excoriated the people of Gubi Mountain for their carelessness in processing tea: "They simply pile up firewood under their regular cooking pan and roast it in that. Before the tea leaves are taken out of the pan, they are already scorched and parched. Immediately, they pack the still hot tea leaves into a large container made of bamboo. Although there may still be some green twigs and purple shoots, they soon wither and turn yellow. Such tea is only suitable for inferior consumption. How could it be fit to enter in tea-tastings and competitions?" As with green tea, yellow tea, made from both tender and older leaves, is immediately fired in a wok at a high temperature without prior wilting. The subsequent, key process in making yellow tea is known as *men huang* ("sealed yellowing"). To make the most renowned yellow tea, *junshan yinzhen* ("Jun Mountain Silver Needle"), which comes from a small island in Lake Dongting in Hunan province, the leaves are fired, cooled, dried, then divided into 3-lb parcels, wrapped in brown packing paper, and left to ferment in boxes for 40–48 hours, upon which the leaves are dried and cooled a second time, placed in the packing paper and boxes for another 20 hours, dried one last time, and finally, having turned a deep yellow color, packaged in wrapping paper and packed in plaster-lined boxes.

According to legend, one of the finest green teas, *biluochun* ("green snail spring"), was given its name by the Kangxi emperor of the Qing (r. 1662–1723), who was served this tea during a tour of southern China in 1699. *Biluochun* is cultivated on a small island in Lake Tai, near the city of

Suzhou, where the tea bushes have been planted among orchards of peach, plum, almond, persimmon, tangerine, gingko, and pomegranate trees, each of which is said to lend its pollen and aroma to the tea leaves. Some 70,000 buds and leaves are required to produce one pound of top-grade *biluochun*, which is infused in water not hotter than 80 °C (175 °F), and drunk in clear glasses to enjoy the delicate, dancing leaves. Kangxi was also fond of milk tea, as can be seen from the "Banquet of a Thousand Elders" held to celebrate his 60th birthday in 1713, at which the 1,800 guests were served tea with cow's milk. Wu Zhenyu, in his *Collected Records from the Yangji Studio*, wrote: "According to old customs, [one of the comestibles the Manchus] esteemed most highly was milk tea. Every day, a certain number of milk cows was provided to supply the emperor and the leading officials. [After the cows] were milked, [the milk] would be handed over to the tea kitchen."

The next great emperor of the Qing, Qianlong (r. 1736–96), was also an avid tea-drinker, who used a special silver scale to weigh the water from different springs around Beijing, drank milk tea with his Manchu brethren, clear tea with his Confucian scholars, and held an annual tea dinner at the beginning of the new lunar year for the country's 18 most illustrious literati. Qianlong was in the habit of inspecting his country disguised as a commoner, accompanied only by a palace eunuch, and according to Chinese tea lore, it was during one of these journeys that Qianlong, to demonstrate his humble status, found himself in the position of having to serve tea to

A Qing-dynasty enameled teacup decorated with a peony, magnolia, and begonia.

his eunuch, who was just about to kowtow to his master when he realized that this would reveal the emperor's identity. Instead, the eunuch thanked Qianlong with a symbolic kowtow by tapping the table with his index and middle fingers — a gesture of thanks that was enshrined and can still be observed when a Chinese person is served tea or some other beverage.

In addition to conferring the mark of imperial prestige upon milk tea, the Manchu court also popularized tea scented with flowers such as jasmine, cloranthus, cassia, honeysuckle, and rose. To this day, Beijing, remains a bastion of devoted jasmine tea-drinkers, although some put this down to the city's hard, acrid, salty, bitter drinking water, which they say is best ameliorated with scented tea. One of the earliest descriptions of how to make scented tea can be found in the *Cloud Forest Hall Collection of Rules for Drinking and Eating*, written in the 14th century by the artist and author Ni Zan:

> Select average quality "small sprout" tea, and select an earthen pot for boiling. First, lay down a layer of flowers, a layer of tea, a layer of flowers, a layer of tea till the pot is full. Then tightly lay down a layer of flowers on the very top and cover it up. Put the pot under the sun and turn it over three times. Pour a shallow layer of water into a saucepan and steam the pot over a slow fire. Steam until the cover of the pot reaches its hottest, then take it out. Wait till it is completely cooled down, then remove the tea from the pot. Take away the flowers, leaving only the tea. Use "lotus seed" paper to wrap up the tea and put it under the sun to dry. The paper should be opened frequently to shake the tea inside, so that it is evenly distributed, and it will be dried easily. If each pot of tea is divided into three or four paper bags the sunning will be easier. Repeat the steaming and drying processes three times, changing the flowers each time. Then the tea will be extremely good.

During the Qing, Beijing people sipped their jasmine tea in a wide variety of tea houses (*chaguan*) at their disposal: *qingchaguan*, which only served tea and organized *chaniaohui*, tea and songbird appreciation parties; *dacha-guan*, big, boisterous tea houses; *erhunpu*, tea houses that sold tea, wine, and food; *hongluguan*, which served Chinese and Manchu-style pastries baked in stoves on the premises; *qichaguan*, where customers played chess while drinking tea; *yechaguan*, country tea houses located in scenic spots such as the Western Hills; and *shuchaguan*, where master storytellers spellbound their audiences with famous tales such as *The Romance of the Three King-doms* and *Journey to the West* during engagements that could last up to three months, bringing customers back every day to hear the next episode. "You have eaten our family's tea. How come you still haven't become a wife in our family?" Wang Xifeng says to Lin Daiyu, the heroine of another famous novel in the teahouse storyteller's repertoire, *Dream of the Red Chamber*.

Tea also played an indispensable part in traditional Chinese mar-riage customs. "To grow the tea bush, one must sow seeds, and the bush cannot be transplanted, for if it is, it will not come back to life. Therefore, a woman who is betrothed is said to 'eat tea,' and tea is given as a betrothal gift, because it symbolizes everlasting faithfulness," the author Lang Ying wrote in the 16th century. In some areas of Hunan province, the *yanchapan*, "salt and tea tray," a tray on which dyed lamp wicks were used to form small sculptures of mythological birds and beasts, with salt and tea filling the spaces in between, was an obligatory betrothal gift. The wedding ceremony itself was known as *dingcha* ("settling tea"). And before consummating their marriage, the newly-weds performed a ritual in the nuptial chamber called *hehecha* ("harmoniously joined tea"), which is still popular in many places: seated on benches facing each other, the groom and bride put their left leg and arm respectively on their counterpart's right leg and shoulder. With the index finger and thumb of their free hands, the couple then forms a square in which a cup of tea is placed, and the wedding guests are invited to drink from it in turn.

In 1578, the great herbal pharmacologist Li Shizhen completed his magnum opus, the *Bencao Gangmu* ("Compendium of Materia Medica"), which expounds on 1,892 herbal, animal, and mineral drugs, and counts as the definitive Chinese herbal pharmacopeia. In his extensive entry on tea, Li Shizhen explained: "Tea is bitter and cold, a yin among yin, has a dampening function, and is best at directing fire downward. Fire leads to a hundred diseases, and by dampening the fire, a clear qi [vital energy] can rise." Li thus recommended tea to young, strong people with lots of fire in their hearts, lungs, spleens, and stomachs, but warned people with *xuhan* [cold-deficiency syndrome] and *ruoxue* [weak blood] from prolonged tea consumption. Taking himself as an example, Li wrote: "When Shizhen was young and his qi vigorous, he had to drink several cups of tea to be satisfied. It produced a light sweat, cleared his muscles and bones, and made him feel very happy. In his middle years, the stomach qi had already been slightly damaged, and he could feel that tea hurt the body, giving him, if not a feeling of nausea and stuffiness in the chest, then a coldness in the abdomen and diarrhea." Li goes on to expound on the dangers of addiction to tea, and in his list of tea prescriptions includes this remedy against "tea addiction," first cited in the *Binhu Collection of Simple Prescriptions*: "When a person was afflicted with this disease, a doctor told him: 'Fill a new shoe with tea, and "eat" it all. Repeat this three times, and you will not "eat tea" again. If a man uses a woman's shoe, and vice versa, the results will be even better.'"

In contrast to the boisterous tea competitions of the Song dynasty, the learned Ming scholars, emulating Lu Yu and the ancient sages, sought peace and quietude way up in the mountains, where drinking alone was considered divine, with one friend delightful, and with two interesting, while a company of seven or eight persons "dispersed" the tea. In the early 16th century, the Ming artist Tang Yin depicted this ambience of utter repose in several well-known tea paintings, such as *Serving Tea* and the *Bamboo Stove*, hailed today as masterpieces of the period. One of these solitary tea masters was Lu Shusheng, who in his article "Record of a Tea House," listed six occasions for having tea:

> On a cool terrace or in a quiet room,
> Before a bright window or next to a low, curved table,
> In a monk's quarters or a priest's courtyard,
> When there's a wind in the pines or a moon over the bamboos,
> Sitting at a banquet chanting poetry,
> Or next to a clear pond holding a scroll.

The Ming and Qing saw an effusion of new teas — Oolong, black, white, and yellow — the transmission of tea deep into Central Asia, and the advent of the European tea trade. Through the years, decades, and centuries, the tea bush was observed and studied, propagated and manured, pruned and picked with greater care than any other member of the vegetable kingdom. The tea-makers who manipulated the leaves learned their deepest secrets, how to conjure forth their most seductive aroma, and how preserve their most salubrious qualities. For the tea traveling thousands of miles to Tibet sown up in hides on yak backs, however, no such refinement was required. The coarse leaves and twigs were simply steamed and pressed into cakes, which by the time they reached Lhasa, under the action of yeast and bacteria, had assumed a dark, purple-brown hue. This was the beginning of the famous, post-fermented Pu'er brick-tea, prized for its digestive properties and mellow smoothness. In the late 16th century, tea, together with Buddhism, was "reintroduced" to the Mongols, who had been deprived of the beverage for two centuries as punishment for their invasion of China, and today, Tibet and Mongolia form the world's axis of brick-tea culture.

Tang Yin's Bamboo Stove. *Through the ages, poets and artists have sipped their tea for its subtle, mysterious effects, praying for a spark from the inner muse.*

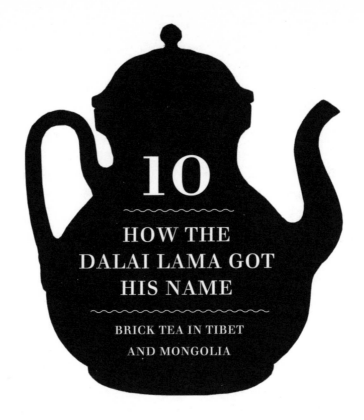

10

HOW THE DALAI LAMA GOT HIS NAME

BRICK TEA IN TIBET AND MONGOLIA

At every turn, the craggy, majestic landscape of the Tibetan Plateau humbles the heart. The mountains here are dotted with the caves of hermits who have traveled far in their meditations. Only such a person could have conceived a work, *The Tibetan Book of the Dead*, that offers instruction and good advice to a departed soul on its 49-day journey through the state of *Bardo* between the lands of death and rebirth. But the dry, thin atmosphere does more than turn the mind toward the spiritual and macabre. It also desiccates the body. At 6,000 feet above sea level, humans perspire and exhale twice as much moisture as they do at lower altitudes, which is why Tibetans must drink large quantities throughout the day. So when bricks of Sichuan tea began making their way up on the plateau, the new herb was readily adopted as an invigorating, refreshing beverage.

The *Tang Guo Shi Bu* ("Supplement of the History of the Tang") relates the following anecdote about Chang Lugong, a Chinese ambassador who went to Tibet in 781. One day, he was boiling tea in his tent, when the Tibetan king asked him:

"What is that?"

"It sweeps away troubles and cures thirst. It's called tea," Lugong replied.

"I have that too," said the king, and brought out his tea. "This is from Shouzhou, this from Shuzhou, this from Guzhu, this from Qimen, this from Changming, and this from Dizhu."

The boastful litany, which includes famous teas from five different provinces, shows how far and wide tea was traded in the Tang. It was also during this period that chapter in a Tibetan book entitled "Sea of Sweet Dew" appeared, describing the characteristics of 16 different teas from China, among them, tea that grows in valleys, tea that grows at the mouths of valleys, and tea fertilized with manure, while "The tea tree that grows in fields watered by urine is called Gru-gu pha-la. Its leaves are numerous and the tree grows at an angle. The infusion of this tea is yellow in color and its flavor is quite astringent, with an aroma like the Majñuśaka (or Mañjuśaka) tree. The best tea from this tree is ground into a fine powder; drinking it can cure diseases of the blood."

According to tradition (as recounted in Chapter 4) it was the Chinese princess Wencheng who converted the founder of the Tibetan empire Srong-tsan Gampo (605–50) and the Tibetan people to Buddhism, but Srong-tsan also married a Nepalese princess who brought the Tibetans into closer contact with the lands south of the forbidding Himalayas. Ministers were dispatched to India to learn Sanskrit, from which a Tibetan script was devised. Later kings supervised grand projects to translate the Buddhist scriptures into Tibetan, and a decree was issued stating that every lama (Buddhist teacher) should be supported by seven households. But during the mid-9th-century reign of Lang Darma, the Tibetan empire disintegrated and the spread of Buddhism ground to a halt. Interest in Buddhism was not rekindled until some 200 years later, this time from Kashmir via western Tibet, where Buddhism was adopted by the rulers of the powerful Guge state. In the following centuries, four main Buddhist schools evolved: *Nyingma* ("The Ancient Ones"); *Kagyu* ("The Oral Lineage"); *Sakya* ("Grey Earth"); and *Gelukpa* ("The Virtuous Ones"). And, as in China, tea followed hand-in-hand with the religion.

In comparison with the Tibetans, tea is curiously absent from the early historical records of the Mongols. Tea is not mentioned in the *Secret History of the Mongols,* compiled in 1240. Nor is it among the drinks listed by the Franciscan missionary William of Rubruck, who sojourned in the Mongol capital Karakorum for several weeks in 1254, and described in detail the four beverages he was offered there: *koumiss*, fermented horse milk, "a pale wine like that of La Rochelle"; "ball," a drink made of honey; "rice beer," which was as sweet and clear as white wine; and *karacosmos*, purified horse milk. One of the rare references to tea among the Mongols during this period is a Tibetan document which states that Khubilai Khan offered the *Sakya* lama 'Phags-pa a number of valuable gifts, including 200 baskets of tea, to thank 'Phags-pa for inventing a new script for the Mongol language (but, since this is supposed to have taken place in 1254, when Khubilai Khan was busy fighting in Sichuan and Yunnan during his campaign to conquer China, some historians have questioned the accuracy of that document).

There was a close, political-ecclesiastical relationship between the Mongol rulers and the *Sakya* lamas, in which political patronage was exchanged for religious prestige, and which continued after the Mongols, as the new rulers of China, had established the Yuan dynasty in 1280. The Mongols made their capital in Dadu, present-day Beijing, received the finest tea in the land from the imperial gardens, and raised the tax on tea to unprecedented levels. The Mongol emperor Hui Zong (r. 1333–67), was so fond of tea that he kept a female servant by his side ready to serve him at all times. One of these "tea-makers" was a Korean beauty by the name of Qi Shi, who became the only non-Mongolian empress of the Yuan dynasty. The *Yin Shan Zheng Yao* ("Essentials of Food and Drink"), compiled by the Mongolian court doctor Hoshoi in 1332, contains the earliest description of the Mongolian use of butter and curd (a hard cheese that is the by-product

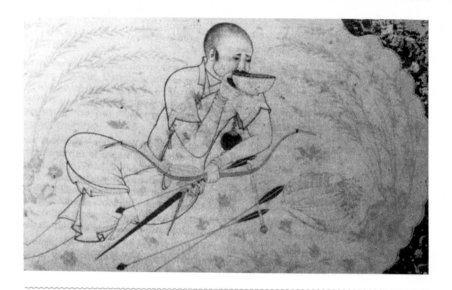

Hulegu Khan, the Mongol warrior who sacked Baghdad in 1258, takes a break with what is probably a bowl of tea.

when distilling old yoghurt into strong liquor, known in Mongolian as *aaruul*) in the preparation of tea. For *chao cha* ("fried tea"), the tea leaves were roasted in a wok until red, then boiled with butter and curd, while *lan gao* ("orchid paste") was prepared by mixing three spoons of powdered tea with flour and butter and then whisking the paste with hot water.

While Tibetan Buddhism had been introduced to Mongolia during the Yuan dynasty, it declined after the Mongols were ousted from power in China, and, according to tradition, was only reintroduced in the 1570s by Altan Khan, chieftain of the Tümed Mongols, who made their capital in Köke-qota ("The Blue City"), or present-day Hohhot, the capital of Inner Mongolia. At that time, the *Gelukpa* lineage, known as the "Yellow Hats" for their Mohawk-like headgear, needed a political ally, while Altan Khan needed the Tibetans to aid his attempts to pressure the Ming into opening trade and allowing the Mongols to purchase tea officially, as they had been barred from this trade from some two centuries. In 1577, Altan Khan invited the Tibetan lama Sonam Gyatso (1543–88), the abbot of the "Yellow Hat" Drepung and Sera monasteries, to a meeting on the shores of Qinghai Lake (Kokonor) in Qinghai province, and requested permission from the Chinese to build a special temple for the occasion. He also requested a golden seal to accompany him on his journey across Chinese territory, and expressed his desire to organize a great tea and horse fair near the temple.

The Chinese agreed: the meeting between Altan Khan and Sonam Gyatso took place at the new temple, built by the town of Xining near Lake Kokonor, in 1578. The Tibetan word *gyatso* means "ocean," and the Mongolian word for ocean is *dalai*. For this reason, Altan Khan addressed Sonam Gyatso as Dalai Lama, and presented him with a seal bearing that inscription. This is how the Dalai Lama got his name. And since Sonam Gyatso was the third incarnation of his lineage, Altan Khan's honorific title was bestowed posthumously upon the previous two incarnations, making Sonam Gyatso the third Dalai Lama (Tenzin Gyatso, the present Dalai Lama, is the 14th). Along with the "re-introduction" of Tibetan Buddhism to Mongolia sparked by this meeting, it also marked the beginning of a renewed alliance between the Mongol rulers and the Tibetan religious dignitaries. That same year, the Mongols received official permission to purchase tea from the Chinese, with the main market situated northeast of Beijing in Kalgan (Zhangjiakou), which later became the main entrepôt for the caravan tea trade with Russia.

In 1642, the fifth Dalai Lama, supported by the Mongol ruler Gushri Khan, defeated the *Kagyu* school, united Tibet and started construction of the present Potala Palace. Eight years later, the 15-year-old Öndür Gegen, who had been recognized as the first "Living Buddha of Urga," the highest Buddhist dignitary in Mongolia, traveled to Tibet, where he received instruction from the Dalai

A Tibetan lama drinks tea.

Lama, took vows from the Panchen Lama, the number two lama in the "Yellow Hat" hierarchy, and "established ceremonial teas and offered offerings in the temples and monasteries." When the 5th Dalai Lama died in 1682, his death was kept a secret for 15 years, until the Potala Palace had been completed. By that time, tea had become an integral part of Tibetan life, both monastic and otherwise. In addition to its invigorating properties, Tibetans soon discovered the excellent digestive properties of tea. Today, farmers prefer their tea without condiments, while nomads most often take their tea with salt and yak butter (see box on p. 134). The pounded tea leaves are boiled in a pot for half an hour, filtered out, and the liquid poured into a long, cylindrical, plunger-type "tea churn." In another pot, fresh milk is brought to a boil. The cream is skimmed off and, together with salt, added to the churn. The housewife sets to work plunging vigorously, and when the sound of the churn turns from "*guadang, guadang*" to "*cayi, cayi*," the tea and cream (butter by now) are said to be well-mixed. Tea is also mixed with barley flour and yak butter to make *tsampa,* the most common breakfast food. "Some Tibetans believe that, when the stomach is empty, water rises from the liver, and should be pressed down with food and tea. So they call this morsel the 'liver-pressing' (*chin-nön*). Others hold the early morning discomfort to be due to worms rising from the stomach, and find that the hot tea with a pinch of food drives them back again," the famous early 20th-century British Tibetologist Charles Bell explained. Bell also related that before eating, a Tibetan will make an offering to the gods by dipping the middle finger of his right hand (thought to be the cleanest, as Tibetans say that babies are born with this finger in their nostrils) in the tea, and then flicking a few drops upwards with the thumb.

In the monasteries and temples, tea was served eight to ten times a day. The refectory, or tea kitchen, attached to each temple had two tea masters, *Japön,* in charge of the distribution of government tea, and the kitchens were equipped with enormous boilers capable of preparing tea for several thousand monks. The cauldron of the great Lhasa temple, for example, was said to hold about 1,200 gallons. Before taking the tea, the lama poured out some of the drink as a libation, and said a grace such as this: "We humbly

A complete set of Tibetan tea utensils: (a) brass teapots, (b) wooden bowl, (c) porcelain bowl with case, (d) brick of tea, (e) copper pot from Kokonor, (f) copper kettle from Tashilumpo, (g) tsampa bag, (h) wooden butter-box, (i) tea churn, and (j) tea strainer.

beseech thee! That we and our relatives throughout all our life-cycles may never be separated from the three holy ones [the Buddha, the Dharma, and the Sangha]! May the blessing of the trinity enter into this drink!" At this point, the Lama would sprinkle a few drops on the ground with the tips of the fore and middle fingers, and continue: "To all the dread locality, demons of this country, we offer this good Chinese tea! Let us obtain our wishes! And may the doctrines of Buddha be extended!"

In March, 1716, the Italian Jesuit Ippolito Desideri, having traveled several months from Kashmir along the northern side of the Himalayan ridge, reached Lhasa, where he received a friendly welcome and settled in at the Sera monastery to study the Tibetan language and Buddhism "from morning to night, only stopping to drink tea." In his theological studies, Desideri went straight to the heart of the matter: the subtle, yet profound difference between the spiritual trajectories of Christianity and Buddhism. It was the Buddhist concept of nirvana, which offered no light at the end of the tunnel, no pot of gold at the end of the rainbow, no God, and no eternal life on the other side of the Last Judgment, but rather postulated an all-encompassing void as the highest truth and destination of all religious endeavor, that troubled Desideri most deeply. During his five years in Tibet, Desideri became so proficient in the Tibetan language that he was even able to compose a theological work in Tibetan entitled *The Essence of Christian*

Perfection, in which he put forth his arguments for a God and against the Buddhist void. In his *An Account of Tibet*, Desideri also describes the Tibetan custom of tea:

> All drink *cià*, let us call it tea, many times a day.... Into a large earthen pot (in the monasteries and convents a huge brass cauldron is used) they put the proper amount of tea with a little water and some *putoà*, which as I have said before, is a white powder of salt earth, and imparts no taste to the tea, but colors it red like good red wine. The tea is boiled until the water is somewhat reduced, when it is beaten up with a whisk as we do chocolate for a long while until covered with froth. It is then strained, more water is added and it is put on the fire again until it boils. Fresh milk is then poured in and good yellow butter with a little salt is added. The *cià* is put into another clean receptacle, again whipped up and then decanted into a wooden teapot ornamented with sprigs of copper and brass, and everyone has three or four cups....

With the advent of a theocratic government in Tibet lead by the Dalai Lama, the Tibetan side of the tea trade also came under his control. From the Tang dynasty until the 17th century, the major tea and horse markets had been located in the grasslands of Shanxi, Qinghai, and Gansu provinces, and the principal route to Tibet had run from Xining over a series of inhospitable mountain ranges to the plateau and on to Lhasa. But during the reign of the Manchu emperor Kangxi, the Chinese government's pastures were bounding with horses, and the strategic importance of the tea and horse trade began to fade. Meanwhile in Tibet, there was large-scale migration from the borders with India and Chinese Turkestan to eastern part of the country, which abuts Sichuan, and which became the home for the majority of Tibetans. Gradually, the center for Chinese-Tibetan trade shifted to the frontier town Dajianlu (Dar-rtse-mdo in Tibetan), present-day Kangding, located in western Sichuan some 150 miles west of Yazhou, the province's principal tea district. In 1693, the sixth Dalai Lama asked the Chinese court to officially open Dajianlu for trade, and in 1701, Dajianlu and Yazhou were connected by the famous 370-foot iron chain suspension bridge erected across the Daidu river at Luding.

While the Yazhou tea district included Meng Mountain, with its famous green tea, most of the tea produced there was the black brick tea destined for Tibet. This tea was manufactured in five standards, and while the highest quality, *Go-mang chu-pa*, consisted only of the best fermented leaves, the lowest quality, *Jong-ma*, was made from the coarse leaves, stems, and branches of the tea bush mixed with the matter of other trees such as the scrub oak, which were finely chopped and steamed in large wooden tubs. The mixture was then spread out on mats and allowed to dry. Rice water was added as an adhesive, and the tea packed, first in small red-paper packages, then into cylinders of bamboo mats, which when filled with tea weighed 20–25 lb each. From Yazhou to Dajianlu, the tea was transported by "a very nationality of porters," the Giama Rongbas, who were able to carry incredible loads – over 300 lb – of tea on their backs, traveling 6 miles per day, including a 3,000 feet ascent to Dajianlu in the final 18 miles. One of these porters is even on record as having carried a safe weighing over 400 lb for a certain Monseigneur Biet to Dajianlu, although he died shortly afterward from the exhaustion of this mind-boggling feat.

At Dajianlu, the bamboo cylinders were opened and the tea carefully sewn up in hides to be transported by yaks to Lhasa — an arduous three-month, 1,300-mile journey. From Tibet, the Dalai Lama's traders brought the finest products of that land: yak hides, lambskins, fox, leopard and lynx skins, rugs, gold, precious stones, musk, deer horns, brown sugar cakes, saffron from Kashmir, soap bars from India, a medicinal plant known as "devil's dung" (*Ferula asafoetida*), and other products. Nevertheless, the total value of these goods was far less than the value of the tea purchased. Instead, most of the tea was paid for with the rupees that the Tibetans had earned through their trade surplus with India. In Dajianlu, the business negotiations between the Tibetans and the Chinese were facilitated by female translators known as *shabao'er*. When the deal was done, the Tibetans commenced their long homeward journey, which, if successful, could be highly lucrative,

Two tea coolies carry 300 lb of brick tea each at 5,000 feet above sea level; photographed in 1908 on the treacherous path between Yazhou and Dajianlu.

TEA IN TODAY'S TIBET

In the Tibetan village Brag mda', a farming community with some 500 inhabitants located in the Dkar mdzes Tibetan Autonomous Prefecture in western Sichuan province, the people purchase their tea in 3-feet-high, 1-foot-wide bamboo containers, each containing six bricks. One such container costs 45 renminbi ($7), and in one year, an average family consumes about 12 containers. One reason for the large consumption is that tea is also given to horses and milk cows. Called *ja lo* ("tea leaf"), this tea is mixed with *tsampa* (barley flour) and butter, and given to the animals the day before they are required to do hard work, such as a carrying a person up a mountain to visit a deity's shrine, or transporting bundles of wheat and barley.

The villagers prepare several kinds of tea for their own use. *Thu ja*, "milk tea," is the common family beverage, and made by adding tea to boiling water, boiling the milk separately, and then adding this to the tea. *Wojoh ja* ("*tsampa* tea") is served to special guests and monks asked to perform special rituals in the home. *Rera ja* ("bone tea") is prepared by boiling pig leg bones, tea, and *tsampa*, and drunk during periods of intensive labor, such as the harvest time. And when a family does not have any milk, it makes do with *ja dongma* ("tea only").

A Tibetan woman with a headdress of stones pours yak butter tea.

as a catty of tea purchased in Dajianlu for 1 copper coin and 3 cents could be sold in Tibet for 25 to 26 copper coins. At the end of the 18th century, some 15 million lb of brick tea per year was transported from Sichuan and Yunnan provinces to Tibet via the path from Dajianlu and the two other major routes from Songpan, also in Sichuan, and Lijiang in Yunnan.

Up till the 19th century, foreign missionaries and explorers had usually been welcomed in Tibet, but when the British took power in India, and with the Russians expanding aggressively in Central Asia, Tibet found itself another square on the chessboard of the Great Game. Warily, the Tibetans closed their doors to all but the old neighbors, and Lhasa became the most distant and mysterious place on earth, the holy grail of the great 19th century European explorers. One of the few who succeeded in visiting Lhasa was the French missionary Père Évariste Régis Huc, who reached that city during a journey in 1844–46. En route to Tibet, he stayed at the Kumbum monastery in Qinghai province, where he recounts a "tea offering for the entire *sangha* [community]" given by a pious pilgrim for the monastery's 4,000 monks, each of whom was served 2 cups of tea, at an expense of 50 taels of silver. Kumbum's most magnificent tea party, however, had been sponsored by the Tartar king of Souniout, who following the annual "Flower Festival," treated the monastery's monks to a "general tea," replete with cakes and butter, that lasted for eight whole days.

By this time, the Mongols had also developed an inordinate thirst for tea. Like the Tibetans, they subsisted on a heavy diet of meat, milk products, and grain, and prized tea for its digestive properties. An ordinary cup of Mongol tea was prepared by breaking a tea brick into pieces with an axe, crushing the tea in mortar, and boiling the crumbs with water and a pinch of soda to extract all the strength and flavor. This infusion was set aside, and cow's or goat's milk boiled with an ample amount of salt. The tea infusion was then mixed with the milk, and some flour and Mongolian-style butter, made by boiling cream at a low heat, added. When this yellow broth had been brought to a boil, it was transferred to a Mongolian teapot – a two-foot cylindrical brass container with a handle on the side and two holes in the soldered lid: one for tea and one for air, and served in simple wooden bowls.

After the commencement of official, direct trade between the Mongols and Chinese in the late 16th century, altogether six trading stations were opened up along the Great Wall separating the two nations. At these markets, the Chinese traded tea for Mongolian horses, which they now needed to combat another nomad people from the north – the Manchus. From Kalgan, the tea was transported to the Mongolian capital Urga, present-day Ulaanbaatar, in long camel caravans, and in the 18th and 19th centuries, tea bricks were so pervasive in Mongolia that they became the country's common currency, collected as tax and used to purchase goods. In 1838, the people of the Minžüürdorž banner submitted a petition to the Sečen Khan and other high-ranking officials, accusing their banner's leader of forcing them to pay his personal debts and the taxes of other people. In the long list of arbitrary, unjust impositions, the petitioners complained that "last winter, the Jasagh borrowed 2,825 bricks of tea and another 10 small pieces of yellow tea from the Chinese merchants in Urga. The total interest amounted to 95 bricks of tea for 3 months. We repaid this loan, including interest, with 595 ounces of silver."

At the beginning of the 20th century, tea was still a common currency, as observed by the Finnish Orientalist Gustav John Ramstedt, who wrote: "To buy mutton or anything else at the market in Urga, a servant carrying brick tea on his back must be brought along. In any case, tea is a more reliable payment method than *hadaken* (a longer or shorter piece of silk). But as pieces of tea easily break off from the brick, and the corners in particular become worn and rounded, the tea brick can not pass through many hands before it becomes useless, and a worn and dirty brick can only be used to make tea. You can therefore say that the Mongolian people in the end always drink up their money."

Today, Tibet and Mongolia form the world's brick tea axis, and are the most vociferous imbibers of the brew. On average, a Tibetan consumes 33 lb of tea per year, a Mongolian 18 lb. And though the brick tea they drink is customarily made from the coarsest leaves, and even twigs, connoisseurs today collect cakes of aged brick tea, known as Pu'er from the region in Yunnan where the best kind is made, and vie for rare vintages in online auctions.

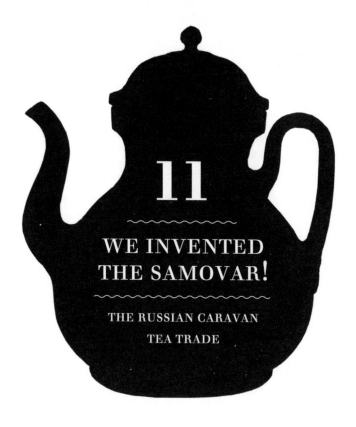

11

WE INVENTED
THE SAMOVAR!

THE RUSSIAN CARAVAN
TEA TRADE

Bounded by a common border 2,600 miles long, separated by histories as disparate as the poles, China and Russia have always had a relationship made up in equal parts of intimacy and loathing, mutual interest and intractable rivalry, understanding and misunderstanding. Yet ever since the two empires first rubbed shoulders in the 17th century, one commodity has run like a red thread through the ups and downs, thick and thin, war and peace. In the 18th and 19th centuries, hundreds of thousands of camels, ox-carts, and sleighs laden with tea trudged their way from China across the undulating Mongolian steppe, through the snowstorms of southern Siberia, over the Ural Mountains, and on to their final destination – the bustling fair of Nizhny Novgorod, Imperial Russia's greatest emporium, situated on the banks of the Volga river 250 miles east of Moscow. From the gilded halls of the Kremlin to the tarred cabins of the country's peasants, tea became Russia's national temperate drink, and the samovar, a metal urn used to boil water, the embodiment of the warm, hospitable Russian hearth. "Ecstasy," as the poet Alexander Pushkin avowed, "is a glass of tea and a piece of sugar in the mouth."

Having freed itself from its vassalage to the Turkic Tatars in the late 15th century, the Russian city-state of Moscow expanded in all directions with irrepressible elan. In 1552, Ivan the Terrible defeated the Tatar Khanate of Kazan just west of the Ural Mountains, and in 1581, Russian forces commanded by the Cossack Yermak Timofeyevich subdued the Siberian Khan on the banks of the Irtysh river on the eastern side of that mountain range. Continuing east, the Cossacks established a string of Siberian fortifications, *ostrogi,* which later grew into the major cities of Southern Siberia. By 1648, the Cossack Semyon Dezhnev had sailed round the easternmost end of Eurasia via the Bering Strait, and in 1652, a Russian outpost named Irkutsk was established due west of Lake Baikal's southern end.

The first Russians recorded to have tasted tea were the Cossacks Vasili Tumenets and Ivan Petrov, dispatched in 1616 by the Tsar as envoys to seek an alliance with the Altin Khan, a Mongol prince from the region around Lake Ubsa Nor in the northwestern corner of present-day Mongolia who controlled the only possible route to China, as the more southern road was barred by the hostile Kalmyks. Departing from Tomsk, the then last Russian outpost in Siberia, Tumenets and Petrov traveled for three weeks over fields and rocky hills to the Kirghiz region, and continued to the lands of the Tabin and the Sayan, where the petty prince Karaskul gave them reindeer flesh for the remaining leg of the journey to the Altin Khan's territory. The Altin Khan was amicable, and having received the Tsar's gifts, treated the envoys to a meal of "ducks and black game, hares and mutton and beef; ten kinds in all.... For drink they brought to table cow's milk parboiled with butter, and in it unknown leaves of some sort."

From the Khan, the Russian envoys learned that the Chinese capital lay a month's journey away at the head of a gulf, was built of bricks, and was so huge it took ten days to ride round it on horseback. Two years later, the Siberian Cossack Ivan Petlin reached Beijing and established direct contact with China, but a letter given to him by the Chinese emperor, with an offer to the Tsar to trade with China, remained untranslated for 56 years for lack of a person in Russia who could read Chinese. In 1638, Russian envoys Vasili Starkov and Stepan Nevierov returned to the Altin Khan, who accorded them a chilly reception, as the Tsar had not seen fit to fulfill the Khan's wish list: a dwarf, a repeating gun with at least five chambers, and a monk from Jerusalem. In the end, however, amends were made, and the Altin Khan even sent a tribute to the Tsar that included 200 *bakhchas* (paper packets, containing about 3 lb each) of tea, despite Starkov's objection that, since tea was unknown in Russia, the Court would have preferred the equivalent in sables.

In 1654, the first official Russian mission to China ended in failure when the envoy Fedor Baikov refused both to kowtow and, it being the time of Lent, to drink a ceremonial cup of tea, prepared in the Manchu manner with milk and butter. Four years later, the second mission received an imperial gift of ten *puds* (359 lb) of tea, but the Russian representatives immediately sold it in Beijing and purchased jewelry with the proceeds instead. However, by 1674, tea had made its way to Moscow, where the Swedish envoy Kilburger wrote that it cost 30 kopeks per lb, and was used "especially to avert drunkenness, if they take it before drinking, or to disperse the intoxication resulting from drink, if they use it after drinking."

Already in October, 1652, the Russians and Chinese had come to loggerheads at the battle of Wuchala in the Amur river valley, when a combined force of Manchu vassals, the pastoral Duchers and the Achans, a fishing tribe on the Amur, attacked the Russians and were defeated, taking 676 casualties according to the Russian leader Erofei Pavlovich Khabarov. In 1665, a group of Polish bandits on the run from justice reached Albazin on the middle reaches of the Amur, where they built a fort and turned the place into a watering hole for sundry adventurers and outlaws. The Manchus attacked Albazin in 1685, and in 1689 the hostilities were concluded with the historic Treaty of Nerchinsk, in which Russia lost its access to the Sea of Japan and agreed to destroy Albazin, but secured its claim to Transbaikalia, the region to the east of Lake Baikal. In 1699, the first official Russian caravan trundled into Beijing, trading furs for gold and silver, cotton cloth, silk and porcelain, but no great quantities of tea, and for the next three decades, these Russian caravans arrived in the Chinese capital regularly every three years – the time it took to make the return journey from Moscow.

In 1712, China dispatched one of its rare embassies to the Mongol Kalmyks, who in the 1660s had emigrated from western Mongolia to the lower reaches of the Volga river on the northwestern side of the Caspian Sea (today forming the only Buddhist state in the Russian Federation, Kalmykia). Reporting on the Russians he encountered along the way, the Qing envoy Tulisen recorded: "Wine is drunk upon all joyful occasions. Whenever a friend or a relation arrives he must always be welcomed with wine. Of the use of tea they are ignorant. ... The Russians are naturally vain and ambitious; but they live together peaceably. They delight in pleasantry and ridicule. They are not much given to quarreling and fighting, but they are fond of litigation." On 2 July, 1714, the delegation called on the Kalmyks at their main camp, where Johann Schnitscher, a Swedish officer in Russian service who was accompanying the Chinese envoys, described the meeting: "After this, they all sat down in a row. Having spoken about things of no major importance, tea was served, mixed with goat's milk. A piece of red, rather small damask, was spread out on the ground, to serve as a table cloth."

The Treaty of Kyakhta in 1727 further defined the Russian-Chinese border, allowed the Russians to build a church in Beijing, secured favorable commercial arrangements for Russia, and established the main market for trade between the two countries in Kyakhta, a Russian outpost south of Lake Baikal on the border with Manchu-controlled Mongolia. Directives from the Russian government stipulated: "The Kyakhta market should be a square with 200 meters on a side. A tower should be erected in each corner. Inside this square market, 32 stalls should be established. ..." Within a year, the Chinese merchants had pooled their resources and built their own market on the other side of the border, named Maimaicheng ("trade town"; in Russian Maimaichin) and separated from the Russians' market only by a wooden fence.

Chinese tea-packers. By 1878, Russian merchants had established six tea factories in the British concession of Hankow, present-day Wuhan.

By this time, the Russian attraction to tea had been duly awakened. On the Chinese side, the Kyakhta tea trade was controlled by the Western Guild Merchants from Shanxi, long known for their business prowess. "East of the river, there are many good merchants, who rarely engage in agriculture and sericulture. There are people older than 30 years who do not know how to plough," the Tang-dynasty historian Li Yanshou wrote in his *Bei Shi* ("History of the North"). Early each spring, the Western Guild Merchants traveled to the Wuyi (Bohea) Mountains in northwestern Fujian province, the center of the black tea region, to purchase their consignments of tea, which were transported via Jiangxi and Henan up to a city northwest of Beijing known as Kalgan (Zhangjiakou). This was the transshipment entrepôt and departure point for the caravans assembled to make the arduous 1,500-mile trek across the desolate Mongolian steppe plateau to Kyakhta.

In the hot summer months, these caravans were made up of several hundred ox-carts, each of which carried about 400 lb of cargo. At nightfall, camp was pitched. The oxen were put out to pasture, the carts arranged in an oval, and watch dogs set loose to keep the highway robbers at bay. During the busier winter period, when forage was scarce, the tea was mostly transported by camels, preferably castrated males, with each animal carrying some 280 lb in baskets made of hemp or woven bamboo, traveling at a thoughtful pace of two or three miles per hour. These caravans, with anywhere from 20 to over 1,000 camels, were run by two different Mongol groups, the Khalkha and the Harchin, which operated in slightly different fashions, as the Khalkha drove their caravans during the day, while the Harchin, employed by Chinese tea merchants, traveled at night.

In Kyakhta, the Russians awaited the arrival of the caravans with powerful binoculars. According to *Zhuye Ting Zaji* ("Miscellaneous Notes from the Bamboo Leaf Pavilion") by the 19th-century writer Yao Yuanzhi, they were able to estimate the size of the consignment by counting the number of carts and animals four to five days in advance, at a distance of 40–75 miles. In 1750, 7,000 *puds* (250,000 lb) of brick tea and 6,000 *puds* (215,000 lb) of Pekoe (loose-leaf tea of finer quality), were traded through Kyakhta. In addition to tea, the Chinese exports included silk, porcelain, gold, silver, tobacco, and, above all, dried Chinese rhubarb, highly prized by the peoples of Siberia, Russia, and Europe for its medicinal and laxative properties. The Russians were primarily trading furs and skins.

Conflicts between the Chinese and Russians occasionally closed trade at Maimaicheng-Kyakhta. During these periods, European Russia turned to the Dutch and English for its tea, while Siberian nomads such as the Buryats bought tea secretly from the Chinese for themselves. But as soon as the market at Kyakhta reopened, the trade in tea continued to grow, as its price fell and popularity spread. By the end of the 18th century, the Russian side of the trade had been formally organized into six major guilds, among which the Moscow Guild traded woolen goods and walrus and sea lion skins for the Chinese merchandise. In 1810, these guilds bartered their goods for 75,000 *puds* (2.7 million lb) of brick tea and Pekoe, almost six times more than in 1750. And in 1818, with trade not yet fully recovered after Napoleon's capture of Moscow, the Russian representative in Kyakhta recorded the arrival of 1,420 ox-carts and 3,450 camels laden with Chinese goods, with tea by now overwhelmingly the major commodity.

Having purchased the tea in Maimaicheng, the Russian merchants transported it across the border to Kyakhta, where the tea chests were reloaded and sown up in *tsebiks* (cowhides) by *tsebikovs*, which became the surname of the people engaged in this profession (to this day, there are still people named Tsybikov living in Kyakhta). In the summer, the tea was transported by land and water from Kyakhta to Irkutsk, by land to Tomsk, by barge to Tiumen, by land again across the Urals to Perm, and then along the Kama and Volga rivers to Nizhny Novgorod. In the winter, the entire 3,800-mile journey, which took anywhere between 100 and 200 days, was undertaken with wagons and horse-sleighs. Along the route, the tea was tested four times, in Irkutsk, Tomsk, Tiumen, and Perm, to ensure its quality.

As the popularity of tea spread among the Russians, rituals and utensils for preparing and partaking of it were evolved through an amalgamation of timeworn traditions and material reality. In public houses known as *traktirs*, the male customers ordered their tea *s polotentsem*, or "with a towel," which they hung around their necks and used to wipe the sweat gushing forth from their brows as they downed the piping hot infusion, served in glasses with metal holders called *podstakannik*. Russian ladies, however, drank their tea in private in porcelain cups, a curious gender discrepancy thus explained by Alexander Dumas in his *Dictionary of Cuisine*:

In Russia, a custom startling to strangers is that men drink tea in glasses and women drink from china cups. Here is the legend behind this custom. It seems that teacups were first made in Kronstadt, and the bottom was decorated with a view of that city. When a teahouse proprietor stinted on the tea, this picture could be seen clearly, and the customer would say to him, "I can see Kronstadt." Since the proprietor could not deny this, he was caught in flagrante delicto. It became customary then, for tea to be served in teahouses in glasses, at the bottom of which there was nothing to see, let alone Kronstadt!

(Above) An elaborate silver samovar from the end of the 19th century, decorated with enamel and lapis stones.
(Opposite) A Russian peasant family gathered round a more simple samovar for a summer tea party.

Tea-drinking also led to the development of the utensil that symbolizes the Russian hearth and home – the samovar, a Russian word that roughly translated means "self-boiling." The origins of the samovar are somewhat obscure, but historians point to precedents such as similar Chinese and Korean food vessels, West European silver hot-water urns, English tea urns or the Russian toddy-kettle, the *sbitennik*. In its basic design, the samovar consists of a large metal container to hold water with a faucet at its bottom and a fuel pipe running vertically through the container's center. Charcoal or pine cones are placed inside the fuel pipe, on top of which a teapot used to brew the *zavarka*, a strong tea concentrate, is positioned. The fuel is kindled with a bellow, bringing water in the container and the *zavarka* in the teapot to boil, and the tea served by diluting the *zavarka* with the boiling water according to taste, usually at a ratio of about one to ten.

In 1778, the gunsmith Ivan Lisitsyn set up the first known samovar workshop in Tula, a town 110 miles south of Moscow with a long tradition in armaments and metal works, and which became the center of the samovar manufacturing industry. The earliest samovars often took their form from traditional Russian copper cups, antique vases, and urns. Early in the 19th century, samovars made with an alloy of copper and zinc known as "tombac" and produced by the Lomov and Vorontsov brothers, also in Tula, enjoyed great popularity. The acquisition of a samovar became a telltale sign of a family's economic status, determined by the metal employed, the fame of the craftsman, and the intricacy of the samovar's ornamentation. Samovars were given the form of cones, balls, jars, wine-glasses, barrels,

eggs, acorns, pears, and even turnips. Many well-off families owned two of them, one for daily use and one for festivities, while ordinary people made do with the mass-produced varieties that came onto the market during the 19th century. For poor peasant families, the samovar was often the sole source of warmth and hope in their dark, lice-ridden huts, so when the taxman came to collect arrears that the destitute peasants could not pay, he took their most treasured possession instead, as portrayed by Chekhov in his short story *Peasants*:

> It was hopelessly dreary in the Tchikildyeev's hut without the samovar; there was something humiliating in this loss, insulting, as though the honor of the hut had been outraged. Better if the elder had carried off the table, all the benches, all the pots – it would not have seemed so empty.

Fyodor Dostoevsky worked on his great novels through the night, sipping cold, weak tea made with his samovar. In 1862, he left St. Petersburg for his first trip to Western Europe, a restless ten-week journey that took him to Berlin, Dresden, Paris, London, Geneva, Florence, Vienna and the roulette tables of Wiesbaden. Upon his return to Russia, he published his travelogue *Winter Notes on Summer Impressions,* a critical examination of Western Europe, which Dostoyevsky believed had betrayed the brotherhood of man for the false comfort of bourgeois materialism. Finding himself insulted by the supercilious glance of the toll collector at the magnificent Cologne Bridge, Dostoyevsky, searching for an emblem of his Russian identity, raged silently: "We invented the samovar!"

One of the most famous samovars in Russian literary circles was presided over by Princess Odoevsky, the wife of Prince Vladimir Fedorovich Odoevsky, a writer and philosopher who was a close friend of Russia's national poet, Alexander Pushkin. In the 1830s, every Saturday after the theater, the prince and princess held an open salon in their house, where the guests, not expected to arrive before 11 p.m., gathered in two small rooms before entering the library, crowned by an enormous silver samovar. Pushkin was a frequent attendee, as well as an avid devotee of tea. In his account of a journey to the Caucasus, he wrote that the primitive, noble savages living there ought to be bestowed the blessing of Russian civilization in the form of the Gospel and the samovar. And in his famous prose poem *Eugene Onegin,* the heroine Tatyana has been waiting impatiently all day for Onegin's reply to her first (and last) love letter:

> Day faded; on the table, glowing,
> and samovar of evening boiled,
> and warmed the Chinese teapot; flowing
> beneath it, vapour wreathed and coiled.

In 1829, 9,670 camels and 2,705 ox-carts laden with tea reached Kyakhta. By that time, Kyakhta was among the most prosperous towns in the whole Russian empire. One of the merchants who amassed a fortune in the tea trade was Vasili Silverstrovich Kandinsky, the father of the famous artist. These rouble millionaires contributed to the construction of two magnificent cathedrals in Kyakhta, the Troitsky sobor and Voskresenskaia tserkov,

Tea sown up in cowhides awaits the long journey from Kyakhta to Europe.

which once rivaled the cathedrals of St. Petersburg in opulence, and are still standing there to this day, dilapidated shells and forlorn testimonies to Kyakhta's bygone days of glory. Officially, the trade was conducted on a barter basis, and the Russians were prohibited from purchasing tea with silver, but in reality silver, in the form of candlesticks and other disguised trinkets, was a common method of payment. Trade disputes were frequent. "The [Chinese] merchants are now holding money vouchers from the foreign merchants to a value of more than 80,000 taels of silver. If they try to prohibit them suddenly, the foreign merchants will not pay out the silver according to the voucher. I am afraid that the merchants' suffering will accumulate, and that incidents may easily occur," the Chinese government's representative complained.

In 19th-century Nizhny Novgorod, the great fair, at which some half of Russia's domestic goods changed hands, was officially inaugurated in late July with the ritual opening of the first *tsebik* of tea to arrive from Kyakhta. After the tea chests had been unloaded at the city's Siberian Wharf, samples were brought to the tea merchants' temporary offices in the "Chinese Rows," where expert "tea-smellers" examined the leaves, deciding which tea could be sold and not on the merit of its aroma alone. At the fair, the agents of the Kyakhta tea merchants used the cash payments received from wholesalers for the tea to purchase furs, velveteen, broadcloth, leather wares, and other goods destined for Kyakhta and the Chinese markets, while the wholesalers distributed their tea to provincial merchants all over Russia.

A new treaty between China and Russia in 1851 opened the Central Asian towns of Tacheng and Ili, on the border between present-day Kazakhstan and China's Xinjiang Uyghur Autonomous Region, to trade, thereby launching a direct westward caravan route to the Russian heartland and beyond. While the staple commodities in the Kyakhta trade were the black Bohea and Pekoe teas from Fujian, the main tea traded via the western route was Zhulan, a fine green tea from Jiande in Anhui province flavored with the shrub *Chloranthus spicatus*. This was destined not for Russia, but for the markets of Western Europe. Following the second Opium War (1857–58), Russian merchants acquired the right to purchase tea directly in Hankow (present-day Wuhan) on the middle reaches of the Yangtze river, thereby bypassing the Shanxi merchants. In 1862, the Kyakhta trade was dealt another blow, when the first "Canton tea," transshipped via London, was traded at Nizhny Novgorod. But while "Canton tea," heavily fired to counteract the months it would spend in a damp, moldy ship hold, soon dominated the mass-market with its lower price, delicate palates with deeper pockets preferred the Kyakhta caravan tea, which was more lightly fired to suit the dry, overland route.

With the opening of the Suez Canal in 1869, the tea purchased in Hankow could be transported to Russia via the Black Sea port of Odessa more rapidly and safely than through Kyakhta, and "Odessa tea" joined the competition at the Nizhny Novgorod fair. When navigation was opened on the Amur river, Russian steam boats carried tea from Hankow up to the Sea of Japan and along the Amur towards Lake Baikal for further transport by land. The Russians established several tea factories in Hankow's British concession, and used machines powered by steam to press the pulverized tea into cakes stamped with the respective company's insignia. In 1872, Ivanov & Co. set up the first brick tea factory in Fujian, pressing tea bricks out of black tea dust previously regarded as a waste product. Three years later, two Russian firms with factories in Fujian produced almost 5 million lb of brick tea destined for the samovars of Russia. While the Russians fared better than the British and the Americans in their relations with the Qing authorities, they were not exempted from the Chinese workers' cries of imperialism and exploitation. On 4 September, 1881, a fire broke out in the Fujian factory of Piatkov, Molchanov, & Co., whose employees refused to assist in putting out the blaze. A crowd gathered at the scene, shouting "Burn up all the foreign devils and their property!" while a group of hoodlums broke open the factory's safe and made off with the cash.

Around this time, Russia's temperance movement, battling the nation's debilitating, age-old craving for vodka, began to adopt tea as a new weapon. The First Moscow Temperance Society built five temperance tearooms, established in deprived districts such as the Khitrov Market, where a visitor was served a pot of tea with three lumps of sugar for 5½ kopecks.

To curtail alcohol consumption, the new State Vodka Monopoly restricted alcohol sales to government stores where no food was served, but according to Dr. A. V. Balov, a critic of the monopoly, this measure had no effect on would-be tipplers, who soon found ways to circumvent the inconvenience: "A customer enters a tearoom and orders tea. After emptying the glass, he retrieves a bottle of vodka from his pocket and pours himself a drink, and then returns the bottle to his pocket," the doctor wrote. Another, more refined method of temperance used by women was to drop a concoction known as "Alkola," a mixture of dandelion root, licorice, bromide, and soda advertised as a sure deterrent from alcohol, into the teacup of their unsuspecting husbands. At the very least, the tea-temperance movement won a symbolic victory when, in the late 19th century, *dat' na chai* ("for tea") replaced *dat' na vodku* ("for vodka") as the common Russian phrase for a tip.

The end of Kyakhta was sealed in 1891, when the first track of the Transsiberian Railroad was laid. An epic endeavor that galvanized the expanding Russian empire, the railroad was built across swamps and permafrost by tens of thousands of convict laborers and conscripted soldiers who, in addition to their back-breaking toil, often had to pay with their lives. Reaching Irkutsk in 1899 and Port Arthur on the Yellow Sea peninsula between Korea and Beijing in 1903, the iron horses rendered ox-carts and sleighs redundant, and pulled down the final curtain on Kyakhta. The market square which for more than a century and a half had bustled with a pidgin of the Chinese, Mongolian, and Russian tongues soon lay abandoned.

Kyakhta's demise, however, did not spell the end of Russia's love affair with tea. Like the English and the Dutch, the Russians sought to end their dependence on Chinese tea, and in 1893, the Popoff tea firm established the empire's first tea garden in the Caucasus near the Georgian town of Batumi. From there, tea cultivation soon spread across the mountains to the region of Rize in Turkey, where tea eventually replaced coffee as the national beverage. The Turks also adopted the Russian samovar, as did the Persians, Afghans, and other people in the Islamic world, whose history of tea will told in the following chapter.

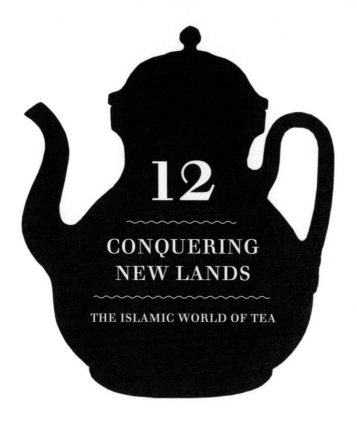

12

CONQUERING
NEW LANDS

~~~~~~~~~~~~~~~~~

THE ISLAMIC WORLD OF TEA

F ollowing the Prophet Muhammed's death in AD 632, Arab forces
spread his religion with awesome swiftness. By 732, they had
already clashed and been defeated by Charles Martel at the battle
of Tours in France, and 19 years later, at the eastern end of their expansion, Arab soldiers stood face to face with a Chinese army for the first and
last time at the Talas river in present-day Kazakhstan. The popular Arabic
proverb "Seek wisdom, even [if] in China," often attributed to the Prophet
(although Islamic scholars question its authenticity), encapsulates the relationship of the Islamic World to China: It's far away, but just might possess
some deep knowledge that would make the arduous journey worthwhile.
And even if it didn't, it did produce desirable commodities like silk, ceramics, and tea. By the 9th century, Arab dhows were trading at the southern
port town of Canton, where the merchant Suleyman noted the tea sold in

the markets, and in the 11th century, the Persian polymath al-Biruni displayed his knowledge of the tea plant.

Then, in 1258, the Mongols sacked Baghdad and put an end to the Abbasid caliphate. Whether they packed tea in their saddlebags on this particular campaign is doubtful; although it has been suggested that the habit of tea-drinking spread to western Asia with the Mongols, evidence for its presence as a beverage in Persia, Mesopotamia or the Levant is scanty before the 17th century. To control the western part of their empire, the Mongols moved their capital to Tabriz, west of the Caspian Sea's southern end, where Rashīd al-Din, the son of a Jewish apothecary who converted to Islam at the age of 30, rose to become one of the most powerful ministers under Ghazan (r. 1295–1304), the seventh Mongol ruler of Persia.

Rashīd al-Din was a prodigiously learned man who, in cooperation with the Mongol emissary Bolad, produced works on the history of Khubilai Khan's reign, the Chinese system of government, and a work on agriculture called *Kitab-i Āthār va Ahyā* ("The Book of Monuments and Living Things"), which, covering the entire continent from China to Egypt, was copied by scribes in both Persian and Arabic, and disseminated around the empire to encourage the development of agriculture. In his section on Chinese agriculture, al-Din provided detailed information on the botany and cultivation on crops such as coconuts, cinnamon, black pepper, sandalwood, oranges, jujubes, mulberry trees, litchi nuts, and an extensive entry on tea, describing its medicinal properties and the efforts of Khubilai Khan to encourage its cultivation in northern China. "There is a special kind [of tea] which they mix with musk, camphor, and other things. ...They grind the leaves in a mill just like henna or sifted flour. Then they roll it in a long piece of paper and stamp it for *tamghâ* [tax revenue] purposes. .... Whoever does sell it without a *tamghâ* will be considered to be at fault. They transport the tea in paper [like this] to all the provinces. This is a big commodity and it has a special taste and [nutritional] value," wrote al-Din.

In Transoxiana (present-day Uzbekistan), which lies between the Syr Darya and Amu Darya rivers that both flow westward into the saltwater Aral Sea, the Mongol empire was supplanted by that of the legendary

Timur (1336–1405), or Tamerlane, himself a member of a Turkicized Mongol subgroup and a Muslim. He set up his capital in Samarqand, and during his 35 campaigns conquered Persia and Georgia, abetted the capture of Moscow, ravaged Baghdad and Damascus, invaded northern India, and created the vast Timurid empire, before dying of a fever just as he was embarking on an expedition to subdue China. Shah Rukh, Timur's youngest son and successor, moved the Timurid capital to Herat in present-day western Afghanistan, refrained from military exploits, built magnificent mosques and theological colleges, and, in 1419, dispatched an embassy to Ming China. In his report to Shah Rukh, the embassy's diarist and artist Ghiyathuddin Naqqash recorded that the delegation, upon leaving China, was stopped and searched by Chinese officials, who wanted to make sure that they were not smuggling any contraband goods, tea in particular, which was a strategic, tightly controlled commodity used by the Chinese in the tea and horse trade with the Tibetans, and illicitly traded on pain of death.

"There are people [ascetics in China] full of wisdom who don't eat and drink much. They have never had cold water for generations, but they only drink boiled water flavoured with tea," wrote the Persian merchant Ali Akbar in the early 16th century. Tea is also listed in a Persian-Chinese trade dictionary from the period, but by 1543, it was still naught but hearsay in Bukhara, the fabled Silk Road oasis located some 130 miles west of Samarqand. From Bukhara, the 16th-century Turkish historian Seyfi Çelebī wrote that the Tibetans imported a leaf they called *cāy* from the Chinese, "of which they make a beverage that is drunk like we drink coffee. If they do not obtain their tea, their characters become as morose as those of opium eaters in Constantinople. ..." That tea had not yet penetrated into Central Asia in any greater quantities is also attested to by the English explorer Anthony Jenkinson, who, traveling east of the Caspian Sea in the middle of the 16th century, noted that the Tatar Turks in his caravan drank nothing but water and mare's milk.

The Bukharans were famous traders, who from their oasis town, strategically located in the heart of Central Asia, traveled east through

An Afghan tea house. Afghans drink "cooling" green tea in the summer, and "warming" black tea in the winter.

the Ferghana valley and over the Pamir Mountains to Kashgar and other Silk Road caravanserais, where they purchased silk, cotton goods, gems, tobacco, and rhubarb, carrying it in caravans to Siberia, Moscow, Persia, and beyond, before returning to Kashgar with merchandise such as hides, woolen cloth, carpets, mirrors, and sal ammoniac. *Dahuang,* dried Chinese rhubarb root, was a particularly valuable commodity which the Bukharans held a virtual monopoly on. Long prized in Europe as a panacea "given with great success in all obstructions of the liver, in the jaundice, in diarrhoeas," *dahuang* was also highly sought after in Russia and Siberia, while in Hindustan people would "gladly exchange for it more than ten times its weight in gold."

In the second of the 16th century, as the Mongol threat finally receded, the strategic importance to the Chinese of the tea and horse trade began to decline. Gradually, the Chinese government loosened its grip on the commodity, allowing private merchants to transport ever larger quantities of tea to the Uyghurs, Kazaks, Kirghiz, Uzbeks, Tajiks, and other people of Central Asia, who following a familiar pattern soon grew addicted to the humble infusion of leaves and twigs. From Bukhara, caravans carried the tea through the Karakum and Dasht-e Kavir deserts some 1,000 miles southwest to the Persian capital Isfahan, where by the first half of the 17th century it had become a part of daily life. In his account of the German state of Holstein's embassy to the Persian Shah in 1638, the secretary Adam Olearius noted the three types of taverns found in Isfahan: *scire chane* ("wine taverns"), where the whoremongers went; *cahwa chane* ("coffee taverns"), where the poets, historians, and storytellers went; and *tsia chattai chane* ("*Cathay* tea taverns"), where persons of good repute went to drink tea, smoke tobacco, and play chess, known in Persian as *shatranj* (from the Sanskrit *chaturanga* ("four arms")), a game in which the Persians according to Olearius even surpassed the Muscovites. "The Persians boil it [the tea] till the water hath got a bitterish taste and a blackish color and add thereto fennel, aniseed, or cloves, and sugar," he wrote. The Hindus in Isfahan, on the other hand, took their tea plain, in insulated cups made of "wood or cane done over with a plate of copper or silver gilt and sometimes of gold, so that the heat not being able to penetrate them, they may hold them in their hands even though the water were boiling."

Wherever Islam conquered, in North Africa, Persia and Central Asia, over-indulgence in alcohol was discouraged in accordance with the Koran. (In 986, the Russians, seeking a religion, briefly contemplated adopting Islam, but, perhaps because of the interdiction on alcohol, decided against it, and in 988 adopted Christianity instead.) And as it was the Buddhists of China who led the opposition to rice beer and adopted the tea plant to abet their meditative journeys, it was the mystical orders of Islam, the Sufis, who by the middle of the 15th century had begun to use coffee to keep awake during their nocturnal ceremonies, as they sought communion with God by freeing their minds through chanting, swirling, and swaying. From its native land in Yemen, coffee spread throughout the Islamic world, and coffee houses sprang up in Mecca, Cairo, Tangier, Istanbul, Baghdad, and Isfahan. Yet no sooner had the popularity of coffee begun to catch on than the Islamic clerics, worried at this worldly distraction from the mosque and religious duties, launched a crusade against it. If it could only be proved that coffee *intoxicated*, then it would be subject to the Koran's explicit ban, and the seditious, immoral coffee houses could be shut down with no further ado. Learned Muslim scholars racked their brains to find the effects of coffee intoxicating, but their arguments failed to carry any force of conviction, and the attempts of the theocratic authorities in Cairo and Mecca to close the coffee houses proved futile. Nevertheless, a religious stigma had been attached to the coffee bean, so when tea from China began to appear more regularly in the markets of Samarqand, Bukhara, and Isfahan in the 17th century, the seeds for a revolution in the drinking customs of the Islamic world were being sown.

As the maritime traffic between Europe and Asia expanded throughout the 17th century, English, Dutch, and Portuguese ships plying the Far East trade carried tea to the ports of call along the way, providing a new route for the beverage's spread around the globe. "Tea likewise is a common Drink with all the Inhabitants of *India*, as well *Europeans* as Natives; and by the *Dutch* is used as such a standing Entertainment, that the Tea-pot's seldom off the Fire, or unimploy'd," wrote the late 17th-century English traveler John Ovington following a voyage to Surat, which, situated some 200 miles north of present-day Mumbai on the western coast of India, was one of its major commercial cities in the 17th century. In other port towns with glimmering names like Batavia, Aden, and Zanzibar, European traders, administrators, and missionaries gathered on their verandas to partake of the exotic new beverage, brewed in Yixing pots and poured in dainty cups of Chinese porcelain, and were soon emulated by the local potentates and wealthy merchants.

In 1662, an English garrison of about 3,000 soldiers on foot and horse arrived in Morocco to take possession of Tangier, a port town near the Gibraltar Strait bestowed on Charles II as part of Catherine of Braganza's dowry. The 19th-century French anthropologist Auguste Mouliéras believed it was during this occupation of Tangier, which lasted until 1683, that the English introduced tea to Morocco, but the first recorded transmission did not occur until 1718, when the English envoy Coningsby Norbury included tea among his gifts to Basha Ahmad, the governor of Tetuan in northern Morocco. Soon, tea was being reexported from London to Morocco in growing quantities. In particular, the Moroccans took a liking to the "cooling" properties of green tea, a preference that suited the English tea merchants perfectly, as green tea gradually fell into disfavor in the British Isles.

Throughout the 18th century, tea remained a rare luxury in Morocco. In his *A Tour from Gibraltar to Tangier, Sallee, Mogodore, Santa Cruz, Tarudant, and Thence over Mount Atlas to Morocco*, published in 1793, the English surgeon William Lemprière provides the first detailed description of the Moroccan tea ceremony:

> Whatever be the time of day, tea is then brought in on a tea-board with short feet. This is the highest compliment that can be offered by a Moor; for tea is a very expensive and scarce article in Barbary, and is only drunk by the rich and luxurious. Their manner of preparing it is by putting some green tea, a small quantity of tansey, the same portion of mint, and a large portion of sugar (for the Moors drink their tea very sweet) into the tea-pot at the same time, and filling it up with boiling water. When these articles are infused a proper time, the fluid is then poured into remarkably small cups of the best India china, the smaller the more genteel, without any milk, and, accompanied with some cakes or sweetmeats, it is handed round to the company. From the great esteem in which this beverage is held by the Moors, it is generally drank by very small and slow sips, that its flavour may be the longer enjoyed; and as they usually drink a considerable quantity whenever it is introduced, this entertainment is seldom finished in less than two hours.

And having been dispatched to treat the eyes of the son of the Sultan Sidi Mohamed ben Abdellah, Lemprière relates this curious conversation:

> His majesty next asked, in a very austere manner, "What was the reason I had forbidden Muley Absulem [the Sultan's son] the use of tea?" My reply was, "Muley Absulem has very weak nerves, and tea is injurious

to the nervous system." "If tea is so unwholesome," replied his majesty, "why do the English drink so much?" I answered "It is true, they drink it twice a day, but then they do not make it as strong as the Moors, and they generally use milk with it, which lessens its pernicious effects. But the Moors, when once they begin to use it, make it very strong, drink a great deal, and very frequently without milk." "You are right," said the emperor, and I know it sometimes makes their hands shake."

Back in Persia, according to one account, the first Russian samovar was given to the governor of Rasht, a town near the southwest coast of the Caspian Sea, in 1821. A girl in his harem learned how to prepare tea with the samovar, and together, the girl and the samovar were offered to the ruler of Persia, Fath Ali Shah. From there, the samovar spread to the nobility and other wealthy families, and eventually all the way to Syria and Jordan. The 19th-century German physician Jacob E. Pollak wrote that tea, having fallen out of use during the chaotic 18th century, was "reintroduced" to Persia in the 1830s with a gift to the Persian crown prince. In 1850, Amir Kabir, chief minister to the Persian shah, granted a monopoly on the production of samovars with an accompanying government subsidy to a master craftsman in Isfahan, but when Amir Kabir shortly after fell out of favor, the craftsman was heartlessly forced to return the government money and close down his business.

By this time, the struggle between Britain and Russia for dominance in Asia, romantically dubbed the Great Game, was being waged intensely by British and Russian adventurers and agents disguised as turbaned Persians and Turks, making maps and surveying potential battlegrounds. With Britain in control of India and Russia making territorial gains in Persia, the rivalry between the two imperial giants focused on Afghanistan, Britain's buffer against a feared Russian invasion of India. In 1829, the master spy Lt. Alexander Burnes departed for a reconnaissance mission up the Indus river, and with great resourcefulness managed to reach Bukhara in the heart of Central Asia. Upon his return, he published the popular account *Travels into Bokhara,* which fully attests to the place tea had acquired in the daily lives of the Uzbek, Iranian, and Afghan people:

Nothing is done in this country without tea, which is handed round at all times and hours, and gives a social character to conversation, which is very agreeable. The Uzbeks drink their tea with salt instead of sugar, and sometimes mix it with fat; it is then called 'keimuk chah.' After each person has had one or two large cups, a smaller one is handed round, made in the usual manner, without milk. The leaves of the pot are then divided among the party, and chewed like tobacco.

In Bukhara's bazaar, Burnes observed the preparation of tea in European tea urns, and describing the trade, related that 950 horse-loads of tea, about 200,000 lb, had been brought there that year across the Pamir highlands from Yarkand, a major caravanserai on the western edge of the Taklamakan Desert in Chinese Turkestan, about 100 miles southeast of present-day Kashgar. Transported to Yarkand from the Chinese heartland "by a tedious journey of many months," the tea was then transferred to bags and sewn up in raw hides, as boxes would not have withstood the remaining journey. All of the tea sold in Bukhara was green, and the best, known as "banca tea," came from a place in China called Tukht in small tin or lead boxes, cost 4 rupees per lb, and tasted better than any tea Burnes had tried in England, as it "retains its flavour from never having been subjected to the close atmosphere in a ship's hold or the sea air."

"I had a long talk with the Yoozbashee to-day about tea," relates Robert Shaw, a young Assam tea planter who, having traveled to Central Asia to investigate a possible new market for Indian tea, found himself caught up in the Great Game, becoming the first Englishman to reach Yarkand in 1868–69. "The quantity drunk is enormous," Shaw continues. "He [Yoozbashee] himself takes part of, at least, eight or ten teapots in a day. A Toork [Turk] who does not consume a teapot full at noon, and another before twelve, is not considered a man." According to Shaw, 10,000 camel-loads of tea, nearly 5 million lb, entered Bukhara annually from China, a 25-fold increase over the quantity cited by Burnes some 40 years earlier.

Every year in the 12th month of the Islamic lunar calender, Persian pilgrims embarked on their Hajj to Mecca, packing enough tea in their bags to last the journey. In this manner, the use of tea was disseminated to the countries and emirates of the Saudi Arabian peninsula, which subsequently found a ready supply of affordable tea in the rapidly growing quantities being exported from India. In his classic 1870s travel book *Travels in Arabia Deserta*, the English poet Charles Montagu Doughty provides a wonderful account of how tea came to be adopted by the bedouins of Saudi Arabia:

> The afternoon was clear; the sun dried our wet clothing, and a great coffee party assembled at Zeyd's tent. He had promised Khalîl [Mr. Doughty] would make *chai* (tea), "which is the coffee-drink, he told them, of the Nasâra. — And good Khalîl, since the sheykhs would taste thy *chai*, look thou put in much sugar." I had today pure water of the rain in the desert, and that tea was excellent. Zeyd cried to them, "And how likes you the kahwat of the Nasâra?" They answered, "The sugar is good, but as for this which Khalîl calls *chai*, the smack of it is little better than warm water." They would say "Thin drink, and not gross tasting" as is their foul-water coffee. Rahŷel drank his first cup out, and returned it mouth downward (a token with them that he would [have] no more of it), saying, "Khalîl, is not this *el-khamr*? The fermented or wine of the Nasâra": and for conscience sake he would not drink; but the company sipped their sugar-drink to the dregs, and bade the stranger pour out more. I called to Rahŷel's remembrance the Persians drinking chai in the Haj caravan. Beduins who tasted tea the second time, seeing how highly I esteemed it, and feeling themselves refreshed, afterward desired it extremely, imagining this drink with sugar to be the comfort of all human infirmities. But I could never have, for my asking, a cup of their fresh milk; they put none in their coffee, and to put whole milk to this *kahwat en-Nasâra* seemed to them a very outlandish and waste using of God's benefit.

Thus the remarkable process which has gradually transformed the Islamic world, homeland of the coffee drink, into some of the most ardent imbibers of tea, was set in motion. In Morocco, the increasingly severe view taken of coffee and tobacco, which were prohibited by the conservative Wahabis, stimulated tea consumption. At the end of the 19th century, a complete ban on tobacco by the Moroccan ruler Moulay Hassan coincided with a boom in tea imports from 430,000 lb in 1880 to 5.5 million lb in 1910. A smallpox

(Above left) A Moroccan poster advertises "Luck" – "green tea imported direct from China"; (Above right) An old man relaxes with a glass of green mint tea.

epidemic in Morocco at the end of the 19th century further boosted the importation of tea, as doctors ordered their patients to fast and only drink an infusion of tea with mint and wormwood. Taken between the five daily calls to prayer, tea wove itself into the fabric of Moroccan life, and evolved into a quasi-sacred ceremony that embodies the country's spirit, for it is in the awareness of movements and phrases endlessly repeated and handed down through the generations that humans find a deep feeling of recognition and resonance – the nearest approximation to what might called culture.

Moroccans make their tea in curvaceous pots of silver, enamelware, or aluminium. The tea is brought to a boil, and mint and a large quantity of broken sugar cone lumps are added. Some tea is poured into one of the glasses and returned to the pot in order to mix the tea, which is then poured into the glasses from a height to produce a foam, and served on a tray together with almonds, pistachios, sweetmeats, and cakes. In the Atlas Mountains, the tea is often perfumed with rosemary and wild thyme, while in southern Morocco, people like to add a pinch of saffron. According to manner of preparation and region, Moroccans distinguish between an array of infusions: *al m'qazoui* is strong, bitter, and black, and appreciated among people in the Sahara both for its digestive properties and its ability to suppress hunger; *al assida* is weaker, sweeter, yellowish green, and served as a dessert. Then there is the *rezza*, a shot of strong green tea served with an espresso-like mousse.

Both Moroccan Muslims and Jews employ tea for various important occasions, such as during the meal following the Jewish circumcision ceremony, and the ritual to celebrate the baby's weaning from breast milk. Compared with their Muslim brethren, however, Moroccan Jews prepare a thinner infusion which contains less tea than mint, and often add orange blossom, verbena, and geranium. In the old days, as the Jewish people are prohibited from making a fire on the Sabbath, they got their tea water on that day from Muslims, who boiled it in pots over open fires. Or else, the wife of the house would place a small pot of water over a lamplight on Friday night, in order to make tea the following day.

In Persia, tea production was initiated at the beginning of the 20th century, when the Persian consul to India succeeded in smuggling some 3,000 Assam tea seedlings back to his country and had them planted in the Lāhījan region on the southwestern side of the Caspian Sea. Iranians commonly drink black tea, which is generally prepared in the Russian samovar style, and served in tulip-shaped glasses, *estakān,* on a saucer. The tea is taken either *pur-rang* ("with much color") or *kam-rang* ("with little color"), and sweetened with lumps of sugar that are alternatively added to the cup, or placed in the mouth, so that the tea can be filtered through the lump.

By contrast, the neighboring Afghans drink both black and green tea. As in Chinese herbal medicine, green tea is classified by the Afghans as "cool," and only drunk during the hot summer months, while the somewhat more expensive black tea is considered "hot" and thus more suitable for the winter months. Each guest is provided with an individual teapot and bowl, which is rinsed with some tea, whereupon an ample amount of granulated sugar is placed in the bowl, and the tea poured. Since no more sugar is added, the tea becomes more bitter with each cup. In Afghanistan, "sugar on the side" tea is taken with candy, or sugar-coated apricot pits, chickpeas (garbanzo beans), or almonds.

In Turkey, tea remained an expensive and exotic commodity until the second half of the 19th century, when the Suez Canal opened up a route for Russian ships carrying tea to Odessa in the Black Sea, allowing also the Turks to import larger amounts of tea, as well as Russian samovars. In 1881, Barbier de Meynard listed green tea, black powdered tea, and export tea in his Turkish-French dictionary. But it wasn't until the final collapse of the Ottoman Empire in 1923, when Turkey lost the port city of Mocha in Yemen and the control over its coffee production, along with the arrival to power of the resolute reformist Atatürk, who derided coffee as "traditional and retrograde," that tea began to emerge as Turkey's new national beverage. Tea seeds were imported from Russian plantations in the Caucasus and planted southeast of the Black Sea in the coastal region of Rize, where the tea plant thrived and production expanded. In addition to adopting the samovar, the Turks developed their own unique tea utensil: the stacked *çaydanlik*, which consists of a lower kettle used to boil the water and heat a smaller top kettle containing a concentrate of strong tea. To drink the tea, the concentrate is diluted with the boiling water to desired strength and mixed with sugar in tulip-shaped *estakān* glasses, held at the rim with the fingertips to avoid scalding. A truly fine cup of tea, say the Turks, has the color of a rabbit's eye.

In this manner, the relative cheapness of tea and its thirst-quenching properties transformed the Middle East from the home of coffee into a staunch bastion of tea-drinkers. By the 1960s, every country in North Africa and the Middle East, except Algeria and Israel, drank more tea than coffee, and the region now absorbs almost one quarter of the world's tea imports. Statistics from the International Tea Committee show that of the 30 leading tea consumption countries, 15 are Muslim countries in North Africa and the Middle East. Among these nations, the Qataris top the list, with an average consumption of 6.9 lb of tea per year per person.

13

APPROVED
BY PHYSICIANS

THE ADVENT OF TEA
IN EUROPE

As we have seen in the previous chapter, the British and Dutch played a crucial role in disseminating tea to the Middle East and northwest Africa. The European story of tea begins in the 15th century, when the rise of the Ottoman Turks in Anatolia blocked the caravan routes from Persia, Central Asia, and India to Europe, disrupting the trade in spices such as cinnamon, cloves, ginger, nutmeg, and above all pepper, to which the European palate had become addicted. The great age of European exploration began with the dream to find a sea route to the riches of the Orient free from troublesome interlopers. As Zheng He's treasure fleet explored the east coast of Africa, the first Portuguese *barchas* and *barinels* began probing the opposite coast of that continent. By 1483, the Portuguese had worked their way down to present-day Angola, before Vasco da Gama rounded the Cape of Good Hope and crossed the Indian

Ocean, reaching Calicut on the southwestern coast of India on 20 May, 1498, where the party dispatched ashore was greeted by two Moors. "May the Devil take you! What brought you here?" one of them asked in Castilian. "Christians and spices," the party replied, greatly astonished to hear their tongue spoken so far away from home.

The Portuguese king Manuel, who dubbed himself "Lord of the Conquest, Navigation, and Commerce of Ethiopia, Arabia, Persia, and India" only to be lampooned as the "Grocer King" by the French king Francis I, had heard of China, so upon the departure of Diogo Lopes de Siqueira for Malacca on the southwestern tip of the Malayan peninsula in 1508, he was instructed by King Manuel to find out everything he could about that country. Siqueria failed in his mission, but when Afonso de Albuquerque captured Malacca in 1511, he met Chinese merchants, and in 1517, Fernão Peres de Andrade paid the first official Portuguese visit to the Chinese city of Canton in the Pearl river delta.

The first European reference to tea appears in the *Delle navigationi e viaggi*, a collection of famous geographical accounts compiled by the Venetian Giambattista Ramusio and published in 1545. In his introduction to Marco Polo's voyages, Ramusio relates a dinner he had attended on the island of Murano, near Venice, with the Persian merchant Hajjī Mohammed, who told him about a Chinese drink with excellent therapeutic qualities called *Chiai*. The Persian believed that if this drink became known in Persia and Europe, their merchants would stop looking for rhubarb, the precious medicinal plant traded across the Eurasian content, and start searching for this herb.

One of the major accounts of the Far East at the time was written by Pedro Teixeira, a Portuguese traveler "much addicted to the study of history," who in 1586 left Lisbon with a fleet dispatched to preempt the British. Having visited Goa, Malacca, and Persia, rounded the globe, and traveled by land from India to Italy, he published his book the *Kings of Persia* in 1610, which contains many interesting digressions on African and Asian ethnology, natural history, and pharmacology. Among them is the following passage:

There is another beverage called *kaoàh*, much used in all Turkey, Arabia, Persia and Syria. It is a seed, very like little dry beans, and is brought from Arabia. It is prepared in houses kept for the purpose. The decoction is thick, nearly black, and insipid. If it has any flavor this inclines to bitterness, but very little. All those who want it assemble in these houses, where they are served it very hot in Chinese porcelain cups, that may hold four or five ounces. These they take into their hands, and sit blowing on it and sipping. Those who are accustomed to drink say that it is good for the stomach, prevents flatulence and piles, and stimulates the appetite.

After the same fashion is the Chinese *cha*, and is taken in the same way, except that *cha* is the leaf of a little herb, a certain plant brought from Tartary, which was shown to me in Malacca. But, because it was dry, I could not well judge of its form. It is proclaimed to be very beneficial, and prophylactic of those disorders which Chinese gluttony might provoke.

In 1579, the creation of the United Netherlands by the union of the seven northern provinces – Holland, Zeeland, Utrecht, Gelderland, Groningen, Friesland, and Overijssel – unleashed a wave of energy that rapidly transformed this small industrious seafaring republic into the world's commercial superpower. In July 1599, Admiral Jacob Corneliszoon van Neck returned from the Far East with a cargo of spices that realized a neat profit of 400 percent. Subsequently, in 1602, the Dutch East India Company was formally established in Amsterdam with a capital of some 6 million guilders, and in 1607, one of its vessels made the earliest recorded shipment of tea by a European nation, from Macao to Java. Two years later, the Dutch purchased tea in the Japanese port of Hirado on the west coast of Kyushu, and it is believed that the first commercial consignment arrived in Europe the following year, although this date remains conjectural.

Close on the heels of the Dutch were the British. The English East India Company had been founded in 1600, and in 1613, it set up a factory in Hirado. When an employee of the factory, William Eaton, was dispatched to purchase timber in Omura, he was attacked during a dispute over prices, and killed his assailant. Writing to his colleague Richard Wickham "in Kyoto or elsewhere," on 22 June, 1616, Eaton relates the unfortunate event,

A European tea buyer inspects a sample in a merchant's office in the port of Yokohama, Japan.

and concludes his letter with the second known reference to tea by an Englishman: "I hope you will remember mee for the chawe I wished you to bye for mee & c. And thus for present I end, praying to the Allmightey God for your good health & welfare. . . ." Eaton must have taken a liking to tea during his ten years in Japan, for three years later, he wrote to the factory's head, Richard Cocks: "I pray you lett my Domingo bye for mee some lickerich, if theare be aney to be had. If not a kind of leafe that they use to put in chaw, w'ch hee knows well enow doth taste lick lickerich etc." The "kind of leafe" referred to by Eaton is indeed licorice (*Glycyrrhiza glabra*), the *kanzo* plant, which contains sugar, and was used by the Japanese to sweeten their tea.

Ironically, the Chinese initially traded their tea for the medicinal herb sage, at a rate of 4 lb of tea for 1 lb of sage. "The Dutch in their second Voyage to China," wrote the 18th-century Scottish physician Thomas Short in his treatise *A Natural History of Tea*, "carry'd thither good Store of dried Sage, and exchanged it with the Chinese for tea; they had three or four Pound of the last for one Pound of the first, calling it a wonderful *European* Herb, possessed of as many Virtues as the Indians could possibly ascribe to their Shrub Leaf. But because they exported not such large quantities of Sage as they imported of *Tea*, they bought a great deal, and gave eight Pence or ten Pence a Pound for it in *China*."

"As tea begins to come into use with some of the people, we expect some jars of Chinese, as well as Japanese tea with every ship," the Dutch

TEA IN TAIWAN

In 1623, the Dutch East India Company established a trading post in southern Taiwan to do business with the island's headhunting (as they believed) Austronesian aborigines, and on 5 December, 1635, Cornelis Caesar, the commanding officer of the Dutch Fort Zeelandia, reported that the *Trouw* had sailed for Persia with almost 15,000 lb of Taiwan tea in its hold. While this is the first record of a tea shipment from Taiwan, with no other evidence of tea manufacturing on the island at the time, historians believe that it was most likely a transshipment from Japan or China. In April, 1661, the Ming-dynasty loyalist Zheng Chenggong (or Koxinga), seeking a base from which to counterattack the new Manchu rulers of China, besieged the Dutch in Fort Zeelandia with 25,000 troops, forcing them to surrender 9 months later. The Zheng family controlled Taiwan for 21 years, before it was defeated by the Manchu general Shi Lang in the great sea battle of the Pescadores, a group of islands in the Taiwan Strait. After the Manchu government's annexation of Taiwan, land-hungry farmers from southern Fujian began venturing across the treacherous "black-water ditch" to settle on the plains of the island's western side, as the aborigines retreated into the mountains. In 1701, the Chinese official Wu Tinghua noted the production of tea in the central Maoluo Mountains. The tea, he wrote, had a very "cold" character, so that the aborigines did not dare to drink it. In 1717, another official recorded: "There is a lot of tea in the Shuishalian Mountains. Its taste and color are like Songluo.... But the road is dangerous, and the aborigines are fearsome, so the Chinese dare not go there to pick [the tea]. Nor do they know how to make the tea. If one could find persons who could manufacture Wuyi tea, and hire the aborigines to pick it and make it, the fragrance and flavor would be very good."

Chinese tea-taster. Oolong tea later became Taiwan's special forte.

East India Company wrote to its Governor General in Batavia in Java in 1637. Tea became the fashionable drink in society in The Hague, and the Dutch introduced the new drink to Germany, where a handful of the leaves cost 15 gold coins at a pharmacy in Nordhausen; to France, where Cardinal Mazarin, chief minister to Louis XIII, became an avid convert; and across the Atlantic to New Amsterdam, later known as New York City.

The shop of Thomas Garway, known as Garraway's from the 18th century onward.

In England, the anonymous *Treatise of Warm Beer*, published in 1641, which discusses the advantages of hot drinks versus cold, does not list tea among the beverages consumed in the country at the time. By 1657, however, Thomas Garway's famous coffee house in Exchange Alley, a center for important business transactions which in addition to coffee served ale, punch, brandy, and arrack (liquor distilled from mainly either rice or the sap of coconut palms), was also offering tea, presented as a miraculous panacea that, among many other things, "...prevents and cures Agues, Surfets and Fevers, by infusing a fit quantity of the Leaf, thereby provoking a most gentle Vomit and breathing of the Pores." On 23 September, 1658, the Sultaness Head Coffee House inserted the first advertisement for tea in a London newspaper, *Mercurius Politicus*, which later recorded that tea, coffee, and chocolate were sold "almost in every street." Samuel Pepys, the famous diarist, gossip, and coffee house habitué, drank his first cup of tea on 25 September, 1660: "And afterwards did send for a Cupp of Tee (a China drink) of which I had never drank before," he wrote. That same year, British parliament set a new tax on tea at 8 pence per gallon (twice the tax on coffee).

In 1662, a royal case of bait and switch was adroitly executed when the waning Portuguese empire sealed an alliance with the rising English through the marriage of the beautiful Catherine of Braganza to the debt-ridden Charles II, who, in addition to trading posts in Tangier and Bombay (Mumbai), was promised £500,000 in cash by the Portuguese, the richest dowry ever brought by an English queen consort. When an English representative arrived in Lisbon, however, he was informed by the Portuguese queen that she would only be able to pay half that sum, and that the reduced payment would be made in bags of spices and sugar, not silver coins. While this unfulfilled dowry bedeviled relations between England and Portugal for many years, Catherine became a beloved queen, and is credited with having brought the drink of temperance into the English royal family, commemorated by Edmund Waller in his 1663 panegyric poem "On Tea":

> The Muse's friend, tea does our fancy aid,
> Repress those vapours which the head invade,
> And keep the palace of the soul serene,
> Fit on her birthday to salute the Queen.

Other than the coffee houses, pharmacies were the main outlet for tea, which was largely viewed as a medicine, and no sooner had the exotic novelty drink from the Far East begun to circulate in Europe than medical professionals aligned themselves in two diametrically opposed camps: one that believed tea to be a panacea for all ills, and one that derided tea as a dangerous foreign herb detrimental to human health. The first salvo was fired in 1635 by the German physician Simon Paulli, who wrote: "As to the virtues they attribute to it, it may be admitted that it does possess them in the Orient, but it loses them in our climates, where it becomes, on the contrary, very dangerous to use. It hastens the death of those that drink it, especially if they have passed the age of forty years."

In 1641, the renowned Dutch physician Nikolas Dirx, under the pseudonym Nikolas Tulp, responded with an equally unequivocal endorsement: "Nothing is comparable to this plant. Those who use it are for that reason, alone, exempt from all maladies and reach an extreme old age. Not only does it procure great vigor for their bodies, but it preserves them from gravel [aggregations of crystals formed in the urinary tract] and gallstone, headaches, colds, ophthalmia, catarrh, asthma, sluggishness of the stomach, and intestinal troubles." Subsequently, the learned doctor Guy Patin of Paris joined the fray, denouncing tea as "the newest impertinence of the century." The Dutch physician Cornelis Decker, popularly known as Dr. Bontekoe (a name he adopted himself from a sign near his father's shop; it means "spotted cow"), outdid everybody in his *Treatise on the Excellent Herb Tea* by recommending up to 200 cups per day. Not surprisingly, the records of the Dutch East India Company reveal that Dr. Bontekoe received a substantial reward for his role in boosting the sales of tea.

Much of the first tea imported to Europe came from Japan, where Portuguese missionaries led by the Jesuit François Xavier had in the 16th century brought about the most dramatic conversion to Christianity since the conversion of Ireland by St. Patrick. By 1582, 150,000 Japanese had converted, worshiping in some 200 churches, and Christian samurai generals went to battle flying crosses on their banners. Then, in 1587, Hideyoshi, the Japanese leader who had ordered Sen Rikyū's *seppuku*, angered by the pomposity of the Portuguese prelates and sensing the entrenchment of an alien force outside his control, suddenly ordered the expulsion of all missionaries and the brutal persecution of all believers. The Japanese displayed as much ingenuity as the Romans had, crucifying Christians upside down in tidal flats, where they were slowly drowned by the incoming tide.

By 1638, the Portuguese had been completely expelled, leaving the Dutch with a monopoly on Japan's trade with the West that lasted until 1853. Alongside the Dutch Company's official business, its meagerly paid employees (who had part of their salary withheld until the expiry of their time in the tropics to prevent desertion) ran a thriving "private" trade, the ships sometimes so laden with their goods that the Company's own cargo had to be left ashore. In the 1680s, there was a big scandal when the Japanese authorities cracked down on the contraband trade in Nagasaki and expelled the Dutch Company's representative Andreas Cleijer, who, wealthy from his little side business, retreated to his opulent house on the Tiger Canal in Batavia. Here, he planted tea seeds brought from Japan, thereby garnering the honor of being the first European to cultivate the tea plant successfully outside its traditional homelands. The realization that tea could be cultivated in Java opened the door for a new colonial endeavor, but the idea was not revived until the 1820s, and tea cultivation in Java did not become an industry in earnest until late that century.

By making Batavia the hub of their Far East operations, the Dutch had put themselves at a decided disadvantage in the burgeoning tea trade with China. Expelled by the Dutch from Java in 1684, the English East India Company made its first importation of tea directly from China to England in 1689. By the early 18th century, the tea trade was centered on Canton, where the English and French had been allowed to establish factories. The Dutch, by contrast, had to wait for the Chinese tea junks to arrive in Batavia, paying higher prices for lower-quality tea.

In 1678, the English East India Company (EEIC) imported 4,717 lb of tea, which glutted the London market. At this time, the Company's most important commodity had shifted from Spice Island pepper to Indian cotton, which threatened the English textile industry. Legislation introduced to curtail the imports of Indian cotton prompted the Company to turn its attention to tea. Subsequently, it was the enormous productivity of the steam-powered British textile industry that devastated its Indian counterpart, and turned India into an importer of British cloth. This in turn spurred the Indian production of opium, which it used to pay for British cotton, and which the British increasingly used to pay for its Chinese tea. Later, in the 19th century, the Indians were compensated for the demise of their cotton manufacturing with the advent of tea cultivation in Assam and elsewhere in India, which provided employment for millions of workers and became India's main export industry.

The EEIC's switch to tea proved fortuitous, for through this trade, it became the wealthiest, most powerful commercial enterprise in the world, able to command armies, challenge nations, make war, form alliances, issue its own money, and run its own courts of justice. In 1702, the EEIC's tea cargo from China was made up of two-thirds Singlo, common green tea; one-sixth Imperial, another kind of green tea also known as gunpowder;

and one-sixth Bohea, the black tea from the Wuyi Mountains in northern Fujian that eventually overtook green tea as the most popular variety. Tea soon became a more important commodity than silk, and in 1721, some 1 million lb reached the shores of England, that is, approximately two fully-laden East Indiamen, which were often constructed with a registered tonnage of 499 tons to avoid the obligation of having to carry a chaplain, required by law on all ships of 500 tons or more.

The first English silver teapot, presented by Lord Berkeley to the Committee of the East India Company in 1670.

With the growing demand, prices fell, although the cost of tea remained exorbitant until well into the 18th century. In 1650, 1 lb of tea in England cost somewhere between £6 and £10, which is the equivalent of £500 to £850 ($975 to $1,650) in today's currency. In 1666, Abbé Reynal of Paris recorded that tea in London cost £2 and 15 shillings per lb, and in 1680, tea was advertised in the London *Gazette* for £1 and 10 shillings per lb, £182 ($355) in today's money. The profits from the tea trade made by the Company were equally incredible. In 1705, the English ship *Kent* carried 62,700 lb of tea from Canton to London, purchased in China for £4,700 and auctioned in England for £50,100, a neat mark-up of some 1,000 percent.

As ballast for these lucrative cargoes, the East Indiamen carried the very utensils needed to prepare and drink the tea: Yixing teapots and porcelain teacups and saucers from Jingdezhen. But no sooner had the vogue for tea begun in Europe than its potters and silversmiths were busy fashioning their own tea utensils, in the first flush of chinoiserie by imitating the Chinese wares, then by adapting the utensils to the esthetic sensibilities of their respective countries. The earliest English teapot made of silver is a tapered pot from 1670, given to the East India Company and now in the

Victoria and Albert Museum. During the reign of Queen Anne (1702–14), pyriform, or pear-shaped, teapots with graceful swan-neck spouts enjoyed great popularity, as did globular silver teapots on a raised foot. These were followed by a fashion for teapots formed as urns or vases on a high foot, lavishly decorated with festoons, ribbon knots, and medallions.

The first European imitation of porcelain, a tin-glazed earthenware known as faience, was created by the Dutch potter Aelbregt de Keiser in 1650. The holy grail, however, was the production of true porcelain, which with its translucent fragility and delicate paintings had become a symbol of prestige and refinement among wealthy Europeans. The Venetians, Florentines, English, and French all tried to uncover its secret, before a brilliant German chemist saved his own life by solving the riddle. The improbable story of Johann Fredrick Böttger began in 1701, when, as a pharmacist's apprentice, he played a simple prank on his friends, fooling them that he had found the philosopher's stone – the substance with the power to transmute base metals into gold. To Böttger's horror, the rumor of his false feat reached the ears of Augustus II, King of Saxony, who took the young man prisoner and ordered him to produce gold on pain of death. Several times, Böttger found himself on the verge of execution, but, supported by the kind minister Tschirnhaus, finally managed to escape the gallows by producing something that Augustus coveted almost as much as women and gold – true porcelain. Böttger's sensational discovery in 1708 spawned the famous Meissen factory, the first European producer of porcelain, but did not earn Böttger his freedom. A sick and broken man, he was not released from his prison until 1714, and was hounded by Augustus to find the philosopher's stone right up to his death five years later.

It was in Queen Anne's reign that the nobility created a scandal by substituting tea for ale at breakfast. The tea, served in porcelain cups not much larger than thimbles, was taken together with another novelty from across the seas, sugar, introduced from the Americas by the Spanish and Portuguese. In 1660, the average annual consumption of sugar in England was 2 lb per person. By 1700, this number, spurred by the vogue for tea (and coffee), had doubled, as the English wrested control over the sugar trade from the Spanish and Portuguese by establishing plantations in their new dominions in the West Indies, where African slaves toiled under inhumane conditions to plant, harvest, and process the sugar to be stirred into high-society teacups.

While milk tea was drunk by the Manchu officials that the Europeans would have encountered, and the Dutchman Johann Nieuhoff had been offered tea with milk at a banquet in Canton in 1655, the honor of introducing this custom to Europe is traditionally ascribed to Madame de la Sablière, who in 1680 served tea with milk at her famous Paris salon, attended among others by the famous fabulist and poet La Fontaine. Jugs for milk or cream began to appear in English tea paintings in the late 17th century, and, in 1698, the formidable Lady Rachel Russell, in a letter to her daughter, reported having come across "little bottles to pour out milk for tea; they call them milk bottles." She also wrote, contrary to contemporary tea wisdom, that green tea was good with milk too.

At the beginning of the 18th century, London had some 2,000 coffee houses, hotbeds of political gossip, intellectual ferment, and grandiose commercial schemes that were also known as "penny universities" for the affordable drinks and worldly knowledge to be acquired there. "He who has trained his mind by an exchange of thoughts in conversation, becomes more subtle and pliable than when he has nourished his mind exclusively by reading. . . . Coffee-houses provided them with a place for the interchange of ideas, and for the formation of public opinion. They were. . . brotherhoods for the diffusion of a new humanism," wrote the English scholar Harold Routh. While tea was sold and served in these all-male establishments, coffee was the most popular beverage, and London the coffee-drinking capital of Europe. But this dominance of coffee was not to last.

In 1717, Thomas Twining opened the city's first tea house, The Golden Lyon, at 217 The Strand, where part of it stands to this very day. Here, ladies, barred from the coffee houses, could purchase their own tea. Twining also pioneered the English innovation of blending different teas, later brought to perfection in famous blends such as English Breakfast. Twining's grandson Richard later explained the genesis of this custom:

In my Grandfather's time – for it is a tale to which I have often willingly attended, whatever the reader may do – it was the custom for Ladies and Gentlemen to come to the shop, and to order their own Teas – The chests used to be spread out, and when my Grandfather had mixed some of them together, *in the presence of his Customers,* they used to taste the Tea: and the mixing was varied till it suited the palates of the purchasers.... Whoever understands Tea, and clears home, for example, twenty Chests of Hyson [the most common Chinese green tea], will find, upon tasting them, separately and acurately, that some have rather too much flavour, and are therefore coarse, some have too little, and are therefore weak.... By making a judicious mixture of these Chests, a better Tea may be got, than any of the Chests, taken singly, could afford. Besides, if this custom were not to be practised, it would be impossible to preserve that similarity of Tea, at any given price, which every Dealer must preserve, if he means to give satisfaction to his customer."

By 1730, London's craze for coffee had dissipated as suddenly as it had caught on, and England's preference for tea been firmly established. One reason why England, contrary to all other countries in Europe (except for Ireland), became a nation of tea drinkers was the monopoly and dominance of the English East India Company, which brought so much tea to the shores of England that it simply flooded coffee out of the market. In his *Coffee, The Epic of a Commodity*, the German newspaperman Heinrich Eduard Jacob offered another theory:

We must not forget that coffee made its appearance as an antidote, when individuals and the nation were given to gross excess in the consumption of alcoholic liquors. But in England it remained a foreigner. It had cultivated an excitability and an acuteness which were not, in the long run, accordant with the English character. 'A man's house is his castle.' Coffee ran counter to this family isolation of the Briton. It was not a family beverage; it made people talkative and disputatious, even though in a sublime fashion. It made them critical and analytical. It could work wonders, but it could not produce comfort. It did not promote sitting in a circle round the hearth, while the burning logs crackled and were gradually reduced to ashes.

As the English abandoned coffee for tea, the French deserted tea for coffee. In his 1694 *Histoire Générale des Drogues*, pharmacist Pierre Pomet tells us that tea, which had been in general use among the French nobility in the latter half of the 17th century, was subsequently entirely superseded by coffee and chocolate. This change in taste exacerbated the already precarious financial circumstances of the French East India Company, a latecomer to the Far East, and together with the Dutch and Danes, a rival to England for the tea trade. While tea consumption in France dried up, the tea boom in England had led to higher taxes, which in turn made smuggling a lucrative business. Henry Phillips, in his *History of Cultivated Vegetables* of 1822, wrote:

> In 1720, the French began to send it [tea] to us by a clandestine commerce, which the high duties created; and this unlawful traffic was carried to so great an extent, that it was not uncommon to meet (even within the memory of the author of this work,) a troop of a hundred horses laden with bags of tea. The farmers in Sussex dared not refuse them a passage through their grounds. So formidable were these gangs of smugglers, that to lie under the suspicion of being an informer, or in any way to give them offence, was as dangerous in Sussex, as it would be in Spain to incur the jealousy of the officers of the Inquisition.

The most notorious tea smugglers were the Hawkhurst gang, known for one of the grisliest murders of the times. In 1746, the Hawkhursters joined forces with the Wingham gang to smuggle more than 11 tons of tea, but the venture went awry when the Winghamers tried to double-cross their accomplices. A sword-fight ensued between the two gangs, in which the Hawkhursters injured seven Wingham men and stole 40 of their horses. With the profits from the illicit trade, the gang's financier Arthur Gray built a magnificent mansion in Seacox Heath in Sussex nicknamed "Gray's Folly," replete with hiding holes for smuggled loot and a bonded store. Then, on 22 September, 1747, customs officers intercepted 2 tons of illegal tea off the coast of Dorset en route to the Hawkhurst gang. Unfazed, the gang raided the King's Customhouse at Poole and absconded with the tea. Daniel Chater, an unlucky villager who had recognized one of the smugglers, was whipped, tied to a horse, mutilated, and then thrown down a well and stoned to death by the gang's members. For these horrendous deeds, the gang's leaders were eventually brought to justice, convicted, and executed.

In a more subtle moral realm, a battle raged in the pious conscience of John Wesley, the founder of Methodism, over the harm to health, wastefulness, and sinfulness of tea-drinking. In August, 1746, after 27 years as an avid tea-drinker, he finally mustered the resolve, took the plunge, and quit his daily cup. "And I have now had sufficient Time to try the Effects, which have fully answered my Expectation: My Paralytick Complaints are all gone: My Hand is as steady as it was at Fifteen.... And so considerable a Difference do I find in my Expence, that... I save upwards of fifty Pounds a Year," he wrote in *A Letter to a Friend, Concerning Tea* in 1748. Convinced that tea was the cause of his hand tremor, and that the consumption of the expensive foreign leaves instead of an indigenous herb constituted an inexcusable waste of resources that could be used to feed and house the poor, Wesley concluded his impassioned remonstration against tea: "Pray earnestly to GOD for clear light, for a full, piercing, and steady Conviction, that this is the more excellent Way. Pray for a Spirit of universal Self-denial, of cheerful Temperance, of wise Frugality...." The spirit of Wesley was indeed willing, but his flesh proved weak, for 12 years later, on the advice of his physician, he resumed his habit of drinking tea, and even owned a half-gallon teapot specially made for him by the famous potter Josiah Wedgwood.

For sheer vehemence in opposing tea, Wesley was no match for the eccentric traveler, merchant, philanthropist and reformer Jonas Hanway, who also opposed the naturalization of Jewish people in England, advocated both whole wheat bread and the uniform paving of London's streets, sought to alleviate the miserable health conditions of young chimney sweepers, and, most famously, introduced the umbrella to England through 30 years of persistent use on the rain-swept streets of the country's capital, to the point where, for a long time, an umbrella was referred to simply as a "Hanway." To his *Journal of Eight Days Journey from Portsmouth to Kingston*, published in 1756, Hanway appended *An Essay on Tea*, a scathing critique that blamed tea-drinking for being "pernicious to Health, obstructing

The famous lexicographer Samuel Johnson, center, a self-professed "hardened, shameless tea-drinker," shares a cup with his equally renowned biographer James Boswell.

Industry and impoverishing the Nation," as well diminishing the beauty of female devotees. "How many *sweet creatures* of your sex languish with a *weak digestion, low spirits, lassitudes, melancholy*, and twenty disorders, which in spite of the *faculty* have yet no name, except the general one of nervous complaints? Let them change their diet, and among other things, leave off drinking Tea, it is more than probable the greatest part of them will be restored to health."

Hanway's denunciation elicited the spirited response of that formidable giant of English letters, Dr. Samuel Johnson, who in his own words also happened to be "a hardened and shameless Tea-drinker, who has for twenty years diluted his meals with only the infusion of this fascinating plant, whose kettle scarcely has time to cool, who with Tea amuses the evening, with Tea solaces the midnight, and with Tea welcomes the morning." While Dr. Johnson conceded that diseases of the nerves were more common than in former times, he refuted Hanway's accusation against tea for being the cause. "The whole mode of life is changed; every kind of voluntary labour, every exercise that strengthened the nerves, and hardened the muscles, is fallen into disuse. The inhabitants are crowded together in populous cities, so that no occasion of life requires much motion; every one is near to all that he wants; and the rich and delicate seldom pass from one street to another, but in carriages of pleasure. Yet we eat and drink, or strive to eat and drink, like the hunters and huntresses, the farmers and housewives of the former generation," he argued, a statement that rings even more true in our virtual times.

Anecdotes of Dr. Johnson's infatuation with tea abound in *The Life of Samuel Johnson*, the famous biography by James Boswell, who first met the Doctor over a cup of tea in the back parlor of Davies's bookshop. Of the enormous learning that was poured into the compilation of his dictionary, Dr. Johnson himself said that it was "a mere hoard kept by a devil, until tea set it in act and use." "I suppose no person ever enjoyed with more relish the infusion of that fragrant leaf than did Johnson," wrote Boswell. "The quantity that he drank at all hours was so great that his nerves must have been uncommonly strong not to have been relaxed by such an intemperate use of it." As his capacity for strong drink was equally prodigious – he once drank 36 glasses of port at Oxford without showing discomfort – posterity may be indebted to tea for the completion of his magnum opus.

While Portugal and the Netherlands were the first European nations to reach the Far East by sea, it was Britain that became the greatest maritime power in the world. Coffee came to Europe slightly before tea, and until the 1720s England was firmly under the spell of the black aromatic beans. But in the 18th century, the British invention of steam power sent shock waves through the world economy, turning India into an importer of cotton, and placing the fortunes of the English East India Company firmly with tea. As tea consumption expanded throughout the century, learned men such as John Wesley, Jonas Hanway, and Samuel Johnson joined the fray to debate the pros and cons of the desiccated leaves. By the beginning of the 19th century, British tea consumption was taxing the country's coffers to the point where a new commodity was needed to replace the depleted reserves of silver. The lot fell upon opium, which led to a war that shaped the course of world history.

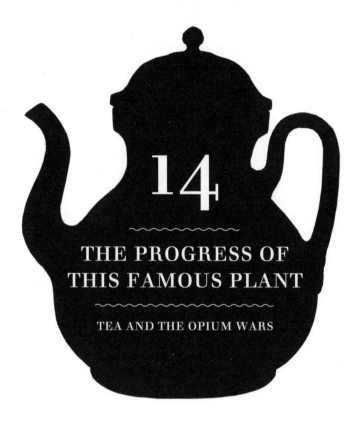

14

THE PROGRESS OF
THIS FAMOUS PLANT

TEA AND THE OPIUM WARS

With the tea trade blossoming and the tonnage of tea imported into Europe growing rapidly each year, there were some attempts, notably by the great Swedish botanist Carl Linnaeus, to bring seeds and tea plants back along with the finished product so that tea could be grown at home. Linnaeus was deeply worried about the silver squandered by Europe to purchase tea and other exotic commodities from China, and Linnaeus wrote himself that he "saw no other cause higher than to close that gate, through which all the silver of Europe was being wasted." Already in 1741, the botanist had concluded that "there is no doubt that tea could grow in Europe and Skåne [Sweden's southernmost province] as well as it does in China and Japan." "Poor Chinese, they will only lose through this more than 100 barrels of gold a year," he mused. However, each time Linnaeus commanded one of his disciples to bring back

"*Potus Theae Camellia Sinensis*" seeds from China, the oil-rich germs rotted and died in the equatorial heat of the homeward sea journey. "If the seeds could be brought from China to Sweden over Russia, they would grow without fail," he wrote. So when his fellow naturalist Pehr Kalm declared his intention to enter China by the northern land route with one of the Russian state caravans, Linnaeus "danced and jumped about" in celebration. But Kalm was unable to bring back any tea plant seeds.

In 1757, the Swedish East India Company sent Linnaeus two Chinese "tea" plants that had survived their long sea journey, but when they flowered in the botanical garden of Uppsala, "the treachery of the Chinese was first revealed. It wasn't the Tea plant, but the herb Camelia," that is, the *Camellia japonica*, the tea bush's more beautiful sister. Then, in 1763, Linnaeus received news from the captain of the ship *Finland,* Carl Gustaf Ekeberg, who, in accordance with Linnaeus's instructions, had planted fresh tea seeds in pots before his departure from Canton. The seeds had sprouted during the journey, and on the ship's arrival in the Swedish port of Gothenburg, Ekeberg found himself with 28 fine tea plants. "But living tea trees! Is it possible? Is it really tea trees? Truly, if it is tea, I shall make Mr. Captain's name more immortal than Alexander the Great's! But I am sure they will never reach Uppsala undamaged. Fate always stands in the way of things too great."

To be sure, the first batch of 14 plants arrived in Uppsala "completely destroyed." The second batch was transported by Ekeberg's wife, who held the plants on her lap during the whole journey to prevent the clumps of earth around their roots from shaking loose. "1763. Linnaeus finally receives tea alive from China... and thus God blessed him also in this respect, that he was given the first honor of seeing living tea brought to Europe through Ekeberg," he wrote in his diary. The tea plants, however, did not fare well in the harsh Swedish climate, and one by one, they wasted away. The last one died in 1781; Linnaeus's good friend A.J. von Höpken offered the following words of comfort: "The tea that comes from China will always be the most desired, as it comes from far away. In this, popular sentiment is peculiar, and cannot be changed."

With few commodities suitable to barter for tea with the Chinese, the English and other Europeans found themselves forced to pay for it with the silver they acquired by selling sugar and other goods to the Spanish, who in Mexico, Peru and Bolivia had gained control over the world's main deposits of that precious metal. In 1730, five English East India Company ships arrived in China carrying 582,112 taels of silver – 97.7 percent of the value of the ships' cargo – and from 1708 to 1760, silver made up 87.5 percent of the English East India Company's exports to China. However, the dominance of silver in the trade was not to last.

The Seven Years War (1756–63), which pitted Britain, Prussia, and Hanover against Austria, France, Russia, Sweden, and Saxony, and put an end to France's colonial aspirations in the Americas, drained the supply of silver to the Far East. By 1764, the English East India Company was so short of funds that it had to arrange a huge emergency loan from private financiers in Macao. The Anglo-American War of Independence (1775–83) further deepened the silver crisis, so that between 1779 and 1785, not a single Spanish silver dollar was transported from Britain to China. At the same time, the tea tax was raised on several occasions to finance the enormous costs of waging war, from 64 percent in 1772 to 106 percent in 1777 and 119 percent in 1784, which in turn pushed the illicit tea business to new heights. According to estimates, during the 1770s, more than 7 million lb of tea were smuggled into England every year, compared with some 5 million lb of declared tea. Some 250 European ships were engaged

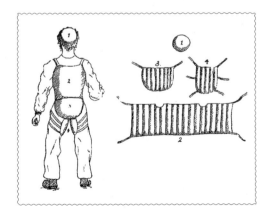

This equipment, depicted in Henry Shore's Smuggling Days and Smuggling Ways, *allowed a tea smuggler to hide some 30 lb of tea.*

A Chinese and a European tea merchant conduct business at a teashop in Canton.

in the business of bootlegging tea to Britain, and among the French, Dutch, Portuguese, Danish, and Swedish ships trading at Canton, around half of the cargoes they carried had Britain's teacups as their clandestine destination.

In place of silver, Indian cotton and above all Indian opium emerged as the new mainstays of England's commerce in the Far East. By the early 1700s, opium was traded, and smuggled, throughout Asia. In 1720, Anders Ljungstedt, the Swedish historian of Macao, recorded the importation there of a few opium chests from the Coromandel Coast on the east side of India. Nine years later, the Chinese emperor, Yongzheng, having learned of opium's pernicious effects, banned the drug, which led the European East India Companies to prohibit the importation of opium to China on company ships. Instead, the trade was passed on to private merchants known as "country traders," who were able to offload opium purchased from the English East India Company in Calcutta by striking deals with corrupt Chinese officials in the Pearl river delta. In 1750, according to the Swede Christopher Braad, opium was sold in Canton at a price of 300–400 taels (24–33 lb) of silver per chest.

With the silver earned from its opium trade, the English East India Company proceeded to purchase ever greater quantities of tea to be shipped back to England. On 13 June, 1767, the Portuguese ship *Bon Voyage* arrived in Macao with a cargo of "nothing but opium." In 1776, the Danes reported a price of 300 Spanish silver dollars for a chest containing approximately 140 lb of opium. Many Chinese colluded with the smugglers, from high officials who turned a blind eye for the right price, to simple fishermen who made some extra cash by guiding the foreign ships into safe, secluded harbors. According to Portuguese records, 726 opium chests were brought to Macao in 1784. By 1828, that number had grown to 4,602.

The long fuse of the 19th-century Opium Wars was lit by the unhappy confluence of two parties profoundly ignorant of each other's history and culture, by the collusion of youthful cupidity with the venality that befalls the old who decline wisdom's grace. The arrival of the Europeans in the Far East dealt China a shock that is still reverberating. For centuries, it had dominated Asia by its sheer size, advanced agriculture, and emphasis on learning. The horse-borne nomads on China's borders might be able to inflict defeat on the battleground, but could never be its superior either in material wealth or cultural sophistication, as attested to by the fact that they were largely forced to adopt Chinese culture in order to rule China. The Europeans, by contrast, presented the autocratic Manchu Chinese officials with a demeanor that utterly upset their view of the world. Here were red-bearded barbarians who gave no hint of vassalage, who had taken the Chinese invention of gunpowder and built cannons far more powerful than any weapon in China's possession, who were full of energy and new ideas, and whose progress in all fields made memorizing the Confucian classics look like a pitiful waste of time. What's more, as if by Faustian design, these avaricious Europeans peddled the very medicine needed to soothe the anguish they caused: opium, the foremost drug of escapism and forgetfulness. Confronted with the overpowering onslaught of enlightenment, capitalism and the Cross, the reaction of China's pampered, corrupt mandarins was to purchase the sedative they were offered, light the pipe, and float away on an evanescent cloud of dreams.

Back in Britain, where little was known of the illicit opium trade conducted on the other side of the globe, dreams were being realized with the immense riches culled from its far-flung colonies: dreams of leisure and pleasure, not only for the aristocracy, but also for the newly wealthy and humble wage earners basking in the glow of the country's burgeoning prosperity. While the London coffee houses had been an all-male affair, its fashionable tea gardens afforded the perfect venue to meet the opposite sex, as well as a place where the whole family could go to enjoy the music of Handel, variety performances, skittle grounds, bowling greens, lantern-lit walks, and hot, refreshing cups of chocolate, coffee, and tea served with bread and butter. The first of London's famous tea gardens, the Vauxhall Gardens, had been opened in 1732, and in 1742, the spectacular Rotunda of the Ranelagh Gardens in Chelsea was unveiled to the public. Some 150 feet in diameter, its entire perimeter wall was lined with a double tier of boxes with refreshment tables, while in its center, an ornate colonnade both supported the domed roof and housed a gigantic fireplace for the colder months. At an admission charge of half a crown, the main amuse-ment at Ranelagh was to dress up and perambulate round the Rotunda in polite conversation, or watch on from one of the boxes while taking tea or coffee with bread and butter, the only refreshments served except on gala evenings. "All was so orderly and still that you could hear the whishing sound of the ladies' train as the immense assembly walked round and round the room," described the poet Samuel Rogers.

In June, 1782, Ranelagh's genteel veneer was pierced by the siren voice of Emma Hart, the most ravishing femme fatale of the era, por-trayed in over 60 paintings by the artist George Romney. The daughter of a Cheshire blacksmith, Emma began her ascent to society's highest echelons as a "tea-maker," caring for the evening tea of rich noblemen, and by 16, had already fallen pregnant and been abandoned by Sir Harry Featherston-haugh (pronounced "Fanshaw") of Uppark in Sussex. Her next lover was the Honourable Charles Greville, younger son of the Earl of Warwick, who on that particular day brought her with him to tea at Ranelagh. Believing he had her safely hid from inquisitive eyes in one of the curtained boxes, he

The palatial rococo Rotunda of the Ranelagh Gardens, designed by William Jones, an East India Company surveyor.

had gone over to call upon some society friends when Emma burst forth from her concealment and sang to the whole gathering, creating a scandalous sensation with her stunning figure and daredevil vivacity. From the hard-up Greville, who "needed to seek a bride worth £30,000 per year," Emma was passed on to his uncle Sir William Hamilton in Naples, where as Lady Hamilton she later made the acquaintance of Admiral Nelson. Following his defeat by the French at Aboukir Bay in 1798, it was Emma who nursed the amputated and blinded Nelson back to health. She became his lover, giving birth to his daughter Horatia in 1801. But when Nelson died in 1805, high society coldly withdrew its protective hand. Emma was left unsupported, succumbed to alcoholism and died in Calais in 1815, her legend immortalized under the epithet of Romney's most famous portrait: "The Tea-Maker of Edgware Road."

In 1784, with America lost and gone after the War of Independence (see Chapter 15), and the smuggling and adulteration of tea having reached epidemic proportions, the English prime minister William Pitt's decisive Tea and Window Act reduced the tax on tea from 119 to 12.5 percent at

THE GENIUS OF JOSIAH WEDGWOOD

Following the demise of the Meissen porcelain factory in the 1750s, the Sèvres factory, near Paris, emerged as the leading producer in Europe, first with its *porcelaine de France*, soft-paste porcelain, and later with a true, hard-paste porcelain known as *porcelaine royale*. But it was the British potter Josiah Wedgwood (1730–95) who broke truly new ground in the history of ceramics with his perfection of the pale cream Queen's ware, invention of the famous Black Basalt and Jasper wares, industrial production methods, and marketing savvy. Ever since the beginning of their quest for true porcelain, European ceramists had been hampered by a lack of the *kaolin*-type clay indispensable to its production. It was in the course of his tireless experiments to make hard-paste porcelain that Wedgwood, in 1768, evolved a hard, vitreous stoneware name Black Basalt, also known as Egyptian ware, which was primarily used to make vases, sculptures, and tea ware. Some 7 years later, he invented an entirely new, hard, fine-grained, durable ceramic material called Jasper for its resemblance to the stone with that name, which could be stained with different metallic oxides that conferred even shades of colors such as yellow, sage green, lilac, and pale blue. Jasper ware was, and still is, extensively used in the production of teapots, teacups, and other tea paraphernalia. Wedgwood was also a pioneer of the Industrial Revolution who crossed the momentous divide from hand-made to machine-made, and greatly boosted productivity by introducing a sharp division of labor, as well as the steam engine and engine-turning lathe, a machine used to produce surface decorations on the various wares. His ingenuity and production-line efficiency posed a severe challenge to other European manufacturers, who hurried to emulate his methods. Meissen even produced a glazed ware named Wedgwoodarbeit. Today, Wedgwood's blue Jasper ware teapot with its white neoclassical decorations has acquired near iconic status in the history of British design.

a stroke, with the revenue thus lost to be recouped by an increase in the curious Window Tax that was levied according to the number of windows in a household. The effects on smuggling were immediate, as the sales of custom-cleared tea leaped from 5 million lb in 1784 to 13 million lb in 1785. Although the wars against Napoleon pushed the tea tax back up to 90 percent by 1806, the Act had dealt the smugglers a blow from which they never really recovered. "We take leave of them with perhaps an unexpected word of thanks on behalf of the tea trade. It was largely due to their clandestine enterprise and cut rates that the habit of tea drinking spread to the remotest corners of the Kingdom, and into the least opulent homes," writes lifetime tea journalist Denys Forrest in his *Tea for the British*.

Adulteration, however, continued unabashed and unabated. The first law against adulterated or fake tea, also known as smouch, was passed as early as 1725, and in 1730, anybody who mixed or stained tea with *terra japonica* (tannin from the vine *Uncaria gambir*), sugar, molasses, clay, or logwood and sold it as "true and real tea" was subject to a fine of £10 per lb. By 1777, when it is estimated that some 2 million lb of dried sloe, elder, hawthorne, birch, and ash leaves were added to 12 million lb of tea annually in Britain, causing "injury and destruction of great quantities of timber, woods, and underwoods," prison had been added to the punishments. Richard Twining, in *Observations on the Tea and Window Act and on the Tea Trade* from 1784, provides a detailed description of that foul business:

> I shall here communicate to the Public a particular account of this manufacture, which I have lately received from a Gentleman, who has made very accurate inquiries relative to this subject.
>
> *Method of making* Smouch *with Ash Tree leaves, to mix with Black Teas.*
>
> When gathered they are first dried in the sun, then baked, they are next put upon a floor and trod upon until the leaves are small, then sifted and steeped in copperas [ferrous sulphate crystal], with sheep's dung; after which being dried on a floor, they are fit for use.... The quantity manufactured at a small village, and within eight or ten miles thereof, cannot be ascertained; but is supposed to be about Twenty Tons in a year....

During the 18th century, both black and green tea were popular in Britain, and tea caddies often came with two inner boxes, one marked "B" for Bohea, the "G" for green. But gradually, Britain became a nation of solely black tea-drinkers. Various reasons for this have been put forward: that the "warming" properties of black tea are more suitable to the country's cold climate, that there is an innate preference for the stronger, more robust flavor of black tea, that milk and sugar go better with black tea, or that green tea was easier to adulterate than black tea. Europeans and Americans expected their fine green teas to have a tinge of blue, and to this end, cheaper green tea was sometimes dyed by unscrupulous producers and merchants. The most common dyes were Prussian Blue, toxic iron ferrocyanide, and verdigris, the poisonous green compound that forms on outdoor bronze statues. The juxtaposition of an anonymous pamphlet that appeared in 1830, *Deadly Adulteration and Slow Poisoning Unmasked, or Disease and Death in the Pot and Bottle*, in which the author lists the lethal adulterants added to tea by the "antemundane subjects of the Brother of the Sun and Moon," that is, the Chinese, and Robert Fortune's *A Journey to the Tea Countries of China*, well illustrates the kind of miscommunication that was common between East and West. Describing the coloring process practiced in China's green tea district, where a fine powder of Prussian Blue and gypsum was added five minutes before the last roasting, Fortune adds:

> I could not help thinking that if any green-tea drinkers had been present during the operation their taste would have been corrected, and, I may be allowed to add, improved.... They [the Chinese] acknowledged that tea was much better when prepared without having any such ingredients mixed with it, and that they never drank dyed teas themselves, but justly remarked that, as foreigners seemed to prefer having a mixture of Prussian blue and gypsum with their tea, to make it look uniform and pretty, and as these ingredients were cheap enough, the Chinese had no objection to supply them, especially as such teas always fetched a higher price!

As the British turned away from green tea, the consumption of black tea grew steadily. "The progress of this famous plant," the critic Isaac D'Israeli wrote at the time, "has been something like the progress of truth; suspected at first, though very palatable to those who had the courage to taste it; resisted as it encroached; abused as its popularity seemed to spread; and establishing its triumph at last, in cheering the whole land from the palace to the cottage, only by the slow and restless efforts of time and its own virtues." Progressive employers in the first factories of the Industrial Revolution offered their workers a tea break as a glimpse of light in the numbing drudgery of their 14-hour work days. Tea has even been accorded an indispensable role in the realization of the Industrial Revolution: without tea, the theory goes, workers would not have had the strength to endure the ear-splitting machines of the "Satanic Mills," and without the antiseptic properties of boiled beverages such as tea, the crowding together in immense cities caused by the migration from field to factory would have unleashed devastating epidemics.

As in Russia, tea was also a crucial tool in the battle against alcohol and inebriation. The very word teetotal seems to connect tea and temperance, although the Oxford Dictionary says that the first syllable of teetotal is actually a doubling of the letter "t" for the sake of emphasis. Nevertheless, the dictionary gives 1834 as the year of the word's coinage, and Preston, the center of the tea-temperance movement, as its birthplace. At the big Christmas tea meeting in Preston in 1833, 1,200 people were served tea from a 200-gallon boiler by 40 reformed alcoholics with the word "temperance" printed on

Poster announcing a tea-temperance gathering in 1850.

their aprons. As the tea-temperance movement gathered force, these big tea meetings, where drunkards took the "vow," became a common phenomenon in industrial towns all over the country, before Charles Dickens poked a hole in the crusade with his satiric description of the Brick Lane Branch of the United Grand Junction Ebenezer Temperance Association in *The Pickwick Papers.*

It was perhaps as a counterpoint to the country's far-flung colonial endeavors, to the heartrending farewells and longing for loved ones gone to distant corners of the globe, that the British developed their unparalleled genius for domesticity – that sublime attempt to banish life's uncertainty with a pair of warm slippers, a crackling log fire, a deep, soft easy chair, a good book, amicable companions, and a steaming pot of Bohea tea. This was the existential ideal that inspired the poet William Cowper in his famous didactic poem, "The Task." At the time of its composition in 1783, Cowper was living in quiet retirement with Mary Unwin at Olney, 50 miles north of London, where their next-door neighbor was no less than Lady Anna Austen. The three spent their evenings together, reading, talking, and singing, when one night, Lady Austen urged Cowper to write a poem in blank verse on the subject of – believe it or not – their sofa, thus setting Cowper to "The Task":

> Now stir the fire, and close the shutters fast,
> Let fall the curtains, wheel the sofa round,
> And while the bubbling and loud-hissing urn
> Throws up a steamy column, and the cups,
> That cheer but not inebriate, wait on each,
> So let us welcome peaceful evening in.

As demand for tea continued to grow, in 1793 George III dispatched Lord Macartney as Britain's first Ambassador to China with the mission to relax trade restrictions, acquire a trading station on an island in the Yangtze river delta, establish a permanent embassy in Beijing, and obtain permission to propagate Christianity. The mission ended in failure, as Lord

Macartney refused to kowtow to Qianlong, who denied the British King's requests in a delusional, conceited letter that would cost China dearly: "As your Ambassador can see for himself, we possess all things. I set no value on objects strange or ingenious, and have no use for your country's manufacture.... It behoves you, O King, to respect my sentiments and to display even greater devotion and loyalty in the future, so that, by perpetual submission to our Throne, you may secure peace and prosperity for your country hereafter...."

Returning from Beijing to Canton by land, Macartney's embassy passed through the tea districts of southern China, where, Macartney wrote, they "were allowed by the Viceroy to take up several tea-plants in a growing state with large balls of earth adhering to them, which plants I flatter myself, I shall transmit to Bengal." There is no record of what happened to these bushes, but the tea seeds collected by the embassy did reach the botanical gardens in Calcutta, where they were successfully germinated under the watchful eye of the famous naturalist and collector Joseph Banks. The following British embassy to China, led by Lord Amherst in 1816, also ended in failure, and on the return journey, their ship *Alceste* was wrecked off the coast of Sumatra. While all the passengers survived, the tea plants brought on the ship were lost.

During the 19th century's first decade, China still enjoyed an annual trade surplus with the rest of the world of some $26 million. From 1800 to 1818, the smuggling of opium held steady at about 4,000 chests per year, but in the 1820s, as the competition between opium producers of Patna, in northeastern India, and the Malwa region south of New Delhi pushed prices down, the consumption of opium in China boomed, reaching 18,760 chests in 1830. From 1828 to 1836, China ran up a trade deficit of $38 million, largely due to the illegal opium trade, which dramatically turned the tide of silver from China to Britain. In this manner, opium became the 19th-century world's single most valuable commodity. The clergy and newspapers such as *The Times* expressed deep moral qualms about the unsavory business, with the future prime minister William Gladstone confessing in his diary: "I am in dread of the judgment of God upon

England for our national iniquity toward China." But the protests never reached the pitch of the anti-slavery movement. In letter to a friend, Dr. William Jardine, the world's kingpin opium trader, cynically summed up the position of the drug runners: "The good people in England think of nothing connected with China but tea and the revenue derived from it, and to obtain these quietly will submit to any degradation."

In the opium debate, the Legalizers, who argued that legalization of the drug would allow the government to gain control over the trade and increase its revenue, were pitted against the Moralists, who believed that utter disregard for a law was not an acceptable reason for its abolition. The Chinese censor Yuan Yulin stated that, if the country continued to sink deeper into the den of opium addiction, "it would mean the end of the life of people and the destruction of the soul of the nation." In July 1838, Lin Zexu, a prodigy of Confucian rectitude who had risen to become governor-general of Hubei and Hunan provinces at the young age of 47, submitted a memorandum on the opium epidemic that stressed both punishment

An opium den in China during the 19th century. Frequented by all social classes, Chinese opium dens varied from the simple to the opulent.

and rehabilitation of addicts, and which so impressed the emperor that he appointed Lin imperial commissioner with sweeping powers to "sever the trunk from the roots."

Having traveled from Beijing to Canton overland in a swift 60 days, on 18 March, 1839, Lin gave the foreigners in Canton three days to turn over their opium stock to the government, reminding them that while China lacked for nothing, they could not live without tea and medicinal rhubarb. "The belief that foreigners, and particularly the English, would die of constipation if deprived of rhubarb was widely held at this time in China. It had its origin, I think, in the practice, so widely spread in early nineteenth-century Europe, of a grand purge every spring, rhubarb-root being often an ingredient in the purgatives used," writes Arthur Waley in his *The Opium War Through Chinese Eyes*. The traders did not give in and so Lin, who later acknowledged that it was only tea that foreigners could not live without, vowed to hold the foreign community in Canton hostage until the opium had been surrendered. When the news reached the British trade superintendent Captain Charles Elliot in Macao, he ordered his warships to move to Hong Kong and departed for Canton, where he commanded the "country traders" to relinquish their opium to the Chinese, pledging full compensation from the British government – an arrangement to which the traders, who had not sold a chest for five months because of the crackdown, willingly acquiesced. Every day, seated in a shady pavilion, the triumphant Lin Zexu supervised the destruction of thousands of chests of opium, which was mixed with lime in ponds and flushed out into the sea.

The situation continued to deteriorate, and on 4 September that year, the first shots of the Opium Wars were fired, when the British fleet, blockaded by Lin and prevented from going ashore for provisions, routed a Chinese junk squadron at Kowloon in present-day Hong Kong. The war itself was an entirely lopsided affair. The British warships, bypass-ing Canton, proceeded north along the coast in order to occupy Chusan (Zhoushan) Island in the Yangtze estuary, where the island's port was taken after a modest nine-minute bombardment in the summer of 1840. In September, Lin Zexu was reprimanded for his utter failure, relieved of his commission and later exiled to Chinese Central Asia for four years. On 20 January, 1841, under heavy pressure from the British, Qishan (Kishen), the new imperial commissioner in Canton, ceded the island of Hong Kong to Captain Elliot, who agreed to return Chusan Island as a sort of compensation. For this traitorous act, Qishan was carried out of Canton in chains, while the British foreign minister Palmerston, angered by Elliot's unauthorized swap, decided to replace him with Henry Pottinger, who arrived in the Far East in August 1841 with a fleet of 25 ships, 14 steamers, 9 support vessels, and 10,000 soldiers, carrying orders to retake Chusan. The island was recaptured on 1 October, and on 13 October, the British forces took Ningbo, a major port town on the Chinese mainland opposite Chusan.

To defend China, the emperor appointed his cousin Yijing, a renowned calligrapher, essayist, and former director of the Imperial Gardens and Hunting Parks. Under his command, 12,000 regular troops and 33,000 militia were organized into a battle force with the objective of retaking Ningbo. A month before they actually launched their attack, a famous painter rendered the expected triumphant battle scene in the exquisite, academic style of the Northern Song dynasty, while Yijing occupied himself for days with a contest to decide which scribe had written the best announcement of the forthcoming victory. The time of the attack was decided in accordance with the divinations of an oracle to take place on 10 March, 1842, at the peak of the spring rain season, when the roads would be a muddy slush. And when the offensive was launched, 60 percent of the troops were retained to shield Yijing and his staff. The front line of the assault was left to 700 Sichuan aborigines wielding long knives, who led the Chinese troops straight into a sickening bloodbath. Continuing their campaign up the Yangtze, the British finally achieved all their goals in the Treaty of Nanking in August, 1842: cession of Hong Kong, a $21 million indemnity, and the opening of five ports – Canton, Amoy, Fuzhou, Ningbo, and Shanghai – for trade.

With its defeat in the Opium Wars, China's doors were forced open, opium flooded across its borders, and the country descended into more than a century of economic hardship, social disintegration, foreign invasions, civil war, revolution, and the collapse of the country's ancient tea industry. Across the Pacific Ocean, some 70 years earlier, tea had played a key role in another event that shaped the course of modern history. The act of defiance perpetrated by a band of Bostonians on the night of 16 December, 1773, as they heaved heavy chests of Bohea tea into the sea, forged the foundation stone for the character and temper of the new republic. The tea itself, however, was soon forgiven, and throughout the 19th century, Americans remained avid drinkers of green tea, which they imported mainly from Japan, and drank iced with fruit punches and spirits.

15

A MASTER TEAPOT MAKER'S MIDNIGHT RIDE

TEA IN AMERICA

The story of tea in the Americas begins with the Dutch, who imported the herb in the middle of the 17th century to their colony of New Amsterdam (present-day New York), where the city's grand ladies did all they could to emulate the aristocracy of the old country, sending out invitations to afternoon tea at which their exquisitely crafted tea tables, caddies, pots, cups, silver spoons, and strainers were proudly displayed. The tables were also adorned with "bite and stir" boxes holding powdered or lump sugar in separate compartments, and an *ooma*, or sifter, filled with cinnamon and sugar that were sprinkled onto the accompanying, piping-hot waffles, pikelets, and puffets. The hostess served several kinds of tea, which, in addition to sugar, was taken with condiments such as saffron or peach leaves.

The famous Quaker William Penn brought tea with him to the colony of Philadelphia, the "City of Brotherly Love," which he founded on the Delaware river in 1682. In Boston, the first tea vendors were Benjamin Harris and Daniel Vernon, who in 1690 took out their licenses to sell tea in public. As in the mother-country, black Bohea was the most popular tea, but green tea was also consumed, evident in the advertisement for "Green and Ordinary teas" put out by the Boston pharmacist Zabdiel Boylston in 1712. Not everybody, however, agreed on exactly what to do with the tea. In the New England town of Salem, for example, the leaves were boiled for a long time to produce an extremely bitter decoction, which was drunk without milk or sugar, whereupon the leaves were eaten with salt and butter. In other places, the tea infusion was discarded, and only the leaves were eaten.

The first regular importations of tea to America began in the 1720s. Legally, the American colonists were only allowed to import tea from Britain, but in reality, about three quarters of the tea was smuggled, mostly from the Netherlands, but also from France, Sweden, and Denmark. When the Swedish naturalist Pehr Kalm visited Albany in 1749, he found that "everybody drank tea for breakfast." In the infant metropolis of New York, the famous London tea gardens of Vauxhall and Ranelagh were given namesakes, albeit on a much smaller scale. Another popular picnic place was the Tea Water Pump Garden, located in Lower Manhattan, close to where the Brooklyn Bridge now crosses the East River. "The demand of the American market for tea was enormous," wrote Sir George Otto Trevelyan in his *The American Revolution*. "The most portable, as well as the most easily prepared of beverages, it was drunk in the backwoods of America as it is drunk today in the Australian bush.... [W]hatever the gentlemen, who rode or drove into a funeral from thirty miles around, were in the habit of drinking, the ladies drank tea. The very Indians, in default of something stronger, drank it twice a day."

While the British colonization of the eastern seaboard proceeded apace, the French, working their way down from Canada and the Great Lakes, claimed the Mississippi river valley, establishing New Orleans in 1718. But in contrast to the British, who formed settled agricultural communities, many of the French colonists were itinerant trappers, and vast swaths of the territories claimed by the French were not buttressed by permanent settlements. In 1748, a group of British colonists founded the Ohio Land Company with the objective of colonizing the valley of the Ohio river, which flows between the Great Lakes and the Appalachian Mountains westward into the Mississippi river. This brought the British into direct conflict with the French, and in 1754, the French and Indian War erupted when British troops led by George Washington clashed with the French at the battle of Jumonville Glen, near present-day Pittsburgh. After a series of stunning defeats, the British eventually gained the upper hand, and at the peace conference in Paris in 1763, the French were ousted from the North American continent as a political and military force.

The removal of the French threat emboldened the colonists, many of whom came from families with a history of several generations in America, and who were losing their blood-ties and emotional bonds to the mother-country. The British, for their part, felt that the colonists should contribute to cover the costs of the French and Indian War, which had been fought for their sake, and also wanted the colonists to set up their own army, something they refused to do. In 1764, to raise revenue from the American colonies, Britain imposed an internal Stamp Tax, which immediately triggered riots and a boycott of British goods among the colonists and forced the British government to withdraw the tax. Mistakenly, the British believed that the Americans had opposed the Stamp Tax because it was an internal tax, and instead imposed a new duty on a few commodities imported from Britain to America – glass, painter's colors, lead, paper, and tea.

Of these commodities, it was tea, the new British national beverage and by far the most important article in the above list, that became the embodiment of the mother-country's despotism. Newspaper articles, town meetings, and handbills competed in formulating the most indignant, inflammatory invective against the "enervating" plant. "Can the spirit of man submit to the insolence of a crew of little dirty tyrants?" one patriot railed in the *Boston Gazette* on 15 August, 1768. "Let us abjure the poisonous baneful plant and its odious infusion – poisonous and odious, I mean, not on account of its physical qualities but on account of the political diseases and death that are connected with every particle of it." Instead of British tea, America's women were urged to drink substitutes such as Labrador tea, a decoction of leaves first used by the Native Americans, and described as having "a very physical taste." Newspapers ran doggerels promoting its use, and printed instructions on how to cure and brew the leaves. Across the colonies, ladies took solemn vows to abstain from tea.

In the spring of 1769, the major American ports – Boston, New York, Philadelphia – concluded a non-importation agreement to protest against the new British taxes. Then, on 5 March, 1770, an event occurred in Boston that brought relations between the city's inhabitants and the British rulers close to the abyss. Hyperbolically christened the "Boston Massacre," it began in the early evening on King Street, when a wigmaker's apprentice by the name of Edward Garrick accused a Captain Lieutenant John Goldfinch of not having paid his bills to Garrick's master. Later, Garrick, who appears to have been drunk, returned to the same place with some companions, and threw insults at Hugh White, the British sentry standing guard in front of the city's Custom's House. The altercation escalated, attracting a crowd, and soldiers were sent to assist White. In the commotion that followed, the British soldiers opened fire, leaving five men dead.

The young artist Henry Pelham made a painting of the event, which was closely copied by Paul Revere, an engraver and patriot who played a major role in the events leading to the American War of Independence, and who was elevated to the pantheon of national heroes by Longfellow's poem "Paul Revere's Ride:"

> So through the night rode Paul Revere;
> And so through the night went his cry of alarm
> To every Middlesex village and farm,
> A cry of defiance, and not of fear,
> A voice in the darkness, a knock at the door,
> And a word that shall echo for evermore!

This elegant, neoclassical teapot, designed in the workshop of the Revolutionary War hero Paul Revere, is fashioned from sheet silver with a riveted, soldered seam at the handle.

Within a few weeks of the shootings, Revere's dramatic print was being disseminated throughout the American colonies, inflaming anti-British sentiment with its emotional and inaccurate depiction of a cold-blooded execution by British soldiers of innocent Bostonians. Revere, while vowing to oppose the importation of tea with his "life and fortune," was also a highly accomplished silversmith who, somewhat ironically, crafted magnificent tea utensils – pots, creamers, sugar tongs, spoons – that are regarded as some of the most outstanding achievements in American decorative arts. His work did not come at a discount. A silver teapot with a wooden handle, made by Revere in 1762, for example, cost £10 16 shillings and 8 pence, at a time when the salary for an ordinary laborer was £30 per year.

In May, 1770, news reached the American colonies that the British government had rescinded all the new taxes except the tea tax. New York was the first to succumb to the temptation of reopening trade with Britain, followed by Philadelphia. By October, the non-importation agreement between the three major American ports had been dissolved, and business as usual with Britain was resumed. During the three following years, known as the "period of calm," the solemn vows to not sell or consume tea were quietly forgotten. Even such a great patriot as John Hancock profited from the resumption of the tea trade, transporting 45,000 lb of taxed tea in his ships from 1771 to 1772.

By the middle of the 18th century, the British East India Company had become the wealthiest, most powerful company in the world, largely due to its monopoly on the tea trade, which generated 90 percent of its commercial profits. But as Britain's predilection for tea grew, so did the government's import duties on tea. The exorbitant tariffs spurred massive smuggling that took a huge bite out of the company's sales. At the same time, the company's stock holders voted to raise their annual dividend to 12.5 percent, even as the company's stock price tumbled from 280 to 239 pence. By the fall of 1772, the English East India Company found itself plunged into a serious financial crisis. It was long overdue on the repayment of a short-term £300,000 loan from the Bank of England, and owed the government over £1 million in unpaid duties and other fees, while in its warehouses, some 18 million lb of surplus tea were gathering mold. To resolve these dire financial straits, in addition to a new, £1.5 million loan from the government, on 10 May, 1773, parliament decided to allow the East India Company to export tea to the American colonies, while retaining the unpopular duty on tea.

"Perhaps no bill of such momentous consequences has ever received less attention upon passage in Parliament," writes the American historian Benjamin Woods Labaree in his *The Boston Tea Party*. By September that year, the East India Company had 2,000 chests containing 600,000 lb of tea ready for shipment to the four American ports of Boston, New York, Philadelphia, and Charleston. When news of the shipment reached America, the "period of calm" was abruptly ended, and American resistance to their high-handed British rulers reawakened with double the force. The decision to allow the East India Company to export tea to the American colonies was viewed as an attempt to make the tea tax permanent and create a precedent for new impositions, as well as to extend the East India Company's trading monopoly to America. "I have told several of the Company that the

Tea and Ships will all be burnt. . . . [A]s I think you will never suffer an Act of Parliament to be so crowded down your Throats; for if you do it is all over with you," wrote one correspondent from Britain to America.

In New York and Philadelphia, the East India Company's designated agents, having been made aware of the people's strong opposition, decided to renege on their commission to receive the tea. In Boston, however, two of the appointed agents, Thomas and Elisha Hutchinson, were the sons of the governor Thomas Hutchinson, who gave them his full support in accepting the shipment. On 3 November, a crowd that included the patriot leaders Sam Adams, Joseph Warren, and John Hancock gathered at Boston's Liberty Tree, a famous elm tree in the town, for a meeting to confront the designated agents, among whom were also Richard Clarke, Edward Winslow, and Benjamin Faneuil. When they failed to appear, a crowd set off for the residence of Richard Clarke, where they wrenched the hinges off the front door and stormed the house, forcing the Clarkes to take refuge behind the heavy door to the counting-room on the second floor. The *Massachusetts Spy* published a letter signed with the pseudonym "Committee Man" which stated that if the designated agents persisted in their intention to receive the tea, "the world will applaud the spirit that, for the common preservation, will exterminate such malignant and dangerous persons."

On 28 November, the *Dartmouth*, nine weeks out of London, entered Boston harbor with 114 chests of tea in its hold. The following morning, a general meeting was called with the notice "Friends! Brethren! Countrymen! The Hour of Destruction or Manly Opposition to the Machinations of Tyranny stares in your Face!" More than 5,000 townspeople attended, and unanimously decided that no duty should be paid and that the tea should be returned to Britain. A contingent of 25 men was chosen to watch the ship and its cargo. On 2 December, the *Eleanor* arrived in Boston with more tea, and 13 days later the two ships were joined by the brig *Beaver*, carrying 112 chests of tea. A notice signed "The People" proclaimed that anybody who attempted to unload the vessels would be treated "as Wretches unworthy to live and will be the first victims of our just Resentment." With the rapidly looming deadline of 17 December, when customs officers according to the rules would be free to seize the *Dartmouth's* tea for non-payment of duties, nerves in Boston were tensed to the breaking point.

On 16 December, a meeting convened at Boston's Old South Meeting House demanded that the captain of the *Dartmouth*, Francis Rotch, depart with his vessel from the harbor, and allowed him to seek permission for this from Governor Hutchinson. When Rotch returned from the Governor's residence in the early evening and announced that the request had been denied, a mob descended on the harbor, shouting "Boston harbor a teapot tonight!" and "The Mohawks are coming!" The day's rain had stopped, and a bright moonlight illuminated the wharf where the three ships lay moored. The perpetrators, crudely disguised as Native Americans, divided into three groups, climbed aboard the vessels and forced the customs officers ashore, then proceeded to break open the tea chests with axes and shovel and pour the tea over the side. One man who secretly filled his coat with tea received a severe beating from the crowd. Soon, the harbor was awash with 90,000 lb of tea.

The destruction of tea belonging to the British East India Company at Boston Harbor, 16 December, 1773.

As news of the Boston Tea Party (as it became known) spread through-out the colonies, tea was destroyed wherever it was found. In Greenwich, the largest, most prosperous town in New Jersey at the time, chests of tea from the *Greyhound*, originally destined for Philadelphia, were burned in the town's Market Square. When a rumor spread that Isaac Jones, an inn-keeper in Weston, Massachusetts, was purveying tea in his tavern, a mob of patriots wrecked his inn and drank all his liquor. And in March, 1774, Bos-tonians had a second tea party, dumping 28 chests of tea from the *Fortune* into their harbor. Later that same month, the British Parliament passed a bill to close Boston Harbor until restitution for the tea destroyed in December had been made. But this punitive action only served to unite the colonies, and on 6 September, 1774, representatives from the 12 American colonies gathered in Carpenter's Hall, Philadelphia, for the first session of the Continental Congress, which decided to ban all imports from Britain and Ireland in retaliation for Britain's blockade of Boston.

It was on the night of 18 April, 1775, that Paul Revere made his famous midnight ride to warn the Massachusetts militia that British troops were marching to confiscate their weapons. At sunrise the next morning, "the shot heard round the world" echoed from Lexington Common, where a group of the militiamen had been confronted by the British troops. In the American War of Independence that erupted, the irregular troops com-manded by George Washington, now fighting for the colonies, battled with the British and their Hessian allies at Princeton, Trenton, Brandywine, and Germantown. In Europe, French volunteers sympathetic to the colonists' cause hurried over the Atlantic under the command of La Fayette. In the fall of 1781, Washington's army, together with La Fayette's French volun-teers, forced the British to evacuate all the major port towns except New York, heralding the war's conclusion. In the ensuing peace treaty, signed in Paris on 3 September, 1783, America's independence was formally recog-nized by Britain.

While, according to a common perception, it was the villainous role of tea in America's road to independence that caused a deep-seated aversion to that beverage and placed the young nation firmly in the coffee camp, tea did not disappear from the American cupboard. After the war, at his estate in Mount Vernon, George Washington "ordinarily, for breakfast, had tea, English fashion, Indian cakes with butter, and, perhaps, honey, of which he was very fond. His evening meal, or supper, was especially light, consisting of, perhaps, tea and toast, with wine."

One of the young men who had fought in Washington's army was a war hero from Boston by the name of Samuel Shaw. Like many other soldiers, Shaw had gone unpaid during his last years of military service, and re-entered civil life deep in debt. It was not long, however, before a golden opportunity presented itself. With its newly won independence, America was able to strike out on its own in the world, which, among other things, meant establishing direct trade with the Far East. In 1783, the Philadelphia merchant Robert Morris, who had made his fortune smuggling tea and been one of the main financiers of the American War of Independence, organized a venture to send the first American ship to China. John Green, a former employee of Morris, was chosen as captain of the vessel, christened *Empress of China,* and Samuel Shaw was offered the position of supercargo – the person responsible for the ship's merchandise. For the maiden voyage, the 360-ton vessel was loaded with 3,000 fur pelts, woolen cloth, lead, cotton, pepper, and no fewer than 30 tons of Virginia and Pennsylvania ginseng. Long prized in China for its restorative properties, ginseng (but of a different species) was also known to the Native Americans, who called it garantoquen and had been using it as a medicine since time immemorial. This raises two equally remarkable possibilities – either the Chinese and the Native Americans discovered the plant independently, or else the latter had brought knowledge of ginseng with them to America when crossing the Bering Strait around 15,000 years ago.

Having set sail from New York on 22 February, 1784, the *Empress of China* arrived six months later in Canton, where the *cohong* ("Chinese guild") merchants immediately snapped up the whole shipment, paying very good prices for the ginseng in particular. With the money earned from these sales, Shaw proceeded to place his purchases, for as he wrote: "The inhabitants of America must have their tea." In all, Shaw purchased 440 tons, mostly the black teas Bohea and Souchong, more than the *Empress of China* could hold, so that another ship bound for America, the *Pallas,* had to carry part of the cargo. The *Empress of China* also brought back 50 tons of chinaware, 3,000 lb of cassia (a cinnamon-like bark), hand-painted wallpaper for Robert Morris and some roosters from Shanghai, which are said to be the forebears of the succulent chicken in today's Bucks County, Pennsylvania. Completing its return voyage in record time, the *Empress of China* saluted New York with 13 guns on 11 May, 1785. Four years later, the American government was ready to levy its own tax on tea: 15 cents per lb for black tea, 22 cents per lb for the green tea Imperial, and 55 cents per lb for Young Hyson, another green tea.

In the 19th century, tea punches, made with cream and sugar, and spiked with liquor, were served on sultry summer afternoons in southern towns like Charleston and Savannah. The earliest recipes used green tea, and with the advent of refrigeration, chilled tea punches became increasingly popular. In 1854, Commodore Perry succeeded in prying open the gate to Japan, and during the second half of the century, Japanese green tea made up the bulk of America's tea imports. One of the first recipes for iced tea appeared in the 1879 cookbook *Housekeeping in Old Virginia*: "After scalding the teapot, put into it one quart of boiling water and two teaspoonfuls of green tea.... Fill the goblets with ice and sugar. A squeeze of lemon will make this delicious and healthful, as it will correct the astringent tendency." And at a reunion of ex-Confederate soldiers held in Missouri in 1890, 15,000 veterans drank 2,220 gallons of coffee and 880 gallons of iced tea to wash down an amazing feast of 4,800 lb of bread, 11,705 lb of beef, 407 lb of ham, 21 sheep, 6 bushels of beans, 60 gallons of pickles, and a wagonload of potatoes. Iced tea is still the favorite tea beverage among present-day Americans.

In its long and winding journey through the centuries, the humble, unassuming tea plant has displayed a mysterious, quixotic knack for appearing at the crossroads where history is being made. In the one-act play of the Boston Tea Party, tea was but the designated prop, the exotic, lucrative commodity that unwittingly found itself the loathsome symbol of tyranny, rapacity, and every injustice that rulers can inflict upon the ruled. In India, which after the loss of America became the new jewel of the British Empire, tea arrived as a double-edged sword – a tool of subjugation as well as a new industry and livelihood. The tea plant thrived in India, and by the back-breaking work of tea planters and laborers, new gardens were established at an astonishing speed. After a mere 50 years, India's infant tea industry was exporting more than its 2,000 year old competitor to the northwest.

The Great American Tea Company, founded in 1859. Later renamed The Great Atlantic & Pacific Tea Company, A&P is still a household name in America.

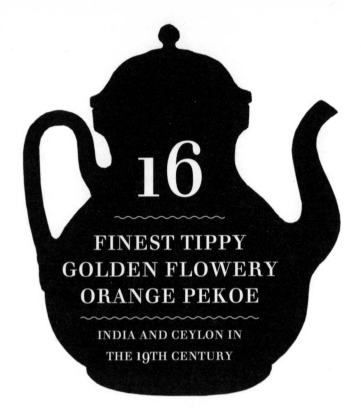

16

FINEST TIPPY GOLDEN FLOWERY ORANGE PEKOE

INDIA AND CEYLON IN THE 19TH CENTURY

At the beginning of the 19th century, the history of tea returned to its southern botanical heartland: the upper reaches of the Brahmaputra river. The way of life among the people here had changed little in the intervening millennia. For centuries, the province of Assam, a 400-mile long, 50-mile wide river plain wedged between the eastern Himalayas and the Naga Hills of Burma, had been the venue of continuous warfare between the Ahom and Kachari Rajas, and the subject of raids by the Naga, Mishmi, Miri, Arbor, Dafta, and Singpho tribes, descending from their fortresses in the surrounding hills. Ruled by the Ahoms from 1228 to 1779, Assam had been occupied by the Burmese in 1779, but soon after a new people from far away with huge beards and powerful weapons began to appear in the valley, desiring to trade and coveting the lush, bountiful land.

In 1823, the British merchant Robert Bruce, carrying a large assortment of goods, traveled up the first stretch of the Brahmaputra valley to the town of Rangpoor, where he made the acquaintance of Beesa Gaum, chief of the Singpho people, one of the tribes in the region with a deep knowledge of the tea plant. Having found wild tea growing around Rangpoor, Bruce signed an agreement with Beesa Gaum to obtain some bushes on his next visit. The following year, war over Assam broke out between the Burmese and the British. Robert Bruce's brother Charles Alexander Bruce, commanding a division of gunboats, was ordered up to a place called Sadiya in deepest Assam, where the Brahmaputra enters the river plain from the Himalayas, not far from Beesa Gaum's home. When the British had driven the Burmese out of Sadiya, the Singpho chief came down from the hills to pay his respects to the new rulers and deliver the tea plants Bruce's brother had ordered. Charles Bruce later noted in his *An Account of the Manufacture of the Black Tea* that:

> The Singphos have known and drank the tea for many years, but they make it in a very different way from what the Chinese do. They pluck the young and tender leaves and dry them a little in the sun; some put them into the dew and then again into the sun three successive days, others only after a little drying put them into hot pans, turn them about until quite hot, and then place them into the hollow of a bamboo, and drive the whole down with a stick, holding and turning the bamboo over the fire all the time, until it is full, then tie the end up with leaves, and hang the bamboo up in some smoky place in the hut; thus prepared the Tea will keep good for years. A good way further east they dig holes in the earth, line the sides with large leaves, boil the Tea leaves, throw away the decoction, put the leaves into the hole, which they cover over with leaves and earth, and then allow the whole to ferment; after which it is taken out, filled into bamboos, and in this manner prepared taken to market. These Singphos pretend to be great judges of Tea.

Already in 1788, Sir Joseph Banks had prepared a memorandum on the possibility of cultivating tea in India, but at that time, the East India Company's immense profits from the China trade had led it actively to discourage all such undertakings. That suddenly changed in 1833, when the Company lost its monopoly on commerce in the Far East and the China trade was opened to free competition. On 24 January, 1834, the first Tea Committee was appointed by the company with the mission to submit "a plan for the accomplishment of the introduction of tea culture into India," which still remained the private fief of the East India Company. At the end of that year, on the evidence provided by Bruce and others, the committee proudly informed the British government "that the tea shrub is beyond all doubt indigenous in Upper Assam." Concurrently, James Gordon, the Committee secretary, was dispatched to China to procure seeds, seedlings, tea manufacturing tools, and expert tea-makers.

In 1836, some 20,000 tea plants raised at the Calcutta Botanical Gardens from seeds obtained by Gordon in China were sent to Charles Bruce, by then Superintendent of Tea Culture, in Sadiya. Another 20,000 plants were dispatched to Kumaon and Dehra Dun in the western Himalayas near Punjab, and 2,000 to Madras on the southeast coast of India. In addition to his experiments with the Chinese tea plants, Bruce started a nursery in Sadiya devoted to the indigenous Assam bush, and continued to discover new tracts of wild tea in the region. From three Chinese tea-makers recruited by Gordon and sent to Assam, Bruce learned the craft of manufacturing tea and later had this curious interview with the tea-makers published:

> "Do you always manufacture the Tea in China in the same way you have the Assam Tea?"
> "The same."
> "Do you know how to make green tea?"
> "No."
> …"How often do you weed your plantations?"
> "Once in the rains and once in the cold weather."

A small sample made by these Chinese tea-makers from Assam tea bushes was sent to Calcutta, where the Viceroy, Lord Auckland, pronounced the tea good. In May, 1838, the first shipment of Assam tea was dispatched in its own cabin aboard the *Calcutta* to London, where eight of the chests, three Assam Pekoe and five Assam Souchong, were auctioned amidst great excitement at the London Commercial Sales Room in Mincing Lane on 10 January, 1839. The first lot was sold at 21 shillings (£68 or $130 in today's money) per lb to a certain Captain Pidding, who subsequently purchased all the remaining chests, reputedly as a publicity stunt for his own brand, "Howqua's Mixture – a blend of '40 Rare Black Teas'."

Within five weeks, a group of London merchants had formed the Assam Tea Company, capitalized with £500,000 in 10,000 £50 shares that sold out in a few days. The East India Company agreed to transfer two-thirds of its Assam tea tracts to the new company without rent for ten years, and more Chinese tea-makers were recruited. The first tasks were to improve the existing tea gardens, get production going, clear new tracts of land for cultivation, and establish a stable line of communication with Calcutta. Steamboats navigating up the labyrinthine, treacherous delta system of the Ganges and Brahmaputra rivers could go no further than Gauhati, located after the bend in the Brahmaputra where it turns east into Assam. From Gauhati to the Assam Tea Company's headquarters in Nazira 200 miles further upstream, the only means of transportation was in a "country boat" – poled and sailed and pulled by coolies against the current – a journey that could take a month.

As a young tea planter fresh off the boat from England, a tea-maker having come all the way from China, or a coolie leaving his family in Bengal, traveling up the Brahmaputra river through the dense Assam jungle must at times have felt like a journey into the heart of darkness. Tigers roamed the forest, and behind every bend, malaria, cholera, and other diseases were waiting to turn the adventure into a one-way passage. At the Assam Tea Company's headquarters in Nazira, almost a 1,000 miles from Calcutta, there were bungalows for the European staff, bamboo huts for the laborers, two tea factory buildings, an experimental tea nursery, rice paddies and plots for wheat, barley, and flax. Wild elephants were captured and domes-ticated in stockades, and then put to work: dragging off felled logs from the tracts being cleared, bringing in the fresh green tea leaves from the scattered fields, and transporting people through the jungle high above the ground, safe from marauding tigers. When the finished tea had been packed in lead-lined boxes, it was loaded onto the "country boats," poled down the Dikhoo river to the Brahmaputra, and then on to Gauhati and Calcutta.

In 1841, Dr. Campbell of the Indian Medical Service brought China tea seeds from Kumaon and planted them at his residence in Darjeeling, beautifully situated in the Himalayan foothills 300 miles due north of Calcutta. In contrast to other places in India where the British initiated tea cultivation, the tea plant was not indigenous to Darjeeling, but Dr. Campbell's experiment soon proved extremely successful. The frost-hardy, small-leafed Chinese plants not only survived in the cold, pristine climate, they thrived, producing exquisitely tender, delicate buds. Under Dr. Campbell's auspices, Darjeeling was developed into a proper hill station with a small European population and a sanatorium for ailing soldiers and government servants. In 1856, the Alubari tea garden was opened by the Kurseong and Darjeeling Tea Company. The plucking season began with the first flush during the rainy season in March, followed by the renowned second flush, considered to produce the finest Darjeeling tea, in June.

Ingenio et Labore, "by ingenuity and hard work," was the motto inscribed on the Assam Tea Company's seal, and by the early 1860s, the commercial success of its indomitable pioneers had attracted the attention of less substantial characters, blinded by dreams of quick riches. The tea planter Edward Money described those heady years of tea mania: "First, we had the wild rush, the mad fever, when every man thought that to own a few Tea bushes was to realize wealth.... New gardens were commenced on impossible sites and by men as managers who not only did not know a Tea plant from a cabbage, but who were equally ignorant of the commonest rules of agriculture." Everybody — retired army officers, doctors, veterinarians, ship captains, pharmacists, shopkeepers, clerks, ex-policemen — wanted to own a tea garden in Assam. New tea companies were established overnight and existing tea gardens were purchased for many times their value. In the district of Cachar, south of Assam, applications for half a million acres of new

Tea party on the lawn in Calcutta, 1890. Mr. and Mrs. Thoby Prinsep and Lady Florence Streatfield are attended by two table servants (in white) and two chuprassis, whose role was to announce new arrivals and add prestige.

tea lands were submitted to the government in 1862–63. At the height of the frenzy, bogus tea gardens with little or no production were palmed off to unwitting speculators in London. By 1865, when it had dawned that the advertised profits were a mirage, these investors sold their estates for whatever price they could get, and the house of cards came tumbling down.

Notwithstanding, tea production in Assam and other regions continued to expand at a rapid pace, propelled by the exemption from duty on tea imported from India to Britain, and by the growing popularity of Indian tea among British consumers, wary of adulterated, unhygienic Chinese tea, and drawn to the strong, robust Assam taste. To plant, manure, and prune the millions of tea bushes, to pluck their leaves, and to wither, roll, ferment, fire, and pack the tea, tens of thousands of laborers were required. The native tribes of Assam, who had often sold their land to the tea companies for a pittance, and had their own paddy fields to attend, were viewed as

Tea-pickers in Ceylon gather by the weighing station at the end of a day's work.

unwilling and unreliable, so the brunt of the workforce had to be brought in from other provinces under conditions only marginally better than slavery. Between 1863 and 1868, more than 100,000 people, most from neighboring Bengal, were imported to work on the tea estates of Assam, between them run by a few hundred British superintendents. Simple, impoverished peasants were lured by unscrupulous agents with false promises and cash advances to sign contracts they could not read, and then placed on crowded steamers going up the Brahmaputra river. Mortality was exceedingly high, and laborers who found themselves deceived and wanting to return home were commonly retained against their will, while captured absconders and poor workers were flogged.

To stem the abuses, the British government in India passed several acts improving the laborers' rights, healthcare, minimum wages, hours of work, and length of contract, but when faced with cold-blooded reality, these benevolent decrees proved quite toothless. In 1868, a government commission dispatched to examine tea cultivation in Assam found that the estate workers there were still recruited through deception, that the laborers were overworked, that the death rate due to overcrowding, poor food, and impure water was appalling, and that the minimum wage was ignored. Worse still, the dearth of labor was so severe that workers in transit to the tea districts were sometimes kidnapped by "coolie raiders" and sold to unscrupulous tea planters. The situation was markedly different in Cachar, where the commission "found conditions in many gardens all that could be desired. Happy and contented, surrounded by their families, earning good wages and possessing numbers of cows and goats; their daily task was light, and when they were sick they were treated with the greatest care." And even in Assam, despite the exploitation and widespread abuses, many laborers chose to settle in the tea districts after their contracts had expired, rather than return to poverty of their home districts.

In contrast to China, where tea cultivation most often was a family business, the Indian tea estates incorporated large tracts of land and hundreds of workers organized on an industrial scale according to the new gospel of efficiency and productivity. After the leaves had been plucked, they were brought to the estate's factory, weighed, and spread thinly on racks to wither for 18–24 hours. The next step was rolling, the most labor-intensive, time-consuming process, in the which the laborers crushed, broke, and twisted the leaves by rolling them with their hands or feet to release the leaves' internal juices and oils and trigger their oxidation. In the 1860s, a Cachar planter by the name of Nelson introduced the first piece of tea machinery, a rolling machine, which rolled the withered leaves between two tables, one fixed and one movable, and reduced the time needed for the process by 75 percent. After oxidation, the next step was firing or drying, which terminates the oxidation process, reduces the water content to a few percent, and stabilizes the leaves' color, fragrance, and flavor. The first drying machine was invented by the tea planter Samuel Davidson, who arrived in Cachar in 1864 at the age of 18 years, and by 1875, had invented a machine that "can dry tea about twice as fast as the charcoal fires can already, but I am raising the chimney by another ten feet and expect it will dry about three times as fast as the charcoaled frames do."

A WHITE-TIPPED TEA FROM JAVA

In 1827, the young Dutch tea merchant and taster J.I.L.L. Jacobson arrived in Java, determined to cultivate tea on that lush island. That same year, the Dutch government imported 500 tea bushes from Japan, which were planted in the Buitenzorg Botanical Garden. From these bushes, Jacobson produced his first samples of green and black teas, but the Japanese variety was found unsuitable for Java's tropical climate, and in the following 6 years, Jacobson undertook several dramatic journeys to procure Chinese tea bushes and tea-makers. In 1832, Jacobson returned from his 5th voyage to China with 300,000 bushes and 12 tea-makers. When 10 of these were killed in an uprising by Javanese coolies, he returned to China one last time, and managed to collect 7 million seeds and 15 tea workers, as well as a large number of implements. By this time, the Chinese government had placed a price on his head, and attempted to seize his vessel, but the young Dutchman eluded his pursuers and returned safely to Java with his priceless cargo. For the next 15 years, Jacobson dedicated himself to the cultivation of tea in Java, publishing the first major European work on the scientific and technical aspects of tea-making, *Handbook for the Cultivation and Manufacture of Tea*, in 1843. After his untimely death in 1848, however, Java's fledgling tea industry foundered, and did not begin to recover in earnest until the 1870s. In 1877, the first shipment of Indonesian tea was auctioned in Mincing Lane, and the following year, tea seeds from Assam were planted in Java with great success. At the turn of the century, Java had become the 4th largest producer of tea in the world. Javanese tea was particularly popular in Persia, as reported by E.G. Foley in his *Report on a Visit to Meshed (Persia)* to the Indian Tea Association in 1901: "The tea which is most liked by Persians and is a great favourite is a white-tipped tea from Java, with a pale straw-coloured liquor and a rather pungent and delicate flavour. . ... The high price of Java tea prevents its being more generally used, as none but the better classes can afford to buy it. If this tea could be sold at a lower price, it would displace the orange-tipped tea throughout Persia, as the Persians are passionately fond of it."

In southern India, tea had been introduced to the Nilgiri Hills, some 50 miles inland from the coastal city of Calicut, by a Dr. Christie in 1832, and to the Travancore Mountains, which run along the western side of India's southern tip, in 1864. At that time, as in neighboring Ceylon (present-day Sri Lanka) across the Palk Strait, coffee, first brought by the Arabs, was the region's main cash crop. In Ceylon's central highlands, hundreds of square miles of dense jungle had been cleared for the cultivation of coffee. But in 1869, Donald Reid, the superintendent at the Galloola coffee plantation in Ceylon, noticed some strange dusty yellow leaves on his coffee bushes. It was the dreaded coffee rust fungus, *Hemileia vastatrix*, which soon spread to southern India. "For some seven or eight years," the journalist John Ferguson wrote in his *Ceylon in the "Jubilee Year,"* "not much was thought of it, save as an inducement to more liberal, careful cultivation; but the scientists called in to investigate, showed that little or no practical check could be offered, and within 15 years... the minute, despised fungus had swept 100,000 acres of coffee cultivation out of existence." The coffee plantations were abandoned, financiers frightened off, and superintendents put out of work.

Many of the planters who chose to stay in Ceylon turned first to the cultivation of the cinchona tree, the bark of which is used to produce quinine, then the most effective antidote to malaria. In the 16th century, Jesuit missionaries had learned the secret of quinine. Later, British botanists managed to smuggle cinchona seeds out of South America, leading to plantations in Java, Ceylon, and India. Quinine was a crucial, highly valued drug that made possible Europe's colonization of malaria-infested tropical countries, and in the 1860s, Ceylon quinine, then the most potent variety, commanded the highest price. Between 1878 and 1883, cinchona plantations in Ceylon expanded from 6,000 to 64,000 acres, and in 1884, production on the island reached a remarkable 11.8 million lb. But the over-supply soon devastated world prices, turning the quinine boom into yet another bust for the planters.

One of the pioneers of the cinchona plantations in Ceylon was James Taylor, a Scotsman who, 16 years old, had arrived at Colombo in 1852 and become superintendent at the Loolecondera estate 18 miles south of

Kandy in the central highlands. In 1867, the first year cinchona bark was harvested at Loolecondera, Taylor planted Assam tea seeds obtained from the Royal Botanical Gardens at Peradeniya on 19 acres of land. His goal was to make a better tea than in Assam and "get it to taste like the China tea sold in the shops." In the beginning, the tea factory was in his bungalow, and the leaves rolled by hand on tables on the verandah. By 1873, he had devised his own mechanical roller, and was selling tea in Ceylon "for well over twice the price we could get for it in London." An indefatigable working man who almost never left his beloved Loolecondera, Taylor spent the only vacation he ever took outside Ceylon in Darjeeling, studying tea. In 1885, when Loolecondera's tea estate had grown to 300 acres, coffee was no longer cultivated. Soon after, cinchona also disappeared. When Taylor died in 1892, just after losing his job for refusing to go on sick leave, 24 men carried his 246-pound body all the way to Kandy, where the simple epitaph on his grave in the Mahaiyawa Cemetery reads: "In pious memory of James Taylor, Loolecondera Estate, Ceylon, the pioneer of the tea and cinchona enterprise, who died May 2, 1892, aged 57 years."

Compared with the miasmic airs, coolie-raiders, and tigers of Assam, Ceylon was a more salubrious and genteel place – after the roads had been built, the jungle of 150-foot trees cleared, the slopes planted, and the bungalows built. The axe men, Kandyan highlanders, began at the bottom of the hill, cut each tree half through, and slowly worked their way up to the top. The highest trees were then cut clean through, and with their weight brought down the other trees on the slope. As the native Sinhalese people refused to work on the plantation estates, Tamil laborers from southern India were imported to plant, pick, and prune the bushes. "One of our greatest advantages is 'free labor.' Close at our shores are the twelve million coolies of Southern India, whose average earnings are between £3 and £4 a year each. Yes, and he is able to live on it, too, and support a wife and family. From this vast source we draw our supply of laborers, and fine, well-trained, diligent fellows they become," wrote the journalist John Ferguson in 1897.

The Tamil laborers were also "free" in a more positive sense, in that they were not indentured or bound by long-term contracts, and many of them

A young Ceylonese tea-laborer sorts the leaves by turning the crank on a wire drum.

returned to their homes in southern India each year for the rice planting season, walking 150 miles along "The North Road," little more than a path through the rugged, inhospitable, malaria-infested jungle from the Kandy highlands to Mannar on the northwest coast, where they boarded small boats for the 20-mile journey across the Palk Strait. Among the Tamil laborers returning from their homes to the estates, "The North Road" served as a merciless quarantine against the cholera in their midst. "The sick were abandoned either on the road or at some of the established halting places. The rest of the gang pressed on and in this way the disease was gradually eliminated," wrote Sir West Ridgeway, the Governor of Ceylon at the time. In 1876, the monsoons of south India failed, causing a famine that drove 167,000 Tamils to seek refuge and sustenance at the plantation estates of Ceylon, and by 1900, the Tamil work force on the tea estates of Ceylon stood at over 300,000, thus laying the foundation for the ethnic conflict between the Tamils and Sinhalese that erupted in a bloody civil war in 1983.

Whereas in Assam, the Assam Tea Company, later joined by the Jorehaut Company, controlled most of the tea production, Ceylon tea was manufactured and sold by individual estates with evocative names such as Bogahawatte, Lover's Leap, and Pooprassie – isolated communities of perhaps 2,000 people, all living for the production of tea. In their free time, the British staff traveled long distances for a game of cricket, fished in the

THE GRADING SYSTEM
FOR INDIAN AND CEYLON TEAS

Whole leaves (bottom to top):
1. Souchong
2. Pekoe
3. Orange Pekoe
4. FOP: Flowery Orange Pekoe
   *This denotes tea made from the end
   bud and first leaf of each shoot.
   FOP contains fine, tender and
   young leaves, rolled with the correct
   portion of tip*
5. GFOP: Golden Flowery Orange
   Pekoe
   *This is FOP with golden tips — the
   very end of the golden yellow bud*

6. TGFOP: Tippy Golden Flowery
   Orange Pekoe
   *This is FOP with a high proportion
   of golden tips*
7. FTGFOP: Finest Tippy Golden
   Flowery Orange Pekoe
   Exceptionally high quality FOP

Broken leaves (bottom to top):
1. Dust
2. Broken Orange Pekoe Fannings
3. Broken Pekoe Orange
4. Broken Pekoe
5. Broken Orange Pekoe

streams, and hunted wild pigs, leopards, elk, and elephant. The most legendary hunter among the planters was Major Thomas Rogers, who killed more than 1,300 elephants before he was struck down by lightning at the age of 41. In the last two decades of the century, with tea production booming, the rough pioneers were gradually supplanted by managers of a finer cloth, accompanied by their wives and entertaining in style.

From the central highlands, the finished tea was transported on bullock carts down the winding road to Colombo, traded among the merchants, and loaded on to ships bound for London. In 1873, 23 lb of tea from James Taylor's Loolecondera reached London, where it was valued at £4 and 7 shillings. The first auction of Ceylon tea, for 980 lb of Orange Pekoe and Pekoe Souchong, was held at the London Commercial Sales Room on 28 October, 1878. "The make of leaf equals the first Indian, but the liquor though of good strength lacks flavour. The Orange Pekoe is a closely twisted even leaf with good gold tip. The Pekoe Souchong is an even blackish leaf," stated a review of the new tea in the weekly *Colonial Empire*. As tea imports to Britain doubled from 88.5 million lb in 1864 to 175 million lb in 1884, Ceylon tea exports caught the wave, growing from 2.5 million lb in 1884 to 15 million lb in 1887. In the historic year of 1889, Indian tea exports to Britain for the first time exceeded Chinese tea exports, with 94.5 million lb Indian tea versus 92.5 million lb Chinese. That same year, Ceylon tea exports to Britain reached 28 million lb. And while the strong and robust Assam teas were considered practically only good for blending, the fine, high-grown Ceylon teas, sold "straight," acquired a reputation for quality and exquisite taste. At the London auctions held on 10 March, 1891, a small consignment of Ceylon tea from the Gartmore estate in Maskeliya consisting only of the finest, most succulent buds, was knocked down by the Mazawattee Ceylon Tea Company at the enormous price of £10, 12 shillings and 6 pence per lb.

The marketing genius Thomas Lipton spent every waking moment conceiving new ways to advertise his brand, so that to this day, his surname remains a synonym for tea.

The sale set off a frenzied, publicity-driven hype for Ceylon's "Golden Tips" which ended on 25 August that year, when tea from Thomas Lipton's Naha-kettia estate set the all-time record at £36 and 15 shillings per lb.

The story of Thomas Lipton and his ubiquitous Yellow Label are inextricably intertwined with Ceylon. Lipton, the son of a grocer who had built an empire selling bacon, butter, and eggs in 300 provision stores across Britain, made his first trip to Ceylon in 1890, when he purchased the Monarakande, Mousakellie, Lyamastotte, and Dambatenne tea estates at cut-price rates, set up his "Lipton's Circus" headquarters in Colombo, and built his own "eagle's nest" on a rocky shelf above a 1,000 foot cliff at his favorite estate, Dambatenne. His plan was to cut out the middleman by producing tea on his own estates and selling it directly to the consumer under the slogan "Direct from the Tea Gardens to the Tea Pot," and his success was beyond all expectations. Through Lipton's skillful advertising, he managed to create the impression that he owned every tea estate on Ceylon. His name became so synonymous with black tea that to this day, in Bamako, the capital of sub-Saharan Mali, the waiters will offer you a choice of "green tea or Lipton's." "If I say that for a period of at least twenty years practically all my spare time – and the only spare moments I had, it seems to me, must have been those spent in bed, on the train, or on board ship at sea – was devoted to thinking out new and original advertising schemes, I will not be overshooting the mark," he wrote in his autobiography. When, en route to the Far East, Lipton's ship, the S.S. *Orotava*, ran ashore in a mist in the Red Sea, forcing the crew to jettison some cargo, Lipton obtained a pot of red paint and a brush from one of the engineers. "Armed with these," he wrote, "I went on deck and, to the vast amusement of the passengers and crew, I painted the words 'DRINK LIPTON'S TEA' on as many bales, cases and crates as I could before they were consigned to the shallow water around the ship. Many of the lighter cases floated ashore all round the coast, and months afterwards I heard of the flotsam and jetsam from the *Orotava* being found by Arabs and other tribes. Whether they had the good sense to follow the advice to drink my tea, I cannot say."

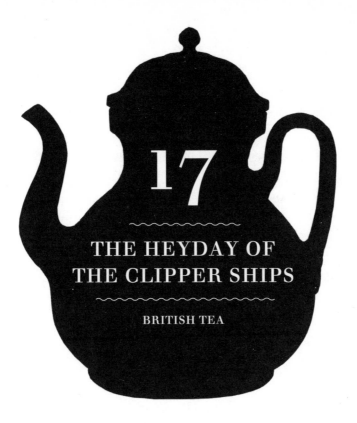

17

THE HEYDAY OF
THE CLIPPER SHIPS

BRITISH TEA

The end of the English East India Company's monopoly on the China trade in 1834 also set in motion the evolution of the tea clippers – the magnificent finale of the commercial sailing vessel's era. Until then, tea and other exotic commodities from the Far East had traveled to Europe in cumbersome, bulging East Indiamen, which could take eight months to complete the return voyage from Canton round the Cape of Good Hope to London. Seaworthiness, size, and stability were the key words revolving in the head of an East Indiaman shipwright. Speed had been not a major consideration. But with the advent of free trade and fierce competition, that all changed.

Historians of shipbuilding trace the tea clipper's origins further back, to the long, low, flush-decked Baltimore clippers that appeared around the time of America's War of Independence. These heavily armed, two-masted ships ranged the seas as privateers, slavers, or flying the cross and bones, and with their characteristically slanted bow, masts, and stern, slight height between the water and deck lines, and multitude of flying kites, the unmistakable silhouette of a Baltimore clipper on the horizon was sure to arouse terror amongst the crew on a potential target.

Equally sharp, and engaged in an equally nefarious trade, the opium clippers picked up their cargo of dark, rich cakes at the government sales in Calcutta, carrying it through the Sunda Strait along the Palawan Passage up to receiving ships in Macao, where the opium was then transferred to smaller vessels, which in turn supplied other clippers stationed all along the Chinese coast from Hong Kong to the Yangtze estuary. The most famous opium clipper was the *Falcon*, purchased in 1836 in Calcutta by Jardine, Matheson & Co. Manned with a crack crew who could "'turn in a dead-eye,' 'gammon a bowsprit,' fish a broken spar, rig a purchase of any given power, knot, point, splice, parcel, and serve," the lavishly fitted *Falcon* roamed the China coast without rest, purveying its illicit goods in exchange for silver in the form of Mexican dollars, which were then used to finance the booming tea trade.

In 1839, the great Aberdeen shipwright Alexander Hall constructed the first British clipper, the 150-ton *Scottish Maid*, which with its bold "Aberdeen bow," leaning 50 degrees to the vertical, was able to compete with the paddle steamers on the run between Aberdeen and London. Nine years later, Hall's firm launched the *Reindeer*, a square-rigged vessel built especially for the tea trade. Sailing from Whampoa on 5 October, 1849, beating down the China Sea against the southwest monsoon, the *Reindeer* arrived with its cargo in Liverpool 107 days later, a source of such satisfaction to its owners Messrs Fear & Vining that they rewarded the ship's captain with a chronometer.

In the same year, the British Parliament repealed the Navigation Laws, opening British ports to foreign competition, in particular to the sleek American clipper ships, which had plied the China trade throughout the 1840s, loading tea in Canton and racing back to New York and Boston via Cape Horn. On 3 December, 1850, the Yankee clipper *Oriental* hauled into

London's West India Docks with 887 tons of tea in her hold, 97 days out of Hong Kong, a feat that caused both excitement and consternation in Britain, and prompted grave predictions of the British Mercantile Marine's demise. Surveyors were sent down to the *Oriental's* dry dock to sketch out the lines of its hull, as an article in the *Times* exhorted its countrymen: "We must run a race with our gigantic and unshackled rival. We must set our long-practised skill, our steady industry, and our dogged determination against his youth, ingenuity, and ardour. It is a father who runs a race with his son. A fell necessity constrains us and we must not be beat."

Throughout the 1840s, Canton remained the main entrepôt for China's tea trade with the Western nations. Most of the black tea favored by the British and other European countries came from the Wuyi (Bohea) Mountain tea district in northwestern Fujian, from where it was carried by coolies in lead-lined chests, one or two at a time, over the mountains to Wukou (Hokow), the bustling emporium of the black tea trade, and then transshipped to Canton and Shanghai. With the scramble of free trade that followed the abolition of the East India Company's monopoly and the opening of new treaty ports after the Opium Wars, the tea began reaching the ports earlier each year. In 1834, the crop did not arrive in Canton before October. By 1848, the first clippers were setting sail from Canton's Whampoa docks at the end of July.

When the tea reached Canton, the Western tea merchants and their Chinese tea men inspected it carefully. If the tea was found to "pass muster," the merchant made an offer to the Chinese tea broker and the purchase was arranged. In 1845, there were 262 foreign males, mostly British and American, registered in Canton's foreign concession, a small area about 1,100 feet long and 700 feet wide southwest of the old city walls of Canton, to which their entry was still barred. Many of them were engaged in the tea trade as buyers and agents. For the British firms, the tea was either bartered against cotton goods and woolens, or, most often, paid for in Mexican silver dollars procured from the Chinese through the sale of opium. When the payment, insurance, freight, and all other financial matters were in place, the ship's ballast arranged, the ironwork down in the hold painted, its woodwork scraped clean, the loading of the tea could commence. Sampans drew alongside the anchored clipper ships, and the tea was hoisted up and lowered down into the hold. The first layer, or flooring chop, consisted of green tea or old tea, shipped at a lower rate and serving as a protection from the bilge water for the rest of the cargo. "When the third tier is completed, the hold, in the estimation of a practical and intelligent seaman, has an appearance worthy of being admired — the surface looks like a splendid deck, flush from stem to stern," averred Captain R. Little of the *John Temperley*.

During the clipper ships' 3- to 4-month passage back to Britain, the physical and mental endurance of the captain and crew were taxed to the very limits. "It required dash and steadiness, daring and prudence to make a crack racing skipper," wrote Basil Lubbock in his *The China Clippers*, "and these are not attributes or character which are often found in conjunction. ... However, there were a few men, who held the necessary qualities of a tea ship commander, whose daring was tempered by good judgment,

The Taeping, *one of the most successful British tea clippers, races home with the new season's tea, every square inch of sail aloft.*

Tea-tasters determining the quality and value of a new shipment in a wholesale warehouse.

whose business capabilities were on par with their seamanship, and whose nerves were cast of iron." One of these giants was Captain Robertson of the *Cairngorm*, of whom it is said that he never went to bed during the homeward run, but catnapped in a deck-chair on the poop deck with one eye open.

Having arrived in Britain, the tea was unloaded with equal dispatch and warehoused along the banks of the Pool of London by companies such as the Red Lion and Three Crane Wharf Ltd. According to rules that remained in effect until 1884, every tea chest landed on British shores had to be opened and its contents poured out on the floor, "with dust arising like a thick, old-fashioned November fog," so that government tea inspectors could examine the tea and customs officers establish the net weight. If deemed necessary, the said tea consignment was then "bulked," or mixed to a uniform quality, before the warehousemen shoveled the tea back into the chests and stamped it down with their hobnailed boots.

Samples of the tea were bored from the chests and sent to the brokers and buyers, where the tea-tasters went to work with their ultra-sensitive olfactory lobes and trained palates. Long rows of little, lidded pots were filled with an equal, small amount of tea from each chest, and water exactly brought to the boil added. After five minutes, the pots were emptied into cups, with the leaves retained by the lids. Working his way down the long rows, the taster took a mouthful from each cup, rolled the tea round his mouth, examined the leaves, spat his mouthful into a spittoon, and informed the accompanying clerk of his price evaluation. In the jargon of the tea-tasters, "agony of the leaves" was used to describe the unfolding of the leaves when boiling water was applied. A tea was said to "stand up" when it held its original color, while "flat" tea was lacking in briskness and pungency, and a "full" tea strong without being bitter.

After the end of the East India Company's monopoly, the quarterly tea auctions were moved from East India House to Mincing Lane and the Commercial Sales Room, a stone structure with a facade "adapted with little variation from the Temple of Minerva Polias at Prienne," and an interior that looked equally like "a suburban railway station and the Bankruptcy Court in Basinghall Street." Mincing Lane became the famous "Street of Tea," and for the next 136 years stood at the heart of the world tea trade, until the London auctions were moved to Sir John Lyon House downstream from Blackfriars Bridge in 1971.

In the 1860s, an article in the trade publication *The Grocer* offered an interesting comparison between the tea brokers and their fellow colleagues, the sugar brokers, who:

> are more florid, solid, jocular, and demonstrative, affect loose coats, light waistcoats, and have on the whole a more jovial, mellower, Christmassy look. The tea men are sharper, more critical, and more subdued sort of persons, with inquiring noses, alert manners, and a general neatness, not to say primness, in dress.…. Where a sugar man would wear plaid trousers and a thick gold Albert chain, a tea man would dress in black or Oxford mixture, and foster his watch with a small briquèt or a hair guard.

After the wholesaler had purchased his tea, it had to be blended to assure a uniform taste from year to year, to suit the individual customers, and to adapt the tea to the water of the region where it was to be sold. The tea blender not only had to be an expert tea-taster, he also had to know everything about tea – the different regions, soils, climates, types of tea – in order to be able to blend them to the desired quality. As tea from India and Ceylon came on to the market, a phenomenon that defied common socioeconomic rules was observed, as people ignored the size of their pockets when it came to purchasing tea. The poor peasants of Ireland, for example, became the most ardent devotees of fine-grade Ceylon and Darjeeling, while industrial workers in northern England drank more expensive tea than in the south. Yorkshiremen preferred tea from Darjeeling and Travancore, while the Scots drank strong Assam, as these teas were able to "get a good grip of the third water" — or in other words, they could be brewed three times. In areas with hard water, such as Yorkshire, highly fired teas gave the best results, while the soft water of Plymouth required a young flowery leaf. The big tea houses even brought in water samples from all over the country for the blenders to work with.

The fine art of tea-tasting was brought into the realm of the exact sciences by the polymath genius Francis Galton (1822–1911), best known as the founder of eugenics, his explorations of southwest Africa, and his contributions to statistics and forensics. A close relation of Charles Darwin and Josiah Wedgwood, he possessed as his governing passion the measurement of all things. And as an ardent tea devotee, Galton devised intricate mathematical formulas and conducted meticulous experiments to determine the physical parameters of the perfect cup of tea, "taking as my type of excellence, tea that was full bodied, full tasted, and in no way bitter or flat." Through his careful observations, Galton was able to conclude that these qualities were only produced when the leaves were steeped in the teapot for 8 minutes in water with a temperature between 180 and 190 degrees Fahrenheit, i.e. more than 20 degrees below the boiling point. "Other people may like tea of a different character from that which I do myself; but, be that as it may, all people can, I maintain, ensure the uniformity of good tea, such as they best like, by attending to the principle of making it, that is to say, to time, and quantities, and temperature. There is no other mystery in the teapot," he firmly concluded.

During the 19th century, Britain's population grew four-fold from 10.5 million in 1801 to 40.8 million in 1911 — an increase that would not have been possible without a safe, boiled beverage such as tea, which played a crucial role in eradicating cholera, the water-borne killer. In those

100 years, official tea imports increased twelve-fold from 23.7 million lb to 295.3 million lb, as the average price of tea fell from 5 shillings and 10 pence (i.e. 70 pence) to 8 pence, in large part due to the faster journeys of tea clippers and steamers. In 1851, 62.5 million lb of tea were exported from Canton, compared to 36.7 million from Shanghai. By 1853, the tide had turned in favor of Shanghai, which that year exported 69.4 million lb, more than twice the exports from Canton. The natural port for the export of Bohea tea, however, was Fuzhou, and with the Treaty of Nanking in 1842, the port was opened to foreign trade. In 1853, as tea shipments to Shanghai were temporarily interrupted by the Taiping Rebellion, the first tea clippers loaded their cargo at Fuzhou's Pagoda Anchorage.

In 1859, Robert Steele & Son, at Greenock on the Clyde river, launched the *Falcon*, a new type of clipper modeled on the lines of brigs which the firm had previously built for the West Indies trade in sugar. At 937 tons, 191 feet long, 32 feet wide and 20 feet deep, the graceful wooden ship had less sheer (the upward slope of a ship's lines toward the bow and stern), less freeboard (the height of a ship's side between the waterline and the deck), lower bulwarks, and a clearer deck than its predecessors, and was noted for her strength in beating to windward, although she was also very fast in light winds. In 1863–64, her second master, John Keay, took her out to Hong Kong in 97 days and then up to Hankow, where she loaded tea at £8 per ton.

A succession of superb vessels followed the *Falcon*. With clipper ship building in America ground to a halt due to the Civil War, the competition was between the great Scottish shipwrights, whose rivalry raised the art of building a clipper ship to its apogee. The Clyde clippers were noted for the lavishness of their fittings – finest Indian teak, mahogany, and gleaming brass as far as the eye could reach, while the Aberdeen ships drew praise for the neatness of their masts, sails, and rigging. In 1863, Steele launched the *Taeping,* the first of the composite tea clippers. Constructed with an iron frame and wooden planks, which were sheathed in copper to prevent the hull from becoming overgrown with weeds and barnacles, these ships could be built longer without increasing weight, were tighter, and delivered their cargoes in better shape.

As the shipwrights toiled over their drawing boards, the demand for tea in Britain was booming. Between 1840 and 1860, the country's per capita consumption of tea doubled. The "new season's tea" became all the rage, and a premium was offered to the first tea clipper returning from China. As Fuzhou was the treaty port closest to the Bohea tea region, tea shipped down the Min river could be loaded there five or six weeks earlier than at Shanghai or Canton, and by 1860, the port had become the starting point for the fabled tea races. Each year in May, the tea clippers began to gather at the Pagoda Anchorage, where they prepared themselves for the race home as they waited for the tea to come down the Min. In Britain, the races elicited great excitement among the general public. Throughout the summer months, the new telegraph wires relayed the latest sightings of the ships from wonderfully distant parts of the globe, as the punters laid their bets and the merchants prepared. When the ships arrived at the Downs at the mouth of the Thames, they often had to wait for a southwesterly wind to be able to enter the river. In Mincing Lane, many tea merchants installed a wind clock marked with the points of the compass and attached to weather vane on the roof. Clerks were detailed to watch the clock through-out the night, and when it veered to the southwest, a mounted messenger was immediately dispatched to awaken the merchant, who hurried to the docks bustling with the crowds that had gathered to greet the first bringer of the new season's teas.

In 1866, it was arranged that nine clippers should sail from Fuzhou on as nearly the same date as possible. Arthur Clark, in his *The Clipper Ship Era* published in 1911, has captured the scene admirably:

> Cargo junks and lorchas were being warped alongside at all hours of the day and night; double gangs of good-natured, chattering coolies were on board each ship ready to handle and stow the matted chests of tea as they came alongside; comfortable sampans, worked by merry, bare-footed Chinese women, sailed or rowed in haste between the ships and the shore; slender six-oared gigs, with crews of stalwart Chinamen in white duck uniforms, darted about the harbour; while dignified master mariners, dressed in white linen or straw-coloured pongee silk, with

pipe-clayed shoes and broad pith hats, impatiently handled the yoke lines.

On shore the tyepans and their clerks hurried about in sedan chairs, carried on the shoulders of perspiring coolies, with quick firm step to the rhythm of their mild but energetic 'Woo ho – woo ho – woo ho!

The broad, cool verandah of the clubhouse was almost deserted. In the great hongs [factories] of Adamson, Bell; Gilman & Co.; Jardine, Matheson; Gibb, Livingston; and Sassoon, the gentry of Foochow toiled by candle light over manifests and bills of lading and exchange, sustained far into the night by slowly-swinging punkahs [fans], iced tea, and the fragrant Manila cheroot.

On 24 May, the *Ariel* loaded its flooring chop of 391 chests and 220 half-chests. Four days later, the Chinese stevedores, working round the clock, packing the chests tightly with big mallets, stowed the last of its 1.23 million lb of tea. Five ships – *Ariel*, *Fiery Cross*, *Taeping*, *Serica*, and *Taitsing* – unmoored from the Pagoda Anchorage within the next three days. The *Fiery Cross* led the way down to Anjer in the Sunda Strait, which was the most trying part of the tea races, with its fickle weather and wind, uncharted reefs, and capricious currents.

By contrast, the stretch between Anjer and Mauritius is where the tea clippers, sustained by the Indian Ocean's steady Southeast trade wind, made their best times. On 24 June, *Fiery Cross* sailed 328 miles in one day, as all five ships sent every possible extra sail aloft – ringtails, spare mizen staysails, Jamie Greens, bonnets, water sails, jib-o'jibs – a total of some 30–40,000 square feet of canvas per ship. "Carpenter making grating for fore-scuttle doorway. Sail maker giving the ringtail 4 feet more roach in the foot – 6½ feet in all. A topgallant stun sail set instead of it meantime," the *Ariel*'s Captain Keay noted in his logbook on 28 June.

The *Fiery Cross* rounded the Cape of Good Hope first, 47 days out of Fuzhou and a few hours before *Ariel*, followed by *Taeping*, *Serica*, and *Taitsing*. By St. Helena, *Taeping*, sailing some 300 miles closer to the African coast, had taken the lead, and on 4 August, *Taeping*, *Fiery Cross,* and *Ariel* all crossed the Equator on the same day. During the stretch from Cape Verde to the Azores, *Taitsing*, sailing magnificently, made up three days on the leading ship, and the four ships passed the Azores within 24 hours. On 5 September, with royal stun sails and all flying kites set, *Ariel* and *Taeping* raced side by side up the English Channel at 14 knots. Early next morning, a pilot boarded the *Ariel* and greeted Captain Keay as the season's first clipper out of China. But *Taeping* received a better tugboat, arrived at Gravesend 55 minutes later and, after a 16,000 mile race that had lasted 99 days, berthed 20 minutes before *Ariel* dropped anchor at the East India Docks.

The clippers brought more and more tea faster than ever into Britain, struggling to satisfy demand, and inevitably, this abundance of tea had a profound effect on the new manners and customs being formed by the forces of empire, urbanization, and industrialization. It was around this time that the Duchess of Bedford experienced a "sinking feeling" late in the afternoon. In the first half of the 19th century, breakfast in well-to-do families was taken at an earlier time than previously, while dinner was gradually moved later and later in the day, from 4 or 5 p.m. in the 1780s to around 8 p.m. in the 1850s. This had given rise to a new meal, lunch, which consisted of cold meats, bread, butter, and cheese. According to British tea lore, the venerable institution of afternoon tea was invented by the Duchess, who, to assuage her low blood sugar level, ordered tea to be served around 5 o'clock with some bread, butter, and cakes. Also known as "5 o'clock tea, "little tea" (for the small amount of food that was served), or "low tea" (because the guests were seated in comfortable armchairs with low side-tables for their teacups), it became one of the most prominent rituals in upper class British life. "The year when Afternoon Tea was served in the august clubs of London, these last sanctuaries of male prerogatives, was an essential date in the history of British society," writes the anthropologist Sidney Mintz.

For the women of the leisured class, it was the perfect opportunity to gather and gossip, and display one's beautiful home and elegant tea utensils. After receiving an invitation via a servant or an informal card, there was no need to answer, and the guests were allowed to come and go as they wished during the gathering. The hostess poured the tea on a small tea table, and the cups were handed out by a gentleman, if present, or by one of the daughters of the house. According to Victorian etiquette, the milk

BESUCHSTEE WITH
KLUNTJE AND CREAM

On the European Continent, where coffee has reigned supreme since the 18th century, the German region of East Frisia stands out as the sole major exception. Situated on the North Sea coast between Denmark and the Netherlands, East Frisia, with its bleak landscape of sand dunes, marshlands, and peat bogs, has traditionally been one of Germany's less prosperous regions. Poor drinking water is a perennial problem, so when tea started to become available in the 17th century, it was readily adopted by the East Frisians as a hot and flavored substitute for plain water. "The water is mostly bad. In the peat bogs it is swampy. In the clay lands it is salty. One therefore makes do with rainwater, which is collected in cisterns. But the East Frisians do not drink water, at least not in its pure form. They have a great love for hot drinks, namely for tea, so that the small province of East Frisia consumes ten times as much tea as the rest of the Kingdom of Hannover," wrote the 19th century temperance propagandist Albert Freiherr von Seld.

For the hard-working, frugal East Frisian peasants, tea had several advantages over coffee. It was cheaper, and did not demand special utensils such as a roasting pan and a grinder. And in times of scarcity, such as during Napoleon's Continental System, weak tea tasted better than weak coffee, making it easier to stretch. From the original, thin decoction of tea leaves, a stronger tea, known as *Besuchstee* ("Visitor's Tea") evolved, which was served to guests with cream and a kind of rock sugar called *kluntje*. "In the course of time, the common enjoyment of tea has led to a refinement of tastes. The East Frisians have learned to make particularly good tea blends, so that 'East Frisian Tea' has become a sought-after commodity in Germany," the writer Erich Schrader observed in the 1920s. By this time, a set ritual for taking tea that united East Frisians from all walks of life had been established. In the East Frisian Tea Ceremony, a special white China with an East Frisian blue decoration is used. First, two pieces of *kluntje* are placed in each cup. The hot black tea is served, and cream or milk added with a special spoon called a *rohmlöppel*. As the cream sinks it to the bottom, it looks like clouds, or *wulkje*. The most important thing to remember is to not stir the cup. In this manner, the sugar remains at the bottom, and the best is saved for last.

shop wisely - buy

Brooke Bond

dividend Tea

In the 1930s, the Brooke Bond Tea Company offered a dividend to everybody who purchased their tea.

or cream was added to the tea, but later the reverse became the fashion. Some preferred hot milk, others cold. The menu for afternoon tea included crustless sandwiches, teacakes, scones, biscuits, shortbreads, simnel cakes, gingerbreads, eclairs, cream jumbles, and macaroons.

Tea permeated every aspect of life in high society. The London season of the select "10,000" ran from April to July, and then from October to Christmas, as they gathered in the capital to dance, visit the Opera, ride their carriages, and drink tea. The fashionable ladies had late breakfasts with tea in their bedrooms, afternoon tea at 5 o'clock, and tea again after dinner. At the Epsom Derby held in April, and the Royal Ascot races in June, the spectators refreshed themselves in the colorful tents with tea and biscuits. From January to March, they retreated to their country estates, where a hot pot of tea was a welcome sight after returning from an afternoon walk in the chilly rain. And during the summers, the ladies and gentlemen brought their portable teasets with them for picnics in the local parks.

High tea, by contrast, began as a working-class meal, and later evolved as a Sunday meal for the upper classes that was easy to prepare when the servants were on their day-off. Farmers, and factory and mine workers seldom had time for tea in the afternoon. Instead, their wives served high tea: a hearty meal of cold meats, bacon, various pies, cheese, potatoes, oatcakes or bread, crowned with a piping hot pot of tea, that was waiting for

The very first photograph of a tea party, taken around 1840 by William Fox Talbot, a pioneer of photography who invented the negative/positive process.

them when they returned home from work in the evening. "A 'High Tea' is where meat takes a prominent part, and signifies what it really is, a tea dinner," Isabella Beeton explained in her *Book of Household Management*. For the very poor, however, tea with bread might have to suffice as the evening meal, while among the wealthy, Sunday high tea included a feast of foods such as cold salmon, pigeon, veal, fruits, cakes, and clotted cream – a special cream made by carefully heating milk and then allowing it to cool while the cream rises to the surface in coagulated lumps.

This period also saw the advent of the big tea brands that dominated Britain's domestic market until the multinational food corporations swal-lowed their businesses in the second half of the 20th century. Already in 1826, the anti-slavery campaigner John Horniman had offered the first pre-packaged tea, wrapped in foil-lined paper with HORNIMAN stamped on the label. With the public increasingly wary of adulterated, artificially colored, and unhygienic loose-leaf teas, a package, label, and standard weight offered a comforting sense of reliability, and with the help of a newly invented packaging machine and brash advertising, Horniman became a household name in Britain.

Another early purveyor of package tea was the temperance reformer John Cassell, who set up the British Hong Kong Tea Company to provide working class families with affordable tea, which was sold in tin-foil packages ranging from one ounce to a pound, making it available to even the poorest. With the profits from his tea business, Cassell soon branched out into publishing, where, not surprisingly, his first magazine was the *Teetotal Times*. Horniman and Cassell were followed by the Birmingham merchant Thomas Ridgway, Brooke Bond from Manchester, the Co-operative movement's Co-op tea, Tetley's, Lipton's and Mazawattee – a combination of the Hindi *mazatha* (luscious) and the Cingalese *wattee* (garden) – which pioneered the use of large, colorful billboard advertisements.

In 1859, swallowed up by expanding suburbs and rendered redundant by new social trends, the last of London's legendary tea gardens, Vauxhall, closed its doors. A couple of decades later, a new fashion swept the country. Britain's first tearoom, or "teashop" may have been in the Aerated Bread Company's bakery shop at London Bridge station. J. Lyons & Co., which had started out in tobacco, picked up on the idea and refined the concept, opening the first Lyon Tea Shop at 213 Piccadilly in 1894. With its cleanliness and smart decor in white and gold, affordable and tasty food, and uniformed waitresses, the establishment was an immediate success, and in the following years, 250 Lyons Tea Shops were opened up around the country. Here, respectable women from all walks of life could take a break from household chores, eat lunch during a day of shopping, or meet a friend for an intimate chat. Glasgow, in particular, became known for its many elegant, affordable tearooms, the most famous of which was (and still is) the Willow Tea Rooms, designed by Charles Rennie Mackintosh with his signature sense of light, colorful decorations, mirrors, panels, friezes, and regal ladder-back chairs.

By the turn of the 20th century, the average consumption of tea in Britain had risen to 6 lb 2 oz per person. In Mincing Lane, the quarterly auctions had become monthly, weekly, and then daily, with Indian teas up for sale on Mondays and Wednesdays, Ceylon tea on Tuesdays, and Chinese, Javanese, and other teas on Thursdays. Ironically, Lipton's, which became the embodiment of British tea around the world, later faded away at home, as other brands captured ever larger market shares with ingenious advertising and innovative new ways of choosing, blending, packing, and distributing their tea. In 1905, as the story goes, a sister of the Birmingham tea merchant John Sumner, Jr. purchased some tea of the Fannings grade, and found that it improved her digestion – Ty.phoo (after the Chinese word for doctor, *daifu*) Tipps was born. Described by the creative marketers as a "leaf-edge tea," "free from injurious gallo-tannic acid," Ty.phoo was sold mostly through chemists, and acquired a reputation for its excellent digestive properties. During World War I, Ty.phoo's popularity was so great that 4,000 doctors joined forces to keep the Fannings from which it was made separate from the government-operated pooling of tea. The renown of Ty.phoo was followed by the even more successful marketing campaign of Brook Bond's PG Tips, or Pre-Gest-Tee (for Pre-digestive tea), which to this day remains the most popular tea in Britain.

In the 19th century, London was firmly established as the capital of the world tea trade, and the British as the world's most ardent tea-drinkers. The race to bring home the new season's tea spurred the evolution of the clippers – the finest sailing ships ever to grace the Seven Seas. In Britain, the venerable traditions of afternoon tea and high tea were deeply inscribed into the daily lives of both the rich and the poor. With the advent of branded package tea, tea became one of the first truly modern consumer commodities, as much dependent on the ingenuity of advertisers and marketers as on the fragrance and strength of the leaves themselves.

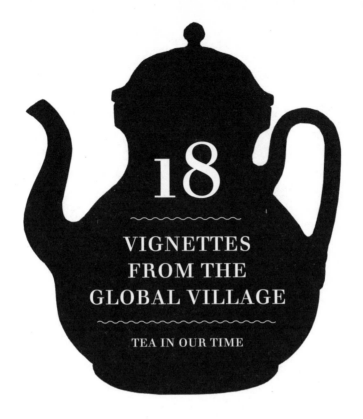

18

VIGNETTES
FROM THE
GLOBAL VILLAGE

TEA IN OUR TIME

At the beginning of the 20th century, Australians were the greatest black tea-drinkers in the world, brewing 7½ lb of the leaves per person a year. Tea had its own ritual in the rough life of an Aussie bushwhacker. You made a neat fireplace with stones, filled it with fallen eucalyptus branches, and built a tripod to hang the "billy" from. The billy, a simple tin can with a metal wire handle, was filled with water from a nearby creek. Usually, a few eucalyptus leaves were allowed to fall into the can. When the billy boiled, one handful of tea was added for every person, with an extra handful for the billy. The smoke from the eucalyptus spread a wonderful scent, giving the tea a special flavor. After steeping for a minute or two, the billy was swung round the head three times to settle the leaves, and the tea served in tin mugs, with milk and sugar if one happened to have these at hand.

Oh there once was a swagman camped in the billabong,
Under the shade of a Coolibah tree,
And he sang as he looked at the old billy boiling,
Who'll come a-Waltzing Matilda with me

The poet Banjo Paterson wrote this song in 1895, perhaps in memory of Samuel "Frenchy" Hoffmeister, a striking sheep shearer, who, having set fire to a woolshed at the Dagworth Homestead, was chased by the farm's owner and three policemen, but shot himself at the Combo Waterhole rather than be captured. In 1903, the popular tune was adopted by the Billy Tea Company as an advertising jingle, and while "Waltzing Matilda" has never managed to become the national anthem of Australia, it has always been the country's most beloved song, a homage to the simple, open life of the Australian bush, and the hard-drinking, tea-guzzling, freedom-loving men who built the land.

While the tea brewed "down under" was one of its more rustic manifestations, the strangely subtle effects of tea have been immortalized in an epiphany that unfolded into one of the great works of modern literature. In the small hours of New Year's night, 1908, the French writer Marcel Proust sat reading in his apartment on Boulevard Haussmann in Paris, still shivering with cold from a late-night walk, when his maid Céline admonished him to take a cup of tea. "When he idly dipped in it a finger of dry toast and raised the sodden mixture to his lips, he was overwhelmed once more by the mysterious joy which marked the onset of unconscious memory. He caught an elusive scent of geraniums and orange-blossom, mingled with a sensation of extraordinary light and happiness. Not daring to move, clinging to the taste on his palate, he pondered, until suddenly the doors of memory opened. The garden of his great-uncle Louis Weil at Auteuil had returned, miraculously preserved by the savour of rusk soaked in tea which his grandfather Nathé Weil would give him when, a child in the summer mornings of the 1880s, he visited the old man in his bedroom," wrote Proust's biographer George Painter. This Zen moment provided the creative key to Proust's masterpiece, *À la Recherche du Temps Perdu,* in which the ordinary tea and biscuit were transformed into the recollected lime tea

In the second half of the 19th century and first half of the 20th, these famous British package tea brands vied for the favor of the nation's housewives.

and madeleine, resurrecting the hidden life of memories "like the Japanese paper flowers which only come to life when we drop them in water."

In his play *Teahouse*, written in the 1950s and one of the great works of modern Chinese literature, the writer Lao She traced the meltdown of Chinese society in the first half of the 20th century through the lives of the colorful habitués of a traditional Beijing tea house. The first act is set in the fall of 1898, after the Hundred Days' Reform Movement by Kang Youwei and Liang Qiqiao to modernize the country's ingrained, backward feudalism had failed. The large room of the Yutai tea house has a high ceiling, square and oblong tables, and traditional benches and stools. Notices warning "Don't Discuss State Affairs" are pasted on the walls. "In the tea houses one could hear the most absurd stories, such as how in a certain place a huge spider had turned into a demon and was then struck by lightning. One could also come in contact with the strangest views; for example, that foreign troops could be prevented from landing by building a Great Wall along the sea coast," Lao She wrote. Act Two takes place in the 1920s, when China was torn by civil strife, and carved into private fiefdoms by feuding warlords. Many big tea houses in Beijing have closed, and half of the Yutai tea house has been turned into a hostel. Traditional snacks such as "noodles with minced pork" are a thing of the past, and even the God of Wealth shrine has been replaced by fashionable advertisements for foreign cigarettes. But the "Don't Discuss State Affairs" signs are still up, in even larger print now. Act Three describes the period in the late 1940s "following the defeat of the Japanese when KMT (Kuomintang, the Chinese nationalists) special agents and American troops were running rampant in Beijing." The tea house is worn and run down, and in addition to the proliferation of "Don't Discuss State Affairs" signs, there is a new notice: "Pay in advance." In the last scene, the proprietor Wang Lifa commits suicide, just as Lao She was driven to take his own life by ranting Red Guards during the Cultural Revolution.

Since the 1880s, China's once thriving tea industry, plagued by exorbitant taxes, inefficiency, government corruption, foreign aggression, and civil war, had been in steep decline, and by the 1940s, it lay in ruins, with no exports recorded for the year 1944. That same year, India and Ceylon exported record amounts to bolster the war efforts of Britain and its Commonwealth allies. "They talk about Hitler's secret weapon, but what about England's secret weapon – tea. That's what keeps us going and that's what's going to carry us through," wrote the historian A.A. Thompson in 1942. If the Americans fought World War II on Coca-Cola, it was tea that fueled the heroic struggle of Britain to defeat the Third Reich. Winston Churchill called tea more important than ammunition, and ordered sailors aboard naval vessels to be issued tea without restrictions. Tea offered warmth, comfort, and a momentary semblance of normality amidst the madness of war. During the Blitz of London, mobile tea canteens moved around the burning, bombed-out streets, serving anybody in need. "In every shelter there was a more or less official tea-taster," wrote Noel Streatfeild, in charge of the canteen teams in southeast London. "In some cases it was the shelter marshal; in others a man or a woman known to be a good taster. We would serve Mrs. Jones with tea, and the shelterers would gather round us. 'What's it like to-night Mrs. Jones?' Sometimes we were rewarded. Mrs.

A Beijing tea house in 1948, on the eve of Mao's ascent to power, captured by the French photographer Henri Cartier-Bresson.

Jones would beam and say, 'Beautiful, ducks'.... On the worst nights she would say nothing. In a ghastly silence, broken only by the roar of the guns overhead, she would hand back the cup. If pressed, she would sometimes offer an explanation. 'Water wasn't boilin',' or, worst insult of all, 'Did you mix some soup in this?'"

The first half of the 20th century also saw the emergence of East Africa as one of the world's major tea-producing regions. The first successful propagation of the tea bush had taken place in the Durban Botanical Gardens, South Africa, in 1850, and in 1886, tea seeds were brought by Dr. Elmslie from the Royal Botanic Garden, Edinburgh, to the Church of Scotland's Mission in Blantyre, Malawi, where the gardener Jonathan Duncan planted the seeds and managed to propagate two bushes, one of which became the mother bush of the tea plantations in Mulanje, Thornwood, and Lauderdale. In the following decades, tea cultivation was introduced to the states now known as Uganda, Tanzania, Kenya, Mozambique, and Zaire. In Kenya, tea is cultivated on both sides of the Rift Valley in the highlands

Tea after a football match in Lhasa, 1937. The British Mission established a team (which included some Tibetans) to play a combined local side, "Lhasa United."

east of Lake Victoria. Until the country's independence from Britain in 1963, virtually all production took place on large estates, but since then, cultivation by smallholders has developed rapidly, and today some 400,000 farmers, growing their tea on plots with an average size of about an acre, account for 61 percent of the country's annual output. In recent years, Kenya has emerged as one of the world's largest tea exporters, with Pakistan, Britain, Egypt, Afghanistan, and Sudan as its major markets.

As the production of black tea expanded in East Africa in the second half of the 20th century, tea was incorporated into the traditional cultures of the region's inhabitants. In the dry plains and semi-deserts of northern Kenya, the Samburu pastoralists, with a current population of about 100,000 people, began drinking tea in the 1940s. "Entering as a visitor to a Samburu home," writes the cultural anthropologist Jon Holtzman, "one of the first things you are likely to encounter is tea. Passing into the small, impermanent, stick-framed dwelling plastered with mud and dung, through a doorway roughly proportional to the stooped height of the owner of the house who has made it with her own hands, you will be seated on a short, simple, hand-carved wood stool and offered tea." In the beginning, the Samburu accorded tea the same sacred properties as tobacco, restricting its use to adults, but as tea, together with sugar, became more available, all age groups were allowed to partake of the beverage. In recent decades, as the Samburu's livestock herds have decreased and their population grown, tea with milk and sugar has replaced pure milk as the major daily staple drink. Two parts of water and one part of milk are blended in a pot over the cooking fire. A handful of tea leaves is added, and sugar mixed in when the brew begins to boil. On special occasions, the tea may be made almost entirely with milk, while families without milk must make do with *turunge* — tea and sugar alone.

The Samburu method of mixing the water and milk even before adding the tea offers "a third way" for Britons divided over the eternal question of whether to pour the tea or milk first. In 1946, the author George Orwell weighed in on that vexing problem in the tenth of his eleven succinct, golden rules for the perfect cup. First, use Indian or Ceylonese tea. Second, use a teapot of China or earthenware. Third, warm the pot beforehand by placing it on the stove. Fourth, make the tea strong. Fifth, put the tea straight into the pot. Sixth, take the teapot to the kettle, as the water should be boiling at the moment of impact. Seventh, give the pot a good shake before allowing the leaves to settle. Eighth, use a cylindrical mug. Ninth, pour the cream off the milk before using it for tea. Tenth, pour the tea into the cup first. "This," wrote Orwell, "is one of the most controversial points of all; indeed in every family in Britain there are probably two schools of thought on the subject. The milk-first school can bring forward some fairly strong arguments, but I maintain that my own argument is unanswerable. This is that, by putting the tea in first and stirring as one pours, one can exactly regulate the amount of milk whereas one is liable to put in too much milk if one does it the other way around." Finally, eleventh, drink the tea without sugar.

Those were the days of the Cold War, when the Communist world's two giants were still united under the alliance sworn by Stalin and Mao,

The ancient, venerable art of tea-tasting relies solely on the acute senses of experienced masters, and their endless search for the perfect cup. After an apprenticeship lasting more than five years, a taster can sample many hundreds of teas every hour.

who bartered tea in return for Soviet tanks. In that bygone era of double agents and assassinations with poisoned umbrella tips, the purportedly best way to detect a Russian spy was to closely observe his eyes as he brought a cup of tea to his lips. Russian men usually drink their tea in tall glasses in metal holders called *podstakannik*, and never remove the teaspoon from the glass. When taking a sip, the spoon is pressed by the thumb against the glass, and one eye instinctively shuts as a precaution against injury by the teaspoon's handle. Dispatched on a dangerous foreign mission, a top-notch Russian agent will surely remember to remove his teaspoon from his cup and place it on the dish, but the reflex of closing an eye, permanently engraved in his central nervous system, will nevertheless give him away.

According to a top-secret Cold War document only recently made public, the British military harbored deep concerns for the country's state of readiness in the event of a Soviet nuclear attack. In particular, it worried over what was known as the "tea situation," with one analyst estimating that 75 percent of Britain's tea supply would be threatened. In the continuous efforts to boost productivity and secure the strategic tea reserve, it was around this time that a revolution in the mechanization of the black tea manufacturing process took place at the Tocklai Experimental Station in northeastern India. Called CTC for crush-tear-curl, the name of the new process evokes all of the brutal efficiency that characterizes life in the modern world. In the CTC process, the old-fashioned, space-consuming bamboo trays and withering racks were made redundant by a continuous withering machine; and the rolling by hand or machine was replaced with the Rotorvane, a cylindrical contraption that minces the leaves into a finished product of fannings or dust. The accelerated CTC process induces a violent oxidation of the tea leaf's catechins and yields a tea that is strong and infuses quickly, but has little aroma to speak of and an acrid flavor, making it difficult to drink without sugar.

On the positive side, the increase in output and lowered prices made possible by the CTC process has opened up new markets in India, Africa, and the Middle East, and brought affordable tea into the lives of legions of new consumers around the world. With the help of fresh milk, copious amounts of sugar, and an army of spices – cardamom, cinnamon, ginger, star anise, peppercorn, and cloves – CTC tea is fashioned into a delicious, invigorating beverage called masala chai, enjoyed everyday by hundreds of millions of people in India's tea houses. In recent years, chai has also acquired an ardent following in the West, with brand names such as Oregon Chai – a strong, sweet tea flavored with vanilla and honey – waiting in the wings to sweep the globe. And in Hong Kong, a city that owes its very existence to the tea plant, the real connoisseurs are the punters who every day retreat to their favorite *cha chanteng* ("tea restaurant") for a steaming cup of *simat naaicha* ("pantyhose milk tea"), which is brewed with CTC tea in pantyhose submerged in kettles by *sifu* ("masters"), who keep their blends a closely guarded secret, and serve their full-bodied brew in special thick cups with sugar and evaporated milk.

Another specialty found only on the menus of Hong Kong's *cha chanteng* is the hot drink *yin-yeung* ("Yin-Yang"), no less than a blend of tea and coffee. In the Middle East, the intimate, intricate relationship between the world's two caffeine beverages is illustrated by the fact that in Iran, the men go to the *qahva*, coffee house, to drink tea, while the men in Turkey go to the *çayhane*, tea house, to drink either coffee or tea. This polarity between the indigenous and imported, rustic and refined, invigorating and comforting, was expressed in a modern debate poem by the Bahraini poet Abdallah Husayn al-Qari, "The Dispute between Coffee and Tea", first published in 1955 and following in a long tradition of debate poems in the ancient languages of Mesopotamia – Sumerian, Akkadian, Aramaic, Syriac – which have pitted against each other such improbable and probable foes as hoe and plow, tree and reed, heron and turtle, vine and cedar, Joseph and Potiphar's wife, Christ and the Pharisees, gold and wheat, and oil-drilling and pearl-diving. In "The Dispute between Coffee and Tea," the poet is lying in bed when the coffee pot and tea kettle sitting on his stove next to him begin to bicker. Coffee disparages tea as "an intruder from Iran" served in "Japanese crockery" from a "Red [Russian] samovar." Tea in turn calls coffee a "slave-girl.... pounded to bits in a mortar, burnt brown like an Indian's daughter," while praising its own "ambergris fragrance." At the climax of the tongue-lashing, coffee threatens war, and rallies her cups, pots, roasting pans, ladles, and mortars. Tea seeks refuge behind the reclining poet, who in the end conciliates the two antagonists.

> And sipping them both, each in turn...
> They kissed, on my lips the two mingled,
> At the touch of each other they tingled!

The tea bag is another 20th-century invention that has changed the way of tea around the world, and has been held up as a potent symbol of our harried times. The first individual tea bag patent was issued to A.V. Smith of London in 1896. In the early 1900s, the New York merchant Thomas Sullivan started sending out tea samples in small silk bags. But instead of opening the bags and pouring out the tea leaves, many customers simply put the entire bag into the pot, and when they complained that the silk mesh was too fine for the leaves to infuse properly, Sullivan started using sachets of gauze instead. Americans adopted the new, no-nonsense invention without a second thought. In Britain, however, tea bags were forced to fight a long-drawn-out, intractable battle against age-old rituals, customs, and preferences. In 1935, Tetley's became the first British tea firm to employ the tea bag, and the going remained a slog; in 1968 tea bags still held less than 3 percent of the British market. By 1971, that share had jumped to 12.5 percent, and from there on it was a walkover, with tea bags now accounting for some 90 percent of the tea consumed in Britain.

In Korea, where tea more or less disappeared with the great purge of Buddhism toward the end of the Koryo dynasty in the 14th century, the beverage experienced a remarkable 20th-century renaissance with the great Korean nationalist, Buddhist monk, and tea master Hyodang Choi Beom-Sul (1904–79), who, building on the work of the 19th-century monk Cho-Ui, reawakened the Korean people's interest in tea. "Like Cho-Ui, Hyodang was a monk deeply marked by the practice of Zen. Like him, he was a faithful friend of persecuted dissidents, a source of consolation in a dark age. Like him, he left behind him a growing community of people, reaching beyond Buddhism, devoted to practicing the Way of Tea as a means of spiritual refreshment, a source of community, a sign of peace," writes his biographer Brother Anthony.

After an adventurous, dangerous life in the service of Korean Buddhism, nationalism, and education, Hyodang resided at the Dasol-sa Temple, where he developed his Panyaro Way of Tea (Panyaro being the Korean transcription of Sanskrit *prajna* ("transcendent wisdom")), in which "the best is drinking tea alone." He also wrote a history of Korean tea, and founded the *Hanguk Chadohoi,* the Korean Association for the Way of Tea. After his death in 1979, his Way of Tea was continued by his wife Chae Wonhwa, who every year travels to the nearby Jirisan (Mount Jiri) to oversee the manufacturing of the exclusive Panyaro tea. First, the newly picked leaves are plunged into near-boiling water and left to drain for a couple of hours. After this, the leaves are simultaneously dried and rolled – turned, rubbed, pressed – in a cauldron over a charcoal fire for up to four hours. The finished tea has an exuberant green color, and unique taste and fragrance. The finer points and secrets of the manufacturing process were transmitted by Hyodang to Chae Wonhwa, who in turn will pass them on only to her chosen successor.

In neighboring Japan, the *chanoyu* art of Sen Rikyū was handed down to the following generations of his family, who true to the manner of squabbling heirs divided his legacy into three schools, the Urasenke, Omotesenke, and Mushanokōjisenke. By the 19th century, the partitioning of *chanoyu* factions had led to the accretion of some 1,000 *temae*, the minute rules for moving the body and handling the utensils when making tea. When showing the tea scoop to the guests, for example, the consummate *chanoyu* devotee was supposed to ensure that the distance between the scoop's tail and the edge of the tatami mat was precisely three stitches in the mat's braided grass straws. And while Urasenke practitioners were to turn the teacup clockwise before drinking, the Omotesenke must turn it in the other direction.

With the Meiji Reformation (which took place in 1868), women were for the first time allowed to practice the *chanoyu* ceremony. It became an important part of the bridal training that Japanese women must undertake before marrying, and by the end of World War II, *chanoyu* had been transformed into a virtually exclusive female preserve. At this time, Japanese intellectuals seeking to regenerate their country's cultural identity put forth *chanoyu* as the complete, integrated expression of traditional Japanese culture. Today, tea in Japan runs the gamut from a bottle of iced Oolong purchased in a vending machine for the evening commute back home, to exclusive teas purveyed by merchants such as the venerable French tea house Mariage Frères, which has shops in Tokyo's busy Shinjuku and Ginza Districts. Although *sencha* – loose-leaf tea steeped in a pot – is the most common way of tea (see box on pp. 108–09), the influence of *chanoyu* continues to smoulder, sending its unobtrusive waves of deep cultural resonance pulsing through Japanese society. The Urasenke school alone is estimated to have around one million *chanoyu* students, with a majority of middle-aged and elderly housewives, who gather with their teachers in small groups to perfect their *temae*. Curiously, after a strenuous, concentrated *keiko* ("training") session of practicing how to whisk green *matcha* ("powdered tea") properly and conduct the formal conversation between the host and main guest, it is common for the women to relax and chat freely over a cup of black tea with cakes.

During its years as a Japanese colony from 1895 to 1945, Taiwan was transformed into a major tea-producer, and in the 1950s and 1960s, it became the main supplier of green tea to northern Africa. As the island joined Asia's economic tigers in the 1970s, Taiwan's tea farmers began making Oolong tea for the burgeoning domestic market, launching a renaissance for Fujian's *gongfu* tea culture. In present-day Taiwan, people sit in the shop of their neighborhood tea merchant late at night chatting and drinking Oolong tea in the *gongfu* manner. After having drunk a few cups and enjoyed

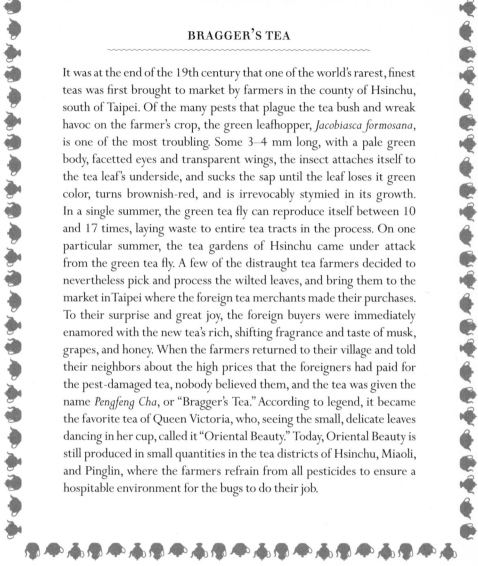

BRAGGER'S TEA

It was at the end of the 19th century that one of the world's rarest, finest teas was first brought to market by farmers in the county of Hsinchu, south of Taipei. Of the many pests that plague the tea bush and wreak havoc on the farmer's crop, the green leafhopper, *Jacobiasca formosana*, is one of the most troubling. Some 3–4 mm long, with a pale green body, facetted eyes and transparent wings, the insect attaches itself to the tea leaf's underside, and sucks the sap until the leaf loses it green color, turns brownish-red, and is irrevocably stymied in its growth. In a single summer, the green tea fly can reproduce itself between 10 and 17 times, laying waste to entire tea tracts in the process. On one particular summer, the tea gardens of Hsinchu came under attack from the green tea fly. A few of the distraught tea farmers decided to nevertheless pick and process the wilted leaves, and bring them to the market in Taipei where the foreign tea merchants made their purchases. To their surprise and great joy, the foreign buyers were immediately enamored with the new tea's rich, shifting fragrance and taste of musk, grapes, and honey. When the farmers returned to their village and told their neighbors about the high prices that the foreigners had paid for the pest-damaged tea, nobody believed them, and the tea was given the name *Pengfeng Cha*, or "Bragger's Tea." According to legend, it became the favorite tea of Queen Victoria, who, seeing the small, delicate leaves dancing in her cup, called it "Oriental Beauty." Today, Oriental Beauty is still produced in small quantities in the tea districts of Hsinchu, Miaoli, and Pinglin, where the farmers refrain from all pesticides to ensure a hospitable environment for the bugs to do their job.

a good conversation, the customer will, most often, feel obliged to recip-rocate the shopkeeper's hospitality by buying some tea. A completely new *gongfu* tea utensil invented by the Taiwanese is the *wenxiang bei* ("smelling cup"), a slender, high cup used in the following way: the tea is poured into the *wenxiang bei*, and covered with a regular teacup as a lid. By pinching the feet of the two cups and turning them over, the tea is transferred to the regular cup, whereupon the *wenxiang bei* is brought to the nose and the tea's lingering aroma enjoyed. In addition to the famous "Oriental Beauty," Taiwan produces several of the world's finest Oolong teas, such as Pinglin Baozhong, Dongding Oolong and Mucha Tieguanyin. Every major Taiwanese Oolong tea has its own annual competitions, but the old tea men complain that in the race to impress the judges with a tea that is beautiful in appearance, teamakers have begun to pick young and tender leaves, which are easier to roll into the desired shape, but which lack the aromatic compounds of the more mature leaves needed to make the most fragrant Oolong.

For all the excesses of the Cultural Revolution, eyewitnesses of the period attest to an incongruous fact: the tea, though packaged in the most unassuming manner, was excellent. Until his death in 1976, Mao Zedong maintained his old habit of rinsing his mouth with green tea instead of brushing his teeth. Under Deng Xiaoping's new policy of reform and opening up, old tea tracts were replanted, tea factories refurbished, research institutes inaugurated, and output boosted from 513 million lb in 1976 to over 1 billion lb in 1986. From the huge, state-run tea plantations, tea cultivation was devolved back to smallholder peasants, who tended their tea bushes with a sharp eye to the bottom line, further increasing, if not quality, then at least productivity, and today, China has recouped its position as one of the world's top tea exporters. Chinese intellectuals, in their attempts to define China's place in the modern world, embrace tea as an integral component of the country's cultural identity, and recent years have seen a greatly renewed interest in the rich heritage of this beverage. China's tea encyclopedia, for example, lists no fewer than 138 different kinds of green tea, cultivated in different parts of the country, each a separate variety of *Camellia sinensis*, and with its own manufacturing process, appearance, fragrance, and taste. At the turn of the 21th century, the capital Beijing was swept by a wave of elegant new tea houses in the Taiwanese style, and following the SARS crisis, Beijing's residents turned from their traditional jasmine tea to green tea, with its lauded medicinal properties. One of the latest fashions in the nightclubs and bars of the capital is a cocktail with distinct Chinese characteristics – Chivas Regal whiskey mixed with sweetened green tea.

Teakettle Junction in Death Valley, California. At every crossroad in history, tea has ventured on a new path, to become both the world's most popular infusion and the common heritage of humankind.

On the opposite side of the Pacific Rim, in the trendy Pearl district of Portland, Oregon, one of the coolest tea cocktails is simply called Matt, that is, jade Oolong tea and vodka with a splash of peach schnapps and a sprinkle of candied ginger. Another is the Genghis Kowboy, billed as "an antioxidant workhorse of extra strength green tea and whiskey served on the rocks." With Seattle the confirmed capital of new-age coffee, its arch-rival Portland has fittingly emerged as the hottest, most creative tea scene in America, offering irreverent blends of black, green, and Oolong teas; intriguing novelties such as green chai latte sweetened with honey-dew melon; politically impeccable decaffeinated, organic, fairtrade, and rainforest-certified teas; Super Irish Breakfast and Double Bergamot Earl Grey, and an endless array of other equally colorful, inventive hot and cold tea beverages. Home of successful franchises such as Stash Tea, Tazo Tea, and Oregon Chai, Portland has also given the tea bag a new life under the name "filterbag," and brought the world the new adjectives "ricey" and "popcorn" to describe the aroma of green tea, as well as the term mojo, for the "vibe that tea emits if you are the least bit psychic." On the East Coast, more traditional purveyors such the Massachusetts firm Upton Tea are tapping into the rapidly growing interest for upmarket teas in America, both by providing excellent estate teas from all corners of the globe, and by educating their customers in the long and venerable tradition of the leaves they are purchasing.

If Portland represents the cutting edge of new age tea, London was until recently one of the last bastions of tradition. On 29 June, 1998, a 319-year era came to a close when the last London Tea Auction was held at the city's Chamber of Commerce and Industry, with the final lot of the day, a single 97 lb chest of Ceylon Flowery Pekoe from the Hellbodde Tea Estate, knocked down by Taylors of Harrogate for a record price of over $40,000. While the tea auction candle no longer flickers in Mincing Lane, Britain's "tea first versus milk first debate," however, continues unabated, and in 2003, following in the footsteps of Francis Galton and George Orwell, the chemistry professor Dr. Andrew Stapley, having spent two months researching the topic, issued his firm conclusion: the milk should go first. "If milk is poured into hot tea, individual drops separate from the bulk of the milk, and come into contact with the high temperatures of the tea for enough time for significant denaturation – degradation – to occur. This is much less likely to happen if hot water is added to milk," Dr. Stapley told *The Guardian* newspaper. In 2005, the British for the first time spent more money on instant coffee than tea, but experts point out that in terms of quantity, tea still holds sway, with an estimated 165 million down-to-earth "cuppas" consumed every day. That same year, an age-old dream finally came true, as Britain's first commercial home-grown tea crop was announced by the Tregothnan Estate in southwest England, where the leaves from some 20,000 tea bushes are harvested, blended, and brought to market at the imposing price of £680 ($1,300) per lb in London's upscale Fortnum & Mason, which caters to refined palates and deep pockets with a range of the world's finest and most expensive teas.

"The English have really carried out a great miracle by replacing the use of coffee with that of tea. They started by giving it as a present to the chiefs, and then, in the spirit of imitation, everybody wanted to drink it. Today, Morocco, all of the Sahara, and part of Central Africa depend on England for tea," wrote the French anthropologist Henri Duveyrier in the 19th century. Among these people are the Tuareg pastoralists, who inhabit the southern fringes of the Sahara Desert in the nations of Niger and Mali, and who for centuries controlled the five main caravan routes across the

Sahara. In their desert perambulations, the Tuaregs became acquainted with the green gunpowder tea first re-exported from Britain to Morocco in the 18th century, and today tea forms an indispensable part of Tuareg life. It marks the beat of the day, concludes every meal, greets every friend, precedes the afternoon nap, and ushers in the night. To visit a Tuareg family and refuse at least one cup of tea is considered highly impolite. In the elaborate, protracted Tuareg tea ceremony, the tea is first put into the teapot and "cleaned" with some boiling water, which is poured out after about one minute. Mint and large amounts of sugar are added, boiling water poured into the pot, and the concoction allowed to steep for three to five minutes. A glass is poured, and then poured back into the pot in order to mix the tea. This is repeated several times. More sugar is added if needed, and when the host deems that the infusion has acquired the proper strength and taste, it is poured into the cups from a height to produce a foam. In the full ritual, which can take a couple of hours, three cups of tea are served. The first, say the Tuareg, is bitter – like life. The second cup is sweet – like love. The third is light – like the breath of death.

As the use of the salubrious tea leaf continues to spread, serious tea-drinkers are becoming more and more demanding of the infusion in their cups, and are asking for tea that is cultivated sustainably and organically, manufactured attentively, sourced ethically, and traded fairly. Meanwhile, advertising executives have already identified the next miraculous medicinal compound in tea. It is called epigallocatechin-3-gallate, EGCG for short, and soon, no doubt, talk shows, websites, magazines, and newspapers will be filled with reports about this new panacea. Such claims should be taken as Lu Yu took his tea, with a pinch of salt. For while nobody denies the beneficial, healing properties of tea, it is not a medicine foremost, but rather a daily ritual, an excuse for a well-needed break, a philosophy, a search for those moments of quietude and companionship when the din of the world subsides and all becomes one. Drink it in that spirit, and health, happiness, and eternal life will follow.

APPENDIX A

THE AUTOBIOGRAPHY OF INSTRUCTOR LU

This is the extraordinary self-written account of the enormously influential founder of the tea cult. It was composed during the second year of the Superior Origin reign period (761), when Lu Yu was 29.

Master Lu's name was Yu and his style name was Hongjian. It is not known where he was from. Some say that his style was Yu and that his name was Hongjian, but it is impossible to know who is right. His appearance was as ugly as that of Wang Can[1] or Zhang Zai[2] and he stammered like Sima Xiangru[3] or Yang Xiong[4], but he was talented and persuasive and had a sincere and trustworthy character. He was narrow-minded and irritable, showing a great deal of subjectivity in his opinions. When his friends reproved him, however, he could be more open-minded and less suspicious. If he were living with another person and got the inclination to go somewhere else, he would leave without saying anything, causing others to suspect that he was born full of anger. But if he had an agreement with another person, he would never fail to keep his word, even if it meant traveling 1,000 tricents through ice and snow over roads infested by wolves and tigers.[5]

At the beginning of the Superior Origin reign period, Lu Yu built a hut by the bank of the Grandiflora stream.[6] He closed his door and read books; he refused to mix with rogues, though he would spend whole days chatting and convivializing with eminent monks and lofty scholars. Often, he would travel back and forth between various mountains and monasteries in his little slip of a boat, clad only in a gauze kerchief, vine sandals, a short shirt of coarse wool, and a pair of underpants. He would frequently walk alone in the wilderness reciting Buddhist scriptures or chanting ancient poems. Striking the forest trees with his staff or dabbling in the flowing water with his hand, Lu Yu might dilly-dally hesitantly from morning until evening and on into the darkness of night after the sun had gone completely down, whereupon he would return home wailing and weeping. So the southerners would say to each other, "Master Lu must be today's Madman of Chu."[7]

An abandoned waif at the age of three, Lu Yu was taken in and raised in the Jingling meditation[8] monastery by the great teacher Jigong. From the age of nine he learned how to write and Jigong revealed to him the occupation of escaping from the world that was described in the Buddhist books. In reply, the lad said to him, "To be cut off from one's brothers, to have no further descendants, to wear a cassock and shave one's head, to call oneself an adherent of Sakyamuni[9] – if the Confucians were to hear of this, would they proclaim it to be filial behavior? Would it be all right if I request that you teach me the writings of the Confucian sages?"

"It's excellent," said the elder, "that you wish to show your filial devotion, but you have no idea at all how great is the meaning of the Way of the tonsure and cassock from the West." The elder obdurately insisted that Lu Yu study the Buddhist canon, and Lu Yu obdurately insisted that he study the Confucian canon. Consequently, the elder feigned not to love the youngster any longer and tested him with a series of demeaning tasks. He had him sweep the monastery grounds, clean out the monks' toilet, mix mud with his feet to plaster on walls, carry tiles on his back and build rooms, and herd 30 head of cattle. At Jigong and around West Lake, there was no paper for the lad to practice writing, so he would trace characters on the backs of the cattle with a piece of bamboo.

One day, Lu Yu asked a learned person about some characters and the person gave him a copy of Zhang Heng's[10] "Rhapsody on the Southern Capital." The lad could not recognize the characters of the rhapsody, but there in the pasture he imitated the little boys who were students. He would sit up straight with the scroll unrolled before him and move his mouth, but that was all. When the elder learned of this, he was afraid that the lad was gradually becoming infected by heretical texts and thus daily growing more distant from the Way. So he confined him to the monastery and ordered him to cut away the overgrown bushes and weeds under the supervision of the head gateman.

From time to time, a character would come to mind, and then Lu Yu would fall into a stupor as though he were lost. He might spend a whole day standing there disheartened like a wooden post and doing nothing. The supervisor thought he was lazy and struck him with a whip. The result was that the lad sighed over the passing of the months and years, fearing that he would never acquire the knowledge that was in books, which caused him to sob uncontrollably. The supervisor thought that he harbored resentment and whipped him on the back until his cane broke. Because he was weary of these labors, the lad escaped from the supervisor and ran away. With only a few extra items of clothing rolled up in a bundle, he joined a variety troupe. While with them, he wrote *Jests* in three chapters. As an actor, he played the role of the phony blockhead clerk who hides a pearl.

Upon finding him, the elder said, "When I think how you have become lost to the Way, how sad it is! Our founding teacher had a saying that, in a 24-hour day, a disciple was only permitted to study two hours of non-Buddhist subjects so that heretical teachings might be overcome. Since there are so many people in our monastery, I'll let you do as you wish now. You may also study miscellaneous subjects and practice your calligraphy."

During the Heavenly Jewel reign period,[11] some people from Chu held a feast in the circuit of Canglang.[12] The district suboffical functionary invited Lu Yu to be the director of the entertainers who were hired for the occasion. At the time, Li Qiwu, administrator of Henan, had been appointed governor of Canglang and was in attendance at the feast. He considered Lu Yu to be someone of extraordinary talent, so he shook his hand and patted him on the back, then personally presented him with his own poetry collection. Thereupon the common people of the Han and Min valleys also considered Lu Yu to be extraordinary.

After that, Lu Yu carried his books to the villa of Master Zou on Firegate Mountain. This happened to be just when the director of the ministry of rites, Cui Guofu,[13] was appointed adjutant of Jingling commandery. Altogether, Lu Yu and he enjoyed each other's company for three years. During this period, Lu Yu was presented with a white donkey, a jet-black pack ox, and a bookcase made of patterned pagoda tree wood. The white donkey and pack ox were given to him by Li Cheng, the governor of Xiangyang;[14] the bookcase of patterned pagoda tree wood was a present from the late vice-director of the chancellery, Lu. Realizing that they are well suited for riding and storing by rural folk, that is why they gave me these items in particular.

At the beginning of the Highest Virtue reign period,[15] refugees[16] from Shaanxi fled south of the Yangtze and Lu Yu also went south at that time. There he developed a friendship with the monk Jiaoran[17] that ignored their difference in age and religious status.

From the time he was young, Lu Yu enjoyed writing, mostly in a satirical vein. If he saw people do something good, he would feel as through he himself had done it; but if he saw people do something bad, he would feel as though he were ashamed of himself. "Bitter medicine is hard to swallow; bitter words are hard to hear" – since there was nothing that he would shy away from saying, the average person kept out of his way. In response to An Lushan's[18] rebellion in the Central Plains, he wrote a poem entitled "Quadruple Sorrow" and, in response to Liu Zhan's insurrection[19] in the region west of the Huai river, he wrote "Rhapsody on the Unclarity of Heaven." All these pieces were inspired by his passionate reaction to current events which caused him to weep and snivel. His other writings include *The Contract Between Ruler and Subject* in three scrolls, *Genealogy of Four Surnames from South of the Yangtze* in eight scrolls, *An Account of Men of Distinction from North and South* in ten scrolls, *A Record of Successive Officials in Wuxing* in three scrolls, *The Classic of Tea* in one scroll, and *The Divination of Dreams* in three scrolls (A, B, C), all of which he keeps in a coarse cloth sack.

Notes: 1. A famous writer (177–217) from the kingdom of Wei during the Three Kingdoms period; 2. A famous writer of the kingdom of Wei (3rd century); 3. The most famous author of rhapsodies (c. 179–118 BC); 4. A noted thinker and language specialist (53 BC–AD 18); 5. A tricent is around 300 paces or approximately ⅓ mile. 6. In the northern part of Zhejiang, it rises in the vicinity of Celestial Eye Mountain (Tianmu Shan) and flows into Lake Tai; 7. Jieyu, an eccentric of the Spring and Autumn period who is noted for having taunted Confucius with a wild song about the phoenix; 8. Sanskrit *dhyana* = Japanese Zen, Chinese Chan; 9. The Buddha; 10. A famous writer (78–139), especially of rhapsodies, and inventor of the Eastern Han period; 11. 742–55; 12. In the modern province of Hubei; 13. A Tang poet and official; 14. In Hubei; 15. 756–57; 16. Escaping from the An-Shi rebellion; 17. A well-known Buddhist poet (730–99); 18. Roxsan the Arsacid, of Sogdian-Turkish ancestry, had been a favorite of the Tang emperor, Xuan Zong, and his "Precious Consort," Yang Guifei (died 756); 19. In 760.

APPENDIX B
A DEBATE BETWEEN TEA AND BEER

During the first decade of the 20th century, a cache of more than 40,000 manuscripts was discovered in a small cave at Mogaoku, outside the remote northwestern Chinese town of Dunhuang in Gansu province. The Dunhuang manuscripts have proven invaluable for the study of medieval Chinese history, religion, society, and literature. Among the manuscripts was found a charming work entitled Cha jiu lun *("A Debate between Tea and Beer"),[1] which is dated to the second half of the 10th century. This must have been a very popular text, since – in whole or in part – it is copied onto no fewer than six different Dunhuang manuscripts. Attributed to the local scholar Wang Fu, it is written in a conspicuously colloquial style, which this translation attempts to reflect. Aside from his mention at the head of the text ("Prefectural Nominee for Advanced Scholar") and on another Dunhuang manuscript dated to 978, where he is identified as a lay scholar, nothing else is known about him.*

A Debate between Tea and Beer is closely mirrored by a Tibetan work entitled The Dispute between Tea and Chang,[2] *which was written by Bon Drongpa sometime during the 17th and 18th centuries.[3] Although the Tibetan work is much longer and more philosophical in its orientation, there are so many resemblances between the two works that one suspects a common heritage.[4] As a matter of fact, this type of dispute between two non-human charac-ters may be traced all the way back to Sumerian literature, where we find debates between* Winter and Summer, Bird and Fish, Sheep and Grain, Tree and Reed, Date Palm and Tamarisk, Hoe and Plow, *and* Silver and Copper.[5] *Since debates between tea and rice beer (or other types of alcoholic beverages) are found in the non-Sinitic popular literature of East Asia (e.g., among the Tai-speaking Bouyei of southwestern China), in Ming fiction, and so forth, it is clear that this was a widespread theme that struck a deeply resonant chord among many different groups.*

I have heard that, when the Divine Husbandman[6] tasted the hundred plants, it was from this that the Five Grains were distinguished. The Yellow Emperor[7] fashioned clothing for people to wear, which was transmitted and taught to later generations. After Cangjie[8] created writing, Confucius was able to explain and cultivate the reasoning for his literati doctrines. It's impossible for me to tell everything from the very beginning in detail, so I shall [merely] present a summary of the essentials. For the moment, let me just ask Tea and Beer, which of you two has merit and distinction? Which of you fellows deserves contempt, and which deserves respect? Today, each of you must set forth your principles. Whoever is more convincing will bring glory to his whole family.

Thereupon, Tea came forth and declared, "You all don't make such a ruckus! Listen to me for a little bit. I am the chief of the hundred herbs and the flower of the ten thousand plants. People honor me by taking my stamens, they esteem me by plucking my buds. They call me the *ming* herb and name me *cha*. I am given as tribute in the residences of the Five Marquises;[9] I am presented to the families of emperors and kings. Timely and fresh, I am offered [to the court]. The glory and splendor of the age, naturally I am respected and honored. What need is there for boasting?"

Thereupon, Beer came forth [and declared], "What ridiculous talk! From ancient times until now, tea has been cheap and beer expensive. A goblet of beer poured in the river [by their commander sufficed to make the soldiers of] the Triple Army [of the ancient state of Chu] all become drunk.[10] When rulers and princes drink beer, they give their courtiers [the opportunity to speak] without fear;[11] when the assembled vassals drink beer, they call out, 'Long live [the Emperor]!' [Beer] pacifies the dead and stabilizes the living, my vapors are enjoyed by the gods. When beer and victuals are offered to others, evil thoughts ultimately vanish. Where there is beer, there are [also beer-drinking] games, [evincing] humaneness, justice, civility, and knowledge. Of course, it is fitting for me to be considered the more respected. Why waste energy making comparisons?"

"Have you never heard tell," Tea addressed Beer, "that a myriad countries come to Fuliang[12] and Shezhou[13] seeking [their teas]? They cross over hills and climb ridges to get the teas of Mount Shu[14] and Meng Ding.[15] In Shucheng[16] and Taihu,[17] they buy male and female servants [to help with their tea service]. In Yuejun, Yuyao, and Hangzhou,[18] gold and silk are used to make bags [for keeping tea]. Like the plain purple robe of the Son of Heaven, [tea] is a rare thing among human beings. [Yet] the merchants come seeking it, their boats and carts jammed one after another. According to this evidence, [it is clear] which of us should be considered inferior."

"Have you never heard tell," Beer addressed Tea, "of Medicinal Beer, Dry Mellow, Worth Brocade and Worth Thin Silk, Grape [Wine], and Nine Times Fermented, all of which are beneficial for health? [As for] Nephrite Beer and Jade Liquor, they are to be found in the cups and glasses of the immortals. [Then there's] Chrysanthemum Blossom and Bamboo Leaf, with whom rulers and princes associate. [In the ancient state of] Zhongshan, there was a brewer [named] Mother Zhao [whose beer] was sweet and delicious, [yet with a] beautiful bitterness. [The legend of a man who] fell drunk on it for three years has been transmitted from antiquity down to the present. [Offering beer shows] respect and deference to one's fellow townsmen and brings harmony to military garrisons. There's no need for you to vainly exert your brain over this, fellow!"

"My *ming* herb," Tea addressed Beer, "is the heart of the ten thousand plants. It can be white as jade or seem yellow as gold. Famous monks of great virtue and hidden recluses in Buddhist temples drink it while making their discourses

because it can dispel dullness and weariness. Tea is worshipfully offered to Maitreya[19] and respectfully presented to Avalokitesvara.[20] Through countless kalpas, the various Buddhas have esteemed it. Beer, [in contrast,] can destroy households and separate families, and [can cause people] to do many depraved and lascivious things. After a person has knocked down three small cups, it causes him to fall deep into sin."

"Three cash for a jar [of tea]," Beer addressed Tea, "[at that rate,] when would one ever become wealthy? Beer can help one make contacts with honorable people, and is admired by dukes and ministers. It induced the lord of Zhao to strum a lute and the king of Qin to beat [a rhythm on] a jug, but you can't even get singers and dancers to come perform for a cup of tea. All you get from drinking tea is a backache, and if you drink too much of it you'll get an upset stomach. If you knock down ten cups of it in a single day, your belly will be as bloated as the big drum for striking the hours at the district magistrate's office. If you drink it for three years, you'll end up looking like a frog nursing a bad case of edema."

"[Like Confucius,]" Tea addressed Beer, "I made a name for myself by the age of 30. Wearing a girdle [at my waist and with] a scarf and comb [for my head, I dress properly as befitting a person of my status]. I leap over seas and vault across rivers to come pay court to the current ruling house. When I am about to arrive in the market stalls, and before I have finished spreading out my wares, people have already come to buy them, so that I have a surfeit of money. Right while we are talking, I have already attained great wealth. There's no need to wait for today or tomorrow [for me to get rich]. You, Beer, can make people muddleheaded and confused.[21] If someone drinks too much [beer], he'll be brawling and wrangling. Out in the streets, he'll implicate innocents and be rewarded with a flogging of at least 17 strokes."[22]

"Haven't you ever noticed," Beer addressed Tea, "that when the ancients and men of talent recite poetry, they always say, 'If you drink up a cup [of beer], it will nourish your life.' They also say, 'Beer is a medicine for dissipating worry.' And they also say, 'Beer can promote wisdom.' These remnants of the ancients have been transmitted down to the present day. Tea is so cheap that you can buy five bowls of it for five cash, whereas beer is so expensive that it costs seven cash for half a cup. Serving beer and giving thanks at the table [promote] civil deference and social intercourse. [Furthermore,] the basis of state music has its source in beer. [If the musicians were to] consume your tea all morning, would they dare to touch their string and wind instruments even a little?!"

"Haven't you heard tell," Tea addressed Beer, "that a young man of 14 or 15 [is advised] not to get near the beer shops? And, sir, haven't you seen the orangutan bird[23] that loses its life because of its fondness for beer? Now, fellow, you claimed that a person will get sick if he drinks tea, and that a person will become wise if he drinks beer. However, whereas I have seen people with alcoholic jaundice and other diseases brought on by drinking beer, I've never heard of people getting tea madness or tea fits.[24] King Ajatasatru[25] killed his parents because of beer, and Liu Ling[26] fell dead drunk for three years because of beer. When a person drinks beer, he will raise his eyebrows and stare at others, brandishing his fists and fighting angrily. In legal accusations, it is only stated that [so-and-so] was brash from being drunk on beer. There has never been a case where someone had words with another person from being drunk on tea. [When someone is arrested for drunkenness,] he cannot avoid begging the jailer and the flogger [for mercy], while the investigators will be asking him for money. A big cangue will be clamped on his neck, and on his back they will toss on a heavy beam. Then he will burn incense and swear off beer, reciting the name of the Buddha and begging Heaven. For the rest of his life, he will drink no more [beer], in hopes that he can avoid [ever again being in such a] horrible position."

Just as the two of them were arguing about who was better, they were unaware that Water was standing by their side.

"You two fellows," Water declared to Tea and Beer, "what's the use of getting so agitated? Who gave you permission to discuss your own merits so audaciously? Your words slander each other, and you are talking heedlessly. One's existence[27] [is dependent upon] the Four Great Elements: Earth, Water, Fire, and Wind.[28] If tea had no water, what would its appearance be? If beer had no water, what would its complexion be? If one were to eat [brewer's] rice yeast dry, it would harm one's stomach and intestines. If one were to eat tea leaves dry, they would slice and scrape one's throat. The ten thousand things[29] all need water, and it is the wellspring of the Five Grains. Above, it corresponds to the symbols of heaven; below, it conforms to the omens [of earth]. The rivers of the realm[30] can flow only when I fill them. In great waves, I can inundate heaven and earth; but I can also dry up, killing fishes and dragons. In the time of Yao,[31] a disastrous [flood lasted for] nine years, and it was simply because of me. All under heaven are moved to revere me, and the ten thousand surnames[32] comply with me. Despite all this, I do not call myself capable and sagacious, so what's the use of you two wrangling over your merits? From now on, you definitely must get along harmoniously with each other. [That way,] the beer shops will prosper and the tea houses will not be ruined. You are brothers forever, as it must be from the beginning to the end."

If people read this book, they will never be harmed by beer fits and tea madness.[33]

Notes: 1. The translation of the word *jiu* presents special difficulties: in this book generally we render it as "rice beer" (and in this appendix and other literary texts often simply "beer"). What we commonly think of as beer is fermented barley malt flavored with hops, but *jiu* is fermented rice, without any flavoring agent (exactly the same as Japanese sake). Functionally, *jiu* often plays a role in Chinese society

and literature that is comparable to that of wine in the West, although the word – with appropriate modifiers – is also used in China to refer to a wide range of alcoholic beverages, including wine, beer, and liquor; 2. *Chang* is Tibetan barley beer. Like Chinese *jiu, chang* is also used in a general sense to refer to any alcoholic beverage; 3. Interested readers may find a complete translation of the Tibetan text, with full annotations, in Bon-grong-pa, *Ja-chang lha-mo'i bstan-bcos* (The Dispute Between Tea and Chang), tr. and annot. Alexander Fedotov and Acharya Sangye Tandar Naga (Dharamsala: Library of Tibetan Works and Archives, 1993); 4. Dunhuang was under Tibetan control from 781 to 847, and there are still many Tibetans living in the region; 5. See Jeremy Black, *et al.*, *The Literature of Ancient Sumer* (Oxford: Oxford University Press, 2004); 6. The mythical founding figure, Shennong; 7. The legendary progenitor of the Chinese people, Huangdi; 8. A god who was supposed to have four eyes, the better to discern the patterns of nature; 9. It was a custom of the Han dynasty (206 BC–AD 220) for rulers to enfeoff five marquises at the same time. Later, the expression "Five Marquises" came to signify the nobility more generally; 10. This is an old tradition going back to later Warring States times (475–221 BC), according to which a military leader would not keep rice beer to himself, but would share it with his troops; 11. A Tang customary expression for when the emperor looked favorably upon his officials. It was influenced by the common Buddhist expression *shi wuwei* ("bestower of fearlessness"); 12. In Jiangxi province; 13. In Anhui province; 14. In Anhui; 15. A peak in Sichuan province; 16. In Anhui; 17. Also in Anhui; 18. All in Zhejiang province; 19. Name of the future Buddha; 20. Sanskrit name (Guanyin in Chinese) of the compassionate savior Bodhisattva; 21. This is a common complaint against alcoholic drinks in Buddhist texts; 22. There are various explanations for why 17 strokes, a number that often occurs in Tang and Song texts. It is usually said that there should actually be 20 strokes (a round number), but the total is reduced for leniency (one less for Heaven, one less for Earth, and one less for the ruler); 23. Orangutans were often said by medieval Chinese to like alcoholic drinks, and it was widely believed that they could be caught by laying out liqor to entice them. It is a mystery how this strange belief about the orangutan was transformed to an unidentifiable bird, a figure that appears in several works of Dunhuang literature; 24. Ironically, despite what Tea asserts here, there are many references in Tang and later works to precisely such illnesses that were said by opponents of tea to be induced by an excess of its consumption; 25. King Ajatasatru was the second incumbent of the throne of Magadha which he secured by killing his father. Originally a follower of the notorious Devadatta, a schismatic opponent of the Buddha, he subsequently repented and became a devout adherent of Buddhism; 26. A famous hard drinker of the Eastern Jin period (317–420); 27. The text actually says *rensheng* ("human existence"), but that obviously requires a slight modification in the context of the present debate; 28. The physical human body, like all things in the universe, is held to be composed of these four *mahabhuta*, a Sanskrit term meaning "Great Element." This Indian conception is closely paralleled by similar ideas about elements or phases of existence in Greek and Chinese cosmology; 29. I.e., everything in creation; 30. The Yangtze, Yellow, Huai, and Ji rivers are specifically named; 31. A mythological ruler of remote antiquity under whose reign there occurred a catastrophic flood that was ultimately controlled by his successor, Yu; 32. All the people; 33. The copyist adds: "Inscribed and copied in his own hand on the 14th day of the 1st month (i.e., 1 February) in the year 972 by Yan Haizhen, fellow of the Academy of Knowledge and Arts."

A GENEALOGY OF WORDS FOR TEA

Here thou, great Anna! whom three realms obey,
Dost sometimes counsel take — and sometimes tea.
Alexander Pope, *The Rape of the Lock*

It is usually claimed that the words for tea in all the languages of the world derive from Chinese. As will be shown in short order, this is true to a large extent. However, like *Camellia sinensis* itself, the genealogy of words for tea has a deeper origin that is to be found in Southeast Asia. (All linguistic terms and concepts used here are given simplified definitions in the notes. Readers who are uninterested in or allergic to phonological description and analysis should simply skip over the section entitled "Phonology" when they come to it.)

To follow all the words for tea that have spread across the entire globe back to their original sources requires painstaking linguistic and philological research. Here we shall present the results of our lengthy investigations in a simplified form that is intelligible to the educated layperson while yet retaining the essential outlines and crucial data of a fuller treatment. Moreover, formal linguistic treatises inevitably employ a bewildering array of signs, symbols, special letters, and diacritical marks. Here we shall dispense with this linguistic apparatus.

By way of preface, it is necessary to make a few general remarks about the nature of Chinese language and writing. Briefly, it is a truism for all the natural tongues of humankind that spoken language comes first, and after that a script is either borrowed or devised to write it (if, that is, it ever gets written at all, since most languages that have existed were never recorded in written form). Furthermore, all languages on earth that are in contact with other languages (and the vast majority of living languages do have contact relationships) borrow more or less freely from each other. Finally, all languages vary through time and space: they are not eternally constant, nor are they uniform at different points on a map.

What makes diachronic and synchronic studies of Sinitic[1] languages especially challenging is that, despite the enormous historical changes experienced by them during the past two millennia or so since the writing system was stabilized, the construction of the individual Chinese characters has remained fundamentally constant. Yet the characters do not provide a clear indication of the sounds of the syllables (most of which are also morphemes[2]) that they are used to write. Rather, most characters provide a combination of semantic and phonetic clues, neither of which is exact, but only suggestive. Moreover, the Chinese writing system is open-ended, with new characters being invented all the time, even up to the present day: there are now more than 100,000 to contend with. All of these features of the Chinese script must be kept in mind as we trace the path of the original etymon for tea up to the present day with its proliferation of seemingly unrelated derivative forms.

Tea, Char, Chai

We may begin our inquiry with the English word "tea" itself, undoubtedly the most common term for this beverage worldwide. Although we now pronounce "tea" as *tee*, 300 years ago it rhymed with "obey," and in some parts of Britain one may still hear it spoken that way. Other languages that have words for tea likewise beginning with the sound "t" include Danish *te*, Dutch *thee*, Estonian *tee*, Finnish *tee*, French *thé*, German *Tee*, Hungarian *tea* (pronounced *teya*), Icelandic *te*, Italian *tè*, Late (scientific) Latin *thea*, Malay *the*, Norwegian *te*, Spanish *té*, and Swedish *te*.[3] Note that, despite their diverse spellings, most of these words are pronounced more or less in the same way as the "te-" part of "tequila." That is understandable, since they all derive from languages belonging to the Southern Min[4] branch of Sinitic that are spoken in the province of Fujian on the southeast coast of China. In particular, the Dutch, English, French, Germans, and others acquired their word for tea from the area around the port of Amoy (Xiamen) where the word for tea is *te* (pronounced as though it rhymed with "eh?").

Also belonging to the *te* family of tea words is Polish *herbata*, although the derivation is not immediately apparent to the untrained eye. *Herbata* most likely comes from Dutch *herba thee* (a minority view holds that it derives from Late Latin *herba thea*, which is perfectly congruent with the Dutch). Other languages that have comparable terms are Cassubian (*arbata/harbata*), Western Ukrainian (*gerbata*), Byelorussian (*garbata*) (*g-* is pronounced as *h-* in both of the preceding terms), and Lithuanian *arbata*.

Pronounced in the second ("rising") tone, *cha* is the word for tea in Modern Standard Mandarin (MSM). Though sometimes with different tonal contours, *cha* is also used to designate tea in other northern and southwestern Sinitic topolects,[5] as well as in Cantonese (*caa4 (tshaa2)*), a large language branch in the far southeast of China. Customarily preceded by the honorific prefix *o-*, *cha* is the term for the favorite non-alcoholic drink of the Japanese. Some other languages whose word for tea is ultimately traceable to *cha* are Portuguese *chá* (pronounced *sha*), Bengali *châ*, Tagalog *tsâ*, Thai *cha*, Tibetan *ja*, Tangut (north China borderland, 11th century) *tse*, Jurchen (northeast China borderland, 15th century) *cha*, and 20th-century English military slang "char."

Just as we can analyze the distribution of words for tea derived from Southern Min *te* as having traveled by sea (initially carried by Dutch ships, then later by English ships) to Europe and America, so can we discern a pattern in the spread of words derived from *cha*. Namely, either they went overland from north and southwest China to bordering regions such as Tibet, or they went by sea in primarily Portuguese ships from Cantonese-speaking ports to countries where the Dutch and the British were not yet engaged in extensive trade.

An intriguing phenomenon is the coexistence in Vietnamese (*trà, chà*) and Korean (*ta, cha*) of both *te* words and *cha* words for tea. We attribute this to their proximity to parts of China where *cha* was used as the word for tea and their coastal location where they could also receive shipments of tea from that part of China where *te* was the word for tea. Italian (*cià*) and English (*chaa*) both initially had *cha*-type words for tea which they respectively received from early travelers and from Portuguese traders around the end of the 16th century and the beginning of the 17th century, but in both cases they were soon displaced by *te*-type words under Dutch influence.

Today, the most rapidly expanding global term for a beverage utilizing the leaves of *C. sinensis* is *chai*. This is an Anglicization of the Hindi-Urdu word *cây*, which the British picked up during the days when the empire possessed India as its most important colony. Often preceded by the word *masala* ("spice"), even when occurring alone nowadays *chai* usually signifies a tea flavored with characteristically Indian spices (e.g., cardamon, cloves, star anise, peppercorn, ginger, cinnamon). It must be noted that this specialized usage is a fairly recent phenomenon that began in North American English during roughly the last quarter of a century, but one that is rapidly spreading in Europe and beyond with the new global marketeers of tea and coffee culture. Older *chai*-type words in numerous other languages which we will mention below simply refer to black tea. For specific historical reasons, English is thus in possession of all three types of tea words: tea, char, and chai. One of the few other languages in the world that maintains both *chai* and *te* types of words for tea is Moroccan colloquial Arabic, where *ashây* signifies generic Middle Eastern black tea, while *atây* specifies green tea (from Fujian or Zhejiang) with fresh mint leaves.[6]

Even to the uninitiated, it is obvious that *chai* appears to be closely related to *cha*, and so it is. Yet, determining how that innocent-seeming *–i* got attached to the end of *cha* has proven to be the most demanding and vexing problem in studying the evolution of words for tea. Many scholars contend that *chai* derives from the Mandarin expression *chaye* ("tea leaves"), with the alleged elision of the final vowel. Given the phonological realities, however, this hypothesis cannot be substantiated. In the first place, *chai* is a single-syllable word, whereas *chaye* is clearly two syllables, even when uttered rapidly. Far more damning, however, is the fact that the *ye* syllable possessed a final *–p* (it still does in southern Sinitic languages like Cantonese) that was not lost in most northern topolects until around the 11th or 12th century, by which time words with the rough phonological shape of *chai* were already in circulation in Central Asia.[7] If persons who spoke a non-Sinitic language heard a Chinese say something like *chayep*, it would have been impossible for them to ignore the final *–p* and reduce those two syllables to *chai*.

A second, though less common, scholarly hypothesis concerning the origins of the word *chai* is that it comes from another Sinitic term, *zhai* ("vegetarian feast"). The idea is that in such non-alcoholic offerings to Buddhist images or monks, tea played a key role and thus came to be identified with the event itself. Unfortunately, this is to take the whole

for a part, nor is it easy to account for the aspiration in *chai* as opposed to its absence in *zhai*. Another piece of evidence that has been adduced in favor of this hypothesis is that, when the Yuan-dynasty Mongol court performed the Tibetan *mang ja* ("tea-offering for Buddhist monks"), the term was rendered into Chinese as *mang zhai*, using two characters respectively meaning "rank growth of grass" and "vegetarian feast." It is obvious from the first syllable that it was chosen purely to represent the sound of the Tibetan. As for the second syllable, we must not lose sight of the fact that it too is fundamentally a transcription, although it cleverly also semantically signifies the event. But this by no means can be used to argue that *cha* ("tea") is equal to *zhai* ("vegetarian feast") or that somehow Tibetan *ja* and Chinese *zhai* fused to become Mongolian *čai*.

In attempting to come up with a more persuasive hypothesis for the origins of the word *chai*, it may be instructive to plot the distribution of those languages which adopted some form of this variant as their word for tea. When we do so, we see a clear pattern emerge: Persian *chây*, Mongolian *čai*, Manchu *cai*, Hindi-Urdu *cây*, Uyghur *chai*, Turkish *çay*, Arabic *shay*,[8] Russian *chai*, Czech *čaj*, Croatian *čaj*, Modern Greek *tsai*, Romanian *ceai*, Slovenian *čaj*, Ukrainian *chai*, and so forth.[9] It is immediately evident that all of these languages are located in a wide band that runs across the center of Eurasia, from the eastern steppe to eastern Europe and southwest Asia. No languages elsewhere adopted a word like *chai* as their primary word for tea, only secondarily from one of the Central Eurasian languages or still more recently from South Asia, as described above.

We may well ask, then, what might have been the mechanism of transmission for this particular variant? A plausible candidate is Persian, which served as the lingua franca of the Mongol empire. It would seem not to be pure happenstance that *chai*-type words for tea went wherever the Mongol conquerors went. Now, it is curious that Persian nouns ending in a long *–â* (as *cha* would have when borrowed into Persian) have so-called "byforms" (i.e., alternative forms) ending in *–i*, which is also often represented as *–y*, hence *châ*/*châi* (or *chây*). Thus, in Persian dictionaries, we have both *châ* and *chây* as entries for tea. This alternation between nouns ending in *–â* and *-ây* is already attested in New Persian texts of the 10th century. It is striking that we find the same phenomenon in Hindi-Urdu, which borrowed the word we now know in English as "chai" from Persian under Mughal[10] influence. A phonological explanation for this phenomenon is that it occurs in languages that do not normally tolerate syllables ending in open[11] *–â*, the final *–y* semivowel[12] or palatal off-glide[13] closing the syllable but sounding like, and in many cases being transcribed with, an *–i*. It is interesting to note that in colloquial Persian one says *châ-î*.

Phonology

We have shown that there are three main groupings of words for tea in virtually all languages: those based on Mandarin or Cantonese *cha*, those derived from Southern Min *te*, and those inspired by Persianate *chai*. There are, however, a few exceptions to be found in several minor languages spoken in Southeast Asia. Remarkably, these languages are situated precisely at the core of the botanical homeland of the tea plant. Before revealing their identity, let us survey the early history of the Sinitic word for tea. We say "word," not "words," because, although they appear and sound quite different in their modern guise, Mandarin-Cantonese *cha* and Southern Min *te* actually come from the same root. (We need not worry about an earlier form of *chai* because the latter is manifestly derived from *cha*.)

How, then, do we explain the phonological relationship between *cha* and *te*? In semi-technical linguistic terms, we may describe what happened thus (focusing only on the initial consonants, which are more important for distinguishing between the *cha* and *te* lineages than are the vowels that accompany them). Both *cha* and *te* go back to a Middle Sinitic (hereafter MS; about AD 600) voiced retroflex stop initial.[14] Historical phonologists transcribe it as *dr-*, but this is just shorthand for a single consonant sound (retroflex *d*). The latter, in turn, goes back to a hypothetical Old Sinitic (hereafter OS; about 600 BC) *dr-*, which would have been a true cluster of a *d-* initial and an *-r-* medial. The Min branch separated off earlier from OS than the other branches (something of an oversimplification of what really happened, but sufficient for our purposes). In Min, the medial *-r-* was lost, so the word for tea ended up having a simple *d-* initial, which eventually devoiced[15] to *t-*, hence *te*, spawning English "tea" and all of its congeners.

Mandarin and languages of the Wu branch like Shanghainese both inherited their words for tea from the MS form with the retroflex stop initial (*dr-*). In Mandarin, such stops all became affricates and aspirated[16] in the process of devoicing, thus yielding *ch-*. In Wu languages, MS voiced initials remained voiced. The retroflex stops, as in Mandarin, became affricates, but dental[17] instead of retroflex. (They might first have gone through a Mandarin-like stage of being retroflex affricates. Thus either *dr-* to *dzr-* to *dz-*, or just *dr-* to *dz-*, where *-r-*, as noted above, is merely a symbol indicating that we have a retroflex sound.) A similar change has occurred in southern Mandarin dialects like Taiwanese Mandarin, where the word for tea is pronounced with a dental initial as *tsha* (pinyin[18] *ca*) instead of *cha*. In some Wu languages, the affricate *dz-* further changed to *z-*. This happened, for example, in the northeastern part of the Wu-speaking area, which includes Shanghai and Suzhou, hence *zo* for tea, but did not take place in other Wu languages, which are conservative in preserving the affricate. For example, in Changzhou the word for tea is *dzo*. In simplest terms, what occurred in the transition from OS to MS was a process of retroflexion, that is, a simple *d-* before *-r-* became retroflex *d-*. In the post-medieval period, the retroflex stop became a sibilant[19] of one kind or another in all the modern vernaculars except Min, whose initial is still a stop (devoiced as *t-*).

The next step backward in our investigation is crucial for recovering the antecedent of the OS initial *dr-* for tea. We mentioned above that the OS initial was *dr-*. As a matter of fact, historical phonologists are not in agreement about the exact quality of their OS reconstructions,[20] which are purely hypothetical, and that is why they mark them with an asterisk. The *dr-* initial sound of the OS word for tea has also been reconstructed as *llr-*, *rl-*, *d-l-*, *d'-*, *d-*, and so forth. While these reconstructions look rather different, they hover around what seems to be an initial that would have had the following properties: a dental lateral liquid[21] (*l*) that was in process of evolving into a voiced dental stop (*d*), perhaps in combination with a clustered *r* flap.[22] We should note that *d* and *l* are very similar, inasmuch as both are voiced dentals. The only difference is that with *l* the air is allowed to escape to the sides of the tongue, whereas with *d* the air is projected forward. This is probably the result of some pre-initial or other feature of the syllable like laxness that is responsible for shutting off the lateral escape of air. Thus, *l* and *d* are very close in their articulation, and it is easy for an *l* to become a *d*. Indeed, there are certain topolects in Central China where, for example, *li* is pronounced as *di*. To summarize, what appears to have happened in OS is that the voiced lateral *l-* became a voiced stop *d-*, with the medial *-r-* subsequently causing the preceding *d-* to acquire retroflex articulation.

As for the vowel of the OS word for tea, historical phonologists reconstruct it as some sort of *-a*.[23] Therefore, we posit the following sequence of changes, all within OS: *la* to *lra* to *dra*. So much for the early evolution of the pronunciation of the Sinitic word for tea. Now we must turn to the graph (or character) that was used to write it.

Writing

Although the tea plant itself is not thorny, the Sinitic nomenclature concerning it is decidedly so. Using only their MSM pronunciations, there are at least eight different characters that are alleged to refer to tea in some form: *tu* 荼 (and two rare variants), *cha* 茶, *jia* 檟, *she* 蔎,[24] *ming* 茗, and *chuan* 荈. The first, as we shall see below, long ago morphed, as it were, into a morpheme that referred only to plants other than tea (mostly bitter), the second is the graph used to write both the MSM and Southern Min words for tea (*cha*, *te*) discussed above, the third and fourth may be dialectal words related to the second, the fifth supposedly signifies especially fine, tender, or otherwise special tea leaves, and the sixth is of ambiguous signification. The first, third, fourth, and sixth occurred in ancient texts, but long ago dropped out of circulation, leading later commentators to expend enormous amounts of energy trying to figure out what they really meant ("tea picked early," "tea picked later," "tea picked last," and so forth), but having no firm basis for their speculations. That leaves only the second and the fifth graphs, *cha* and *ming*, still in common use today. We shall return to them below.

As is obvious to anyone who has seen the first two graphs, *tu* 荼 and *cha* 茶, side by side, the second was created by removing a single, small, horizontal stroke from the unobtrusive central portion of the former, making them devilishly (and probably intentionally) difficult to distinguish. This transformation of *tu* into *cha* occurred by the mid-Tang period (i.e., around the middle of the 8th century), and many authorities believe that it may well have been Lu Yu, the founder of the Chinese tea cult, who created the new graph, *cha*, out of the ashes of the old one. To what purpose? This is a conundrum that has puzzled scholars for over a millennium.

We believe that Lu Yu (or whoever may be held responsible for the excision of the tiny, offending stroke) was motivated by at least four mutually reinforcing factors: 1. phonetically, the morpheme signifying tea (*cha*) had changed to such an extent north of the Yangtze that it no longer seemed appropriate to write it with the old graph that meant basically "bitter vegetable" (*tu*; south of the Yangtze, along the Fujian coast, the old pronunciation persisted, even for the altered character); 2. semantically, the morpheme for tea had radically evolved from "bitter vegetable" to "leaves for making a flavorful infusion"; 3. culturally, tea-drinking had developed from a barbaric southern practice into an acceptable, even desirable, northern custom; 4. personally, whoever it was that invented the new character must have been a proponent of tea as a beverage and hence wished to promote it among the general populace by providing it with a fresh, clean slate, free of all the old barbaric, bitter-vegetable stigmas associated with *tu*.

Thus, there were abundant linguistic and socio-psychological grounds for someone to make *cha* out of *tu*, and that is exactly what happened. It was a stroke (if we may) of genius, in effect a kind of marketing technique, such as modern corporations frequently resort to when they launch a product by giving it a new name, when in fact it may be no more than an old item rechristened and repackaged. Whatever the exact mix of motivations, the graphic change from *tu* to *cha* was successful, since shortly afterward tea-drinking experienced explosive growth within China and swiftly spread beyond its borders to neighboring countries.

To restate a key point of this section that may not have been brought out with sufficient clarity, the graph that has been used to write *cha* ("tea") since the mid-8th century did not exist before then. Prior to Lu Yu's time, the graph for *tu* had to do double duty both for various types of "bitter vegetable" (as well as some sort of grass or rush) and for tea. Consequently, one could not be blamed for confusing, or even equating, the two.

Ethnobotany

It is not entirely clear what plant or plants *tu* signified in the first texts where it occurs, those supposedly compiled between approximately the 6th and 3rd centuries BC. Early commentaries generally refer to it as a kind of *kucai* ("bitter vegetable"), while modern scholars refer to it in translations of the *Shi jing* ("Poetry Classic"; occurs nine times) and *Chu ci* ("Elegies of the South" (i.e., Chu); occurs twice) as "sow

thistle," "a weed," "rush wool," "rush flower," "bitter herb," "bitter vegetable," and so on. Indeed, it seems possible that the graph *tu* may have been used to refer to several different plants, and since a few of them can be located in the south, it is conceivable that one of them may have been what we now know to be the tea plant. However, it is essential to note that, in no text written before the Han period – specifically, prior to Wang Bao's "Contract for a Youth," *c.* 59 BC (see pp. 30–31) – is *tu* described in such a fashion that we could reasonably recognize it as potentially referring to tea. Furthermore, we should recall that Wang Bao's "Contract" is a securely southwestern text. It would not be in the least bit odd if the first attested occurrence of the word for tea in Sinitic were clearly linked to the southwest, which at that time was inhabited largely by non-Sinitic peoples. To be sure, the young slave in Wang Bao's text possesses certain characteristics (e.g., his beard and his name) that lead one to believe he himself may well have been ethnically non-Sinitic.

As late as AD 543, it is evident that the nomenclature for *tu* was still very much in a state of flux. In the earliest, most important, and most complete Chinese agricultural manual that is extant, Jia Sixie's *Qi min yao shu* ("Essential Arts for Regulating the People"), which dates to that year, there is a section at the back which is entitled "Fei zhongguo wu chan zhe" ("Products Not Native to the Central Kingdom"). Since the "central kingdom" or "central state" was located in the north, the title itself is of extraordinary importance for our inquiry. Item no. 53 in this section of the *Qi min yao shu* is *tu* ("bitter vegetable"). Most interestingly, item no. 95 is also *tu*, but here the character has a "wood/tree" signifier ("radical") added to the left to emphasize the woodiness of the plant, which means that it may well have been the tea tree that Jia Sixie (a northerner from Shandong) was referring to. That it indeed was the tea tree is borne out by the quotations of earlier texts that follow, one of which has to do with this plant's property of causing one to sleep less and one which refers to a place called Fuling in the south that was famous for the excellence of its *tu* already by about the 4th century AD and that was renowned for its superior *cha* ("tea") later on.[25] All of this proves several things that are pertinent to our inquiry: 1. tea had not yet become an acceptable drink in the north by the mid-6th century; 2. *tu* signified both "bitter vegetable" and "tea" at this time; 3. people were uneasy about the ambiguity of the two quite different meanings of *tu* and so created another character for the tea tree; 4. the sound of the name of the tea plant had evidently not diverged dramatically enough by this time to warrant tampering with the *tu* phonophore (sound-bearing element) itself, hence all that was necessary was to stick on a semantic element indicating "wood, tree" to ensure that readers would not mistake it for the *tu* that meant a type of bitter vegetable or grass.

Because tea-growing in China initially developed in a part of the country – the southwest – that was originally populated by non-Sinitic peoples, and because the vocabulary relating to tea was confused and unstable until around the mid-8th century AD, it is a reasonable assumption that the word for tea may have been borrowed into Chinese from an indigenous language. The pre-Sinitic inhabitants of the southwest belonged mainly to two linguistic families, Austro-Asiatic (hereafter A-A) and Tibeto-Burman (hereafter T-B). It is remarkable that the word *la* ("leaf") is common to many A-A and T-B languages. Since we have previously shown that the earliest form of the Sinitic word for "bitter vegetable; tea" was also **la*, we may suspect that it was borrowed from A-A or T-B. Our suspicion of borrowing is based, among other considerations, on the following grounds: firstly, it is more likely that a general term would be borrowed with a restricted meaning than vice versa; and secondly, historical research documents that northern Sinitic peoples learned how to utilize the tea plant from southern, non-Sinitic peoples. The question is, then, whether they borrowed it from A-A peoples or T-B groups. In the following paragraphs, we shall demonstrate that ultimately the Sinitic word for "tea" (*cha* from *dra* from **la*) may be traced back to an A-A source, although we do not preclude the remote possibility that it may have been acquired through a T-B intermediary.

The original inhabitants of the botanical homeland of tea were A-A. The A-A family of languages consists of three sub-families: Mundaric, Mon-Khmer (henceforth M-K), and Khasi-Khumic. A-A is the oldest of the four major linguistic groups inhabiting the South Asian subcontinent (A-A, Dravidian, Indo-Aryan, Tibeto-Burman), and it is undoubtedly in South Asia that A-A originated. From there, members of all three sub-families of A-A moved eastward into Southeast Asia. Coupled with linguistic data and archeological finds, it is evident from genetic research that their roots in the region go back 10,000 or more years. It was not until around 1,000 years ago that T-B peoples started moving into the region from the north. Still later, Tai speakers began to enter the region from the east in large numbers. Sinitic speakers, mostly political and military figures until recent times, have been making forays into the northern borders of the region for approximately 2,000 years.

All three main sub-families of A-A share an archaic etymological root **la*, meaning "leaf." When the M-K sub-family entered the core of the botanical homeland of tea in what is now northeastern Burma, northwestern Laos, and the southwestern edge of Yunnan, they brought with them derivatives of the proto-root **la*. Naturally enough, the M-K speakers applied words derived from this etymon to the leaves of the tea plant. Extensive ethnobotanical fieldwork carried out among the inhabitants of the region reveals that tea is central to the cultures of all M-K peoples in the region. Furthermore, analysis of their religious, social, cultural, dietary, and medicinal practices pertaining to tea indicates that tea has been highly valued and extensively utilized over a very long period of time.

When Sinitic, T-B, and Tai speakers successively came into contact with A-A speakers as they impinged from the north and east, they borrowed the A-A word for "leaf/tea,"

together with the basic knowledge of how to exploit the plant as a resource. Among non-M-K groups of the region such as the Dai (who speak a Tai language), *la* is a general term that can refer to ten or more plants used to make beverages, not just tea. This corroborates the evidence which indicates that other groups moving into the region borrowed the old A-A word *la* which originally meant simply "leaf" in general and only later came to refer more specifically to tea leaves and the plant from which they are taken.

In particular, it is the Palaungic division of Northern M-K, whose speakers are situated mainly in the region where the valleys of the Irawaddy, the Salween, and the Mekong converge, one of the world's richest botanical storehouses, that was most intimately associated with the early development of tea usage. These are the Lamet in northwest Laos, the Palaung and Wa in northeast Burma, and the Wa, Blang, and De'ang along the southwestern border of Yunnan. Like other M-K speakers, they share some form of the ancient **la* root for "leaf/tea." But they also have a more specialized word for fermented or sour tea, which is referred to in various of their languages and dialects as *meng, myâm, myan, mem, mi:n,* and so forth. This quintessentially Palaungic type of fermented tea, which we shall refer to by the general name *myem*, is of particular cultural significance. Among the Wa of northern Burma and southwest Yunnan, for example, tea purchased from elsewhere is called *la*, whereas wild tea gathered in the hills is called *miiem* (or *mîam*). Furthermore, when a local religious officiant (the *moba*) uses tea in a ritual, he refers to it as *miiem*, not *la*. The Lamet, a M-K-speaking population of swidden (slash-and-burn) farmers in northern Laos, chew quids of fermented tea leaves, called *meng*, that are packed tightly in coarse bamboo tubes buried just outside their villages. It is most likely that this word has been borrowed into Thai as *miang* ("fermented tea"). Since other M-K groups from Laos to northern Burma also refer to fermented or sour tea leaves as *meng* or a similar name, it is evident that this is a term that is authentically M-K in origin and that it is of long duration. We believe it is self-evident that Sinitic *ming* ("fine, tender, special tea"; OS **mi"eng*) is a borrowing of this M-K botanical and cultural term. Whereas the meaning of the M-K term is precise, the signification of Sinitic *ming* has always been comparatively vague.

T-B languages frequently combine the A-A proto-root *la* for "leaf" with their own term *pa* ("leaf used for economic purposes") to form compounds like *la-pa* for "tea" but such bisyllabic forms do not show up in Sinitic. Moreover, it is telling that the Burmese, who are extremely fond of fermented tea leaves, refer to them not by the special (virtually sacred) M-K term *myem*, but by the doubly composite, constructed T-B expression *laphet thoke* or *lephet thote* ("[tea] leaves mixed"). Consequently, we may conclude that Sinitic *tu/cha* and *ming* were both borrowed from A-A, not T-B. It is undoubtedly not an accident that the only three of the eight graphs that supposedly meant "tea" in antiquity to have survived, namely those for *tu, cha,* and *ming*, were all used to write loanwords from M-K languages. Finally, purely on chronological grounds, it is necessary to opt for A-A over T-B as the source of the Chinese loanwords *tu/cha* and *ming*, since Sinitic peoples would have been in contact with M-K speakers long before T-B speakers had acquired A-A *la* as their word for "tea," often in combination with *pa* ("leaf").

Although *myem* has a special place in the cultural practices of the northern M-K peoples, they also dry, wither, roast, and infuse tea. However, historically they have only done this on a small scale, quite literally for household consumption. The northern M-K peoples in the botanical heartland of tea did not develop tea production on a large scale as a commercial enterprise. This was left for the Chinese to accomplish once they had learned the basics of tea processing and tea consumption from M-K peoples. It was the Chinese who made tea into a commercial product that would, with the help of the Dutch, the British, and others, ultimately attain worldwide dimensions, and it was the Chinese who gave the word tea and its congeners to countless modern languages. Consequently, it is fitting that the current scientific designation of the tea plant be *C. sinensis*. Given what we now know concerning the Southeast Asian botanical and linguistic heritage of tea, however, it is perfectly understandable that more neutral designations, such as *C. thea* ("tea camellia") and *C. theifera* ("tea-bearing camellia"), are still preferred by some specialists.

Conclusion

From its native habitat in the northwestern part of Southeast Asia, southern East Asia, and the northeasternmost corner of South Asia, tea traveled outward across the face of the earth as an item of trade and tribute (primarily the former). As is often the case with other unique economic and cultural products that migrate from their place of origin around the globe (coffee, chocolate, tobacco, karaoke, *barbat/pipa/biwa*, sitar, X-ray, and so on), the word for tea went along with the object. When tea moved into new territories and was absorbed into different languages, not only were the modes of preparation and customs of drinking modified, so too was the term for tea transformed.

Just as the trade routes for tea may be traced, so may the paths of transmission for the various types of words for tea be tracked. Not surprisingly, the two systems – economic and linguistic – closely coincide. Of the three main branches of the family of tea words, *te*, *cha*, and *chai*, the first commenced its voyage from the southeast coast of China where Min topolects were spoken, the second went overland from northern China to neighboring territories, but also by sea from Canton in the south, while the third journeyed by pack animals (camels, horses, mules, but also often humans) and carts across steppes and deserts and over mountains. To study the history of words for tea is thus what might be called an exercise in geolinguistics. In the end, goods produced and named by human beings, from start to finish, are ineluctably linked to the land. The evolution of tea usage is a prime example of the intimate interface between *Homo sapiens* and Mother Earth.

Notes: 1. "Sinitic" refers to the entire group of related languages spoken by the ethnos that has come to be known as Han in modern times. The language group has a history of more than two millennia and includes, among many others, numerous varieties of Mandarin, different types of Cantonese, Shanghainese, and countless other languages, dialects, and sub-dialects, a considerable portion of which are mutually unintelligible. It should be noted that there are also many unrelated non-Sinitic languages within the current political borders of the Peoples Republic of China: Mongolian, Tibetan, Turkic (Uyghur, Kazakh, Kirghiz), Tai (Zhuang, Dai), and scores of others; 2. A morpheme is the smallest unit of meaning in a language; 3. This list is by no means intended to be exhaustive, but merely representative. The same is true of the two lists of words related to *cha* and *chai*; 4. Southern Min is a branch of the Sinitic group that includes the majority language of Taiwan (which is very close to the language of Amoy (Xiamen) on the mainland), Teochew, Hainanese, and so forth; 5. The word "topolect" means exactly the same thing as the Chinese term *fangyan* ("speech form characteristic of a place"); 6. Both with the Berber prefix for masculine nouns, a-; 7. In his *Kitâb al-saydana fî al-tibb* ("Book on Pharmacy and Materia Medica"), the eminent Choresmian scholar and scientist, al-Biruni (973–1048) gives a clear, detailed description of tea, calling it *jây* in Arabic script (equating to *chây* in Persian); 8. Arabic lacks a *ch* sound, so words borrowed into that language which have that sound are written with *sh* or *j*; 9. All the words in this list that are spelled *chây*, *čai*, *cai*, or *caj* all sound essentially the same as chai; 10. The Mughals ruled India roughly from the early 16th to the mid-19th century. It is intriguing to note that, like the name "Mughal," the word "mogul" also derives from "Mongol." In any event, the name of the Mughals reveals their ultimate origins as powerful conquerors from the steppe to the north; 11. That is to say, syllables that end in a vowel rather than with a consonant, in which case they would be closed; 12. Also called "glides," "semi-vowels" are vowel-like sounds that do not constitute the nucleus of a syllable, but join with a full vowel to do so (e.g., [w-], [y-]); 13. A "palatal" sound is made with the blade of the tongue near to or touching the hard palate (the roof of the mouth). In this instance, an "offglide" is a "glide" (see note 12) that follows a full vowel and brings the articulation to a position of rest; 14. Middle Sinitic and Old Sinitic are hypothetical stages in the historical development of the Sinitic language group. A "voiced" sound is uttered with the vocal cord vibrating. A "retroflex" consonant is produced by curling the tip of the tongue above the alveolar (gum) ridge or even back to touch the palate. A "stop" is a consonant in which there is a stage when the breath passage of the vocal tract is completely closed. An "initial" is a sound that comes at the beginning of a word or syllable; 15. A "devoiced" consonant is one that has lost its voicing (see the beginning of note 14); 16. An "affricate" is a consonant that begins as a stop (see note 14), for example [t] or [d], but ends as a fricative (a consonant characterized by frictional passage of the breath through a narrowing of some portion of the vocal tract, e.g., [s], [z]). An "aspirated" consonant is one that is accompanied by a strong burst of air; 17. A "dental" consonant is one that is articulated with the tongue against the upper teeth; 18. Short for Hanyu Pinyin, the official romanization (i.e., romanized transcription) of MSM in the People's Republic of China; 19. A "sibilant" is a hissing or buzzing sound like [s], [sh], [z], [zh], and so on; 20. When historical phonologists attempt to determine what Chinese characters would have sounded like at some point in the past, they are engaged in the process of reconstruction; 21. A "lateral" is a sound produced when air is blocked by the middle of the tongue but allowed to flow out through the side(s). "Liquid" consonants are articulated without friction and can be prolonged like vowels; examples are certain types of [l] and [r] sounds; 22. A "flap" is produced by a single, energetic bouncing of the tongue against the palate or alveolar ridge; 23. The quality of the vowel only began to change substantially in the medieval period, during which it evidently experienced a major bifurcation into –a words and –u words, though with many dialectal variants; 24. When a mid-9th century Arabic traveler in China described what was obviously tea, he called it *sâkh*. Orientalists have assumed that this is a medieval transcription of *cha*, but have been mystified by the final consonant, since *cha* has never had such an ending. If we assume, however, that *sâkh* is a transcription of the rare term *she* for tea, then it would fit fairly well, since the latter is pronounced *siek* in Fuzhou and *suhg* or *saq* in Shanghai; 25. Fuling was in the area of Jingdezhen (site of the most famous kilns in Chinese history), in present-day Jiangxi province.

ACKNOWLEDGMENTS

This volume is the product of our joint efforts over the past three years. The origins of the book, however, go back much earlier. Victor's fascination with tea began during the period 1965–67 when he served as a Peace Corps volunteer in Nepal. It was here that he became deeply enamored of *masala chai* (milk tea with sugar and Indian spices). In the winter cold and at high altitudes, a cup of tea would quickly warm him up, like a pleasant furnace. Oddly enough, on a blazing hot summer day, when he was dripping with perspiration and exhausted from carrying a heavy pack along trails that rose and fell thousands of feet within a distance of a few miles, a hot cup of tea would somehow serve both to soothe and to reinvigorate him. It was also reassuring to know that he could sip the scalding tea without fear of contracting dysentery and other illnesses that were spread by drinking unboiled water.

Victor's devotion to Indian tea was deepened by several trips to Darjeeling, that "diamond island" of the finest teas on earth. There, shrouded in the damp mists that are so conducive to the cultivation of great tea, he imbibed the atmosphere of this charming town nestled in the high foothills of the eastern Himalayas that possesses the perfect conditions for producing tea leaves with ineffably flavorful qualities. Victor's attachment to Darjeeling tea has lasted for half a century, right up to the present day, although he now realizes that the rich, malty teas of Assam and Ceylon are also highly satisfying. Not only did his experience in the Peace Corps turn Victor into a lifelong fan of tea, it also guided him to a career as a professor of Buddhist Studies and Sinology. His involvement in the former led to a keen realization of the intimate relationship between tea drinking and Buddhism, while his pursuit of the latter introduced him to the important place of tea in Chinese culture. While Victor appreciated the crucial role played by China in making tea a beverage that is drunk almost everywhere in the world, he was also deeply troubled by the mixing of myth, legend, and fact in virtually all accounts of the early history of tea. Consequently, already more than two decades ago, he resolved to write a book that would set the record straight, and began to collect massive amounts of material on tea with that goal in mind.

Always nagged by the compelling need to write a book about tea, but never finding time from his teaching and other duties to produce it by himself, Victor was delighted to make the acquaintance of Erling Hoh, a journalist who first met Victor when researching an article on the mysterious, lost "Roman" town of Lijian in China's Gansu province, and who had written on such diverse topics as Egypt's new Bibliotheca Alexandrina, cormorant fishing in China, and a cold winter Sunday spent with the colorful characters of Speaker's Corner in London's Hyde Park. Somehow or other, Erling's natural inquisitiveness, writing skills, and dedication to thorough research automatically led to the collaboration that has resulted in this book.

Erling's path to tea was rather different from Victor's. His first memory is of the brown-glazed, earthenware "Betty Brown" tea pot that his grandmother used in her house in Rotebro, a suburb north of Stockholm. Among the intellectuals and poets that populated Ovandahls Konditori in the university town of Uppsala, the coolest tea was Lapsang Souchong. In the mid-1980's, he shared delicious chai with student radicals in the tea houses of Benares, while at the time, Taiwanese Oolong tasted nothing but bitter. It was not until he returned to Taiwan in 2001 that he began to appreciate the island's rich tea culture, and embarked on a more serious study of the topic. Subsequently, he visited the Brahmah Tea Museum and Fortnum and Mason's wonderful tea department, both in London, and made journeys to the Pu'er tea tracts of Yunnan province, the Oolong tea districts of Wuyi and Anxi, and the green tea regions of Zhejiang, Anhui, and Jiangsu, where, on a dusty November afternoon, he had the good fortune to enjoy a glass of *biluochun* in a simple hut by the dilapidated temple of the monks who first produced this great tea.

Our collaboration over the last three years has been entirely pleasurable for both of us. When we decided to embark on this project in earnest, the sharing of the labor was effortless. Victor knew what he had to do, and Erling set to the work of composing the narrative. Most of the time we followed our parallel paths of research and writing. Fortunately, however, we were also able to meet face-to-face for extended discussions in Stockholm and Philadelphia, which kept the slowly growing manuscript coherent and integrated. By far the most important and intense period of our collaboration were the weeks we spent together in the far north of Sweden at Erling's retreat, where he leads a life that would make Tolstoy proud, chopping wood and cultivating potatoes between bouts at the computer. Since the sun never really sets there in summer, we almost literally worked day and night, sleeping only when compelled to do so by sheer tiredness, and arising as soon as we were rested. We tended to spend the mornings poring over the tea library we had assembled in the previous years, the afternoons debating over the meanings of texts and the interpretation of events, and the evenings assimilating the discoveries of the day. Of course, the rhythm of our activity was punctuated by many cups of tea that kept us alert and content.

The list of people whom we wish to thank is a long one. And even though we shall name many individuals who contributed to the making of this book, the number of those who helped in one way or another, but who shall remain anonymous, is far greater. Above all, we want to express our deep gratitude to Colin Ridler, our editor at Thames & Hudson, for his vision and acuity in helping us transform a mass of facts and ideas into a viable volume. Without his guiding hand, we might still be wallowing in a mountain of ill-digested data. During the final stages of turning our burgeoning manuscript into an actual book, Ben Plumridge performed heroic feats of pruning and shaping. His meticulous attention to detail and consummate thoroughness have contributed immeasurably to making this a much better work than it would have been otherwise. Another essential role was played by Louise Thomas, who served as picture editor. Her resourcefulness and capability made the difficult task of choosing and acquiring suitable illustrations seem easy. We also wish to thank Celia Falconer for seeing the book through production, Therese Vandling for design and layout, and all the other staff at Thames & Hudson working behind the scenes to make this book a reality.

We also need to acknowledge our debt to Thomas Lee Mair, who joined us as cook, woodcutter, fisherman, and boon companion during our stint together in northern Sweden. But Thomas's contributions to this endeavor go beyond those glorious days amid the forests and lakes of that mountain fastness. An excellent researcher in his own right, Thomas checked many sources and discovered many important and interesting details that we might never have found on our own. In addition, he also acquired many valuable items for our tea library.

We would also like to thank Anthony Addison, Thomas Allsen, Christoph Anderl, Urs App, Kathlene Baldanza, Ahmad Bashi, Robert S. Bauer, William Baxter, Christopher Beckwith, Mark Bender, Ross Bender, James Benn, Rostislav Berezkin, Heike Bödeker, David Branner, Francesco Brighenti, Josh Capitanio, Michael Carr, Abraham Chan, Frank Chance, Linda Chance, Che-Chia Chang, S.K. Chaudhuri, Alvin Chia, Hugh Clark, W. South Coblin, Luke Collins, Carol Conti-Entin, Nicola Di Cosmo, Patricia Crone, Pamela Crossley, George van Driem, Michael Drompp, Mark Elliot, Johan Elverskog, Joakim Envall, Wayne Farris, Magnus Fiskesjö, Philippe Forêt, T. Griffith Foulk, Piet Gaarthuis, Naga Ganesan, Hank Glassman, Peter B. Golden, Carrie Gracie, David Graff, Patricia J. Graham, William Granara, Alvin Grundström, Natasha Gunchenko, William Hanaway, Zev Handel, William C. Hannas, Stevan Harrell, John E. Herman, Wilma Heston, Wolfhart Heinrichs, Birgitta Hoh, Hsu Der-sheng, Juha Janhunen, Åke Johansson, Matthew Kapstein, Artur Karp, Gaetano Kazuo Maida, Brian Keeley, John Kieschnick, Leonard van der Kuijp, Hiroshi Kumamoto, William LaFleur, Lin Chang-kuan, Pär Linder, Peter Lorge, Joseph Lowry, Pavel Lurje, Philip Lutgendorf, Timothy May, Laëtitia Marionneau, John McRae, John N. Miksic, Pardis Minuchehr, David Morgan, Susan Naquin, Ruji Niu, Jerry Norman, Steven Owyoung, Roger Pearson, Peter C. Perdue, Rodo Pfister, Frances Pritchett, S. Robert Ramsey, Donald Ringe, Paula Roberts, Staffan Rosén, Morris Rossabi, Laurent Sagart, Harold Schiffman, Susanne Schönström, Axel Schuessler, Tansen Sen, Paul Sidwell, Nicholas Sims-Williams, Prods Oktor Skjærvø, Marie-Christine Skuncke, Jonathan Smith, Elliot Sperling, Brian Spooner, Krishnan Srinivasan, Jan Stenvall, Devin Stewart, Hoong Teik Toh, Joost Tenberge, Michele Thompson, Tseng Yu-hui, James Unger, Urban Vännberg, Geoff Wade, Justin Watkins, Daniel Waugh, Julie Wei, Julian Wheatley, Endymion Wilkinson, Jack Wills, Christian Wittern, Frances Wood, Jonathan Wright, Duan Xingyan, Livio Zanini, and Peter Zieme.

A big thanks is due to Mark Nesbitt of Kew Gardens for his great help in weeding out scientific errors. Any that may still remain are the sole responsibility of the authors. Victor extends his special gratitude to the Swedish Collegium for Advanced Study (SCAS), to Gayle Bodorff for her incisive critique of and suggestions for the manuscript, and to Li-ching Chang for constant understanding. Erling would in particular like to thank Kit Ping for her unswerving support, the friendly staff at the Sorsele Public Library for helping him to retrieve many obscure tomes from the storerooms of Sweden's university libraries, and Eva and Stig Vännberg for bringing light and warmth to the long Arctic winter.

SOURCES OF ILLUSTRATIONS

1 Sentosa Leisure Management Pte Ltd; 2 Östasiatiska Museet, Stockholm; 3 Percival David Foundation of Chinese Art, London; 17 From Captain James Cook, *Voyage to the Pacific Ocean*, London, 1785; 19 From Joseph-François Lafitau, *Moeurs des Sauvages Ameriquains*, Paris, 1724; 21 After E. Coffman; 25 From Franz Eugen Köhler, *Medizinal-Pflanzen*, Germany, 1887; 37 National Palace Museum, Taiwan; 43 National Museum of Natural Science, Taiwan; 45 Chaohua Publishing Company, Beijing; 47 Sentosa Leisure Management Pte Ltd; 49, 50 National Palace Museum, Taiwan; 52–53 Famen Monastery, Fufeng, China; 58, 60 National Palace Museum, Taiwan; 61 Liao Dynasty Tomb, Xuanhua Hebei, China; 64 Victoria & Albert Museum, London; 66 After Edward Chalmers Werner; 73 Li Gonglin, *Five Horses and Grooms*; 77 National Palace Museum, Taiwan; 89 Seikado Library, Tokyo/Werner Forman Archive; 91 From Ukers, 1935; 96 After a painting by Hasegawa

Tohaku; 102 From Sadler, 2001; 103 From A.W. Franks, *Japanese Pottery*, London, 1880; 109 Fukuoka City Museum; 111 National Palace Museum, Taiwan; 114, 117 From J.G. Houssaye, *Monographie du Thé*, Paris, 1843; 119 National Palace Museum, Taiwan; 123 Art Institute of Chicago; 127 British Museum, London; 128 Tiziana and Gianni Baldizzone/Corbis; 130 From Rockhill, 1891; 132 Royal Geographical Society/Alamy; 134 Michael S. Yamashita/Corbis; 144 Ivory and Art Gallery, Tel Aviv; 145 B. Avanzo/Library of Congress, Washington, D.C.; 147 British Museum, London; 154 Marai Shah/AFP/Getty Images; 161 *right* From Raji, 2003; Photo: Michel Lebrun; 168 © The Board of Trustees of the Royal Botanic Gardens, Kew, Richmond; 169 From Ukers, 1935; 173 By courtesy of the Board of Trustees of the Victoria & Albert Museum, London; 179 The Print Collector/Alamy; 183 British Museum, London; 184 From Houssaye, 1843; 187 *The Inside View of the Rotunda in Ranelagh Gardens with the Company at Breakfast, c.* 1751, Engraving; 188 The Wedgwood Museum, Barlaston; 191 Grimsby Local Studies Collection/North East Lincolnshire Council; 194 British Museum, London; 202 Yale University Art Gallery/Art Resource, NY/Photo Scala, Florence; 205 Currier & Ives/Library of Congress, Washington, D.C.; 209 Library of Congress, Washington, D.C.; 215 India Office Library and Records, British Library, London; 216 George Grantham Bain Collection/Library of Congress, Washington, D.C.; 221 Michael Maslan Historical Photographs/Corbis; 223 The Art Archive; 228 Mansell/Time & Life Pictures/Getty Images; 229 Frank Leslie's Illustrated Newspaper, 1876; 237 Courtesy of Brooke Bond; 238 Science & Society Picture Library; 243 From Ukers, 1935; 245 Henri Cartier-Bresson/Magnum Photos; 246 By permission of the British Library, London; 248 Gilbert M. Grosvenor/National Geographic/Getty Images; 255 Luis Castañeda/The Image Bank/Getty Images.

SOURCES OF QUOTATIONS

Unless otherwise noted, all translations are by the authors. Some spellings and transliterations in translations and quotations from other sources have been adjusted where otherwise they might cause confusion.

7 Adams: diary entry, 17 December, 1773; 9 Sen Rikyū: tr. D. Hirota; 17 Cook: *The Journals of Captain Cook on His Voyages of Discovery*, ed. J.C. Beaglehole, 1967; 19 Bartram: from the *42nd Annual Report of the Bureau of American Ethnology*, 1924–25; 22 Montesquieu: *Lettres Persanes*; 33 Guangya dictionary: tr. P.J. Smith; 38–39 Wang Su: *Memories of Loyang*, tr. W.J.F. Jenner; 48–50 *The Classic of Tea*: tr. F.R. Carpenter; 72 Ma Yuan: tr. P.J. Smith; 74 Song Qi: tr. P.J. Smith; 75 Su Che: tr. P.J. Smith; 98 Rodrigues: tr. M. Cooper; 99 Nambō Sōkei: tr. D. Hirota; 107 Chinese poem: tr. D.T. Suzuki; 108 Japanese poem: tr. A.L. Sadler; 120 Ni Zan: from the *Hawai'i Reader in Traditional Chinese Culture*, ed. V.H. Mair, 2005; 129–30 Tea ceremony: from Waddell, 1939; 134 Tea in today's Tibet: as related by Lhundrum, a student of Kevin Stuart; 136 Ramstedt: *Sju Resor I Östern*, 1961; 138 Envoys: quoted in Baddeley, 1964; 139 Kilburger: quoted in Smith and Christian, 1984; 140 Tulisen: quoted in Staunton, 1821; 140 Directive: from *Chaye Zhi Lu* by Deng Jiugang, 2000; 143 Dumas: quoted in Ivanov, 2001; 147 *Eugene Onegin*: Penguin edition, tr. C. Johnstone; 150 Balov: quoted in Herlihy, 2002; 155 Olearius: *The Voyages and Travels of the Ambassadors...*, tr. J. Davies, 1662; 156 Ovington: *A Voyage to Surat in the Year 1689*, 1696; 165 Vasco da Gama: quoted in Diffie, 1977; 166 Teixeira: *The Travels of Pedro Teixeira*, tr. W.F. Sinclair, 1902; 166–67 Eaton: quoted in Farrington, 1991; 169–70 Garway, Pepys, Waller, Dirx: quoted in Ukers, 1935; 175 Russell: quoted in Pettigrew, 2001; 175 Routh: quoted in Jacob, 1935; 176 Twining: *Observations on the Tea and Window Act...*, 1784; 179–80 Johnson: *Literary Magazine*, 1757; 181–82 Linnaeus: quoted in Koerner, 1999 and Drake, 2002; 186 Rogers: quoted in Ukers, 1935; 193 Macartney: quoted in Forrest, 1973; 193–94 Gladstone: quoted in Hanes, 2002; 194 Jardine: quoted in Wakeman, 1978; 203–04 EEIC: quoted in Labaree, 1964; 224 Lipton: *Leaves from the Lipton Logs*, 1931; 227 *Times*: quoted in Clark, 1911; 228 Little: quoted in *The Stowage of Ships and their Cargoes* by R.W. Stevens, 1869; 230 *The Grocer*: November, 1864; 236 Seld: *Little Known Lands and Very Well Known People. Writings for the Pleasure and Erudition of the More Mature Youth and the People*; 236 Schrader: quoted in Kaufmann, 1989; 238 Beeton: quoted in Pettigrew, 2001; 243–44 Lao She: tr. J. Howard-Gibbon; 244 Thompson: quoted in Pettigrew, 2001; 244 Streatfeild: *Tea on Service*, 1947; 247 Orwell: *Evening Standard*, 12 January, 1946; 249–50 al-Qari: quoted in Holes, 1996; 256 *Guardian*: 25 June, 2003; 259–62 Appendix B is tr. from *Dunhuang Bianwen Jiaozhu* ("Collated and Annotated Dunhuang Transformation Texts"), ed. Huang Zheng and Zhang Yongquan, 1997, pp. 423–33.

BIBLIOGRAPHY

Allsen, T.T. 2001. *Culture and Conquest in Mongol Eurasia.* Cambridge: Cambridge University Press.

Anderson, J. 1991. *An Introduction to the Japanese Way of Tea.* Albany: State University of New York Press.

Aubaile-Sallenave, F. 2005. "Le Thé, un Essai de sa Diffusion dans le Monde Musulman." In S. Bahuchet, and P. de Maret (eds.), *El Banquete de las Palabras: La Alimentación de los Textos Árabes.* Madrid: Consejo Superior de Investigaciones Científicas, 153–91.

Avery, M. 2003. *The Tea Road: China and Russia Meet Across the Steppe.* Beijing: China Intercontinental.

Baddeley, J.F. 1964. *Russia, Mongolia, China.* New York: Burt Franklin.

Ball, J.D. 1904 (4th ed. rev.). *Things Chinese.* London: Murray.

Ball, S. 1848. *An Account of the Cultivation and Manufacture of Tea in China.* London: Longman, Brown, Green, and Longmans.

Bawden, C.R. (tr.). 1961. *The Jebtsundamba Khutukhtus of Urga: Text, Translation and Notes.* Wiesbaden: Otto Harrassowitz.

Bell, C. 1928. *The People of Tibet.* Oxford: Clarendon.

Benn, C. 2002. *Daily Life in Traditional China: The Tang Dynasty.* London: Greenwood.

Benn, J.A. 2005. "Buddhism, Alcohol, and Tea in Medieval China." In R. Sterckx (ed.), *Of Tripod and Palate: Food, Politics and Religion in Traditional China.* New York: Palgrave Macmillan, 213–36.

Blofeld, J. 1985. *The Chinese Art of Tea.* Boston: Shambala.

Bodart, B.M. 1977. "Tea and Counsel: The Political Role of Sen Rikyū," *Monumenta Nipponica,* 32.1, 49–74.

Boswell, J. 1792 (2 vols.). *The Life of Samuel Johnson, LL.D.* London: Charles Dilly.

Boxer, C.R. 1948. *Fidalgos in the Far East 1550–1770: Fact and Fancy in the History of Macao.* The Hague: Martinus Nijhoff.
——1965. *The Dutch Seaborne Empire 1600–1800.* London: Hutchinson & Co.

Brinkley, F. 1903–04. *Japan: Its History and Culture.* London: T.C. & E.C. Jack.

Bruce, C.A. 1838. *An Account of the Manufacture of the Black Tea, as Now Practised at Suddeya in Upper Assam....* Calcutta: G.H. Huttmann.

Brunot, L., and E. Malka. 1939. *Textes Judéo-Arabes des Fès.* Vol. XXXIII. Rabat: L'institut des Hautes Études Marocaines.

Burnes, A. 1973. *Travels into Bokhara: Together with a Narrative of a Voyage on the Indus.* London: Oxford University Press.

Burton, A. 1997. *The Bukharans: A Dynastic, Diplomatic and Commercial History 1550–1702.* New York: St. Martin's.

Butel, P. 1989. *Histoire du Thé.* Paris: Les Éditions Desjonquères.

Cammann, S.V.R. 1951. *Trade Through the Himalayas.* Princeton: Princeton University Press.

Campbell, D. 1735. "A POEM upon TEA. Wherein its Antiquity, its several Virtues and Influences are set forth, and the Wisdom of the sober sex commended in chusing so mild a Liquor for their Entertainments. Likewise, the reason why the Ladies protest against all Imposing Liquors, and the Vulgar Terms used by the Followers of *Bacchus.* Also, the Objections against TEA, answered; the Complaint of the Fair Sex redress'd, and the best way of proceeding in Love-Affairs. Together with the sincere Courtship of DICK and AMY, &c." Printed, and sold by Mrs. Dodd; J. Roberts; J. Wilcox; J. Oswald; W. Hinchliff [and 5 others] in London.

Carpenter, F.R. (tr.). 1974. *The Classic of Tea.* By Lu Yu. Boston: Little, Brown and Co.

Cave, H.W. 1900. *Golden Tips: A Description of Ceylon and Its Great Tea Industry.* London: Sampson Low, Marston and Co.

Ceresa, M. 1993. "Discussing an Early Reference to Tea Drinking in China: Wang Bao's *Tong Yue,*" *Annali di ca Foscari, Rivista Della Facoltà di Lingue e Letterature Straniere Dell'Università di Venezia,* 32.3, 203–11.

Chan, H. 1979. "Tea Production and Tea Trade under the Jurchin-Chin Dynasty." In *Studia Sino-Mongolica: Festschrift für Herbert Franke,* Münchener Ostasiatische Studien 25. Wiesbaden: Franz Steiner Verlag, 109–25.

Chang, K.C. (ed.). 1977. *Food in Chinese Culture: Anthropological and Historical Perspectives.* New Haven: Yale University Press.

Chang, T.T. 1933 (rpt. 1969). *Sino-Portuguese Trade from 1514 to 1644: A Synthesis of Portuguese and Chinese Sources.* Leiden: E.J. Brill.

Chen, H., and S. Lin. 2001. *Formosa Oolong Tea.* Taipei: Maotouying.

Chow, K., and I. Kramer. 1990. *All the Tea in China.* San Francisco: China Books and Periodicals.

Clark, A.H. 1911. *The Clipper Ship Era: An Epitome of Famous American and British Clipper Ships, Their Owners, Builders, Commanders and Crews, 1843–1869.* New York: G.P. Putnam's Sons.

Coe, S.D., and M.D. Coe. 1996. *The True History of Chocolate.* London and New York: Thames & Hudson.

Cooper, M. (tr., ed., and annot.). 1973. *This Island of Japon: João Rodrigues' Account of 16th-century Japan.* Tokyo: Kodansha International.

Cousins, D., and M.A. Huffman. "Medical Properties in the Diet of Gorillas – An Ethnopharmacological Evaluation," *African Study Monographs,* 23 (2002), 65–89.

Creel, H.G. 1965. "The Role of the Horse in Chinese History," *The American Historical Review,* 83.3, 647–72.

Crossley, P.K. 1997. *The Manchus.* Cambridge, MA: Blackwell.

Curtin, J. 1908. *The Mongols.* Boston: Little, Brown and Co.

Davidson, J.W. 1903. *The Island of Formosa: Past and Present.* London and New York: Macmillan & Co.

Desideri, I. 1937. *An Account of Tibet: The Travels of Ippolito Desideri of Pistoia, S.J., 1712–1727.* F. de Filippi (ed.). London: G. Routledge & Sons.

Diffie, B.W., and G.D. Winius. 1977. *Foundations of the Portuguese Empire 1415–1480*. St. Paul: University of Minnesota Press.

Dikötter, F., L. Laamann, and X. Zhou. 2004. *Narcotic Culture: A History of Drugs in China*. London: Hurst & Co.

Doerfer, G. 1967. *Türkische und mongolische Elemente im Neupersischen, unter besonderer Berücksichtigung älterer neupersischer Geschichtsquellen, vor allem der Mongolen- und Timuridenzeit*. Band III: *Türkische Elemente im Neupersischen*. Wiesbaden: Franz Steiner.

Doughty, C.M. 1923. *Travels in Arabia Deserta*. London: Cape.

Douglas, C. 1899. *Chinese-English Dictionary of the Vernacular or Spoken Language of Amoy, with the Principal Variations of the Chang-chew and Chin-chew Dialects*. London: Presbyterian Church of England.

Drake, G. (tr. and annot.) 2002. *Linnés Avhandling Potus Theae 1765*. By C. Linnaeus. Uppsala: Svenska Linnésällskapet.

Duveyrier, H. 1864. *Les Touâreg du Nord: Exploration du Sahara*. Paris: Challamel Ainé.

Eden, T. 1958. *Tea*. London: Longmans, Green.

Elverskog, J. 2003. *The Jewel Translucent Sūtra: Altan Khan and the Mongols in the Sixteenth Century*. Leiden: Brill.

Elwood, E.S. 1934. *Economic Plants*. New York and London: D. Appleton-Century Co.

Etherington, D.M., and K. Forster. 1993. *Green Gold: The Political Economy of China's Post-1949 Tea Industry*. Hong Kong: Oxford University Press.

Evans, J. 1992. *Tea in China: The History of China's National Drink*. New York: Greenwood.

Farrington, A. 1991 (2 vols.). *The English Factory in Japan, 1613–1623*. London: The British Library.

Ferguson, J. 1887. *Ceylon in the "Jubilee Year."* London: John Haddon & Co.

Fitzpatrick, A.L. 1990. *The Great Russian Fair: Nizhnii Novgorod 1840–1890*. London: Macmillan.

Fitzpatrick, F.L. 1964. *Our Plant Resources*. New York: Holt, Rinehart, and Winston.

Forrest, D.M. 1967. *A Hundred Years of Ceylon Tea. 1867–1967*. London: Chatto & Windus.

———1973. *Tea for the British: The Social and Economic History of a Famous Trade*. London: Chatto & Windus.

Fortune, R. 1847. *Three Years' Wanderings in the Northern Provinces of China*. London: John Murray.

Furber, H. 1976. *Rival Empires of Trade in the Orient 1600–1800*. Minneapolis: University of Minnesota Press.

Galton, F. 1914–30 (4 vols.). *The Life, Letters, and Labours of Francis Galton*. Karl Pearson (ed.). Cambridge: Cambridge University Press.

Gardella, R. 1994. *Harvesting Mountains: Fujian and the China Tea Trade, 1757–1937*. Berkeley and Los Angeles: University of California Press.

Gilmour, J. 1888. *Among the Mongols*. London: Religious Tract Society.

Gilodo, A.A. 1991. *Russian Samovar*. Moscow: Sovetskaja Rossija.

Glamann, K. 1958. *Dutch-Asiatic Trade 1620–1740*. The Hague: Martinus Nijhoff.

Gompertz, G.St.G.M. 1958. *Chinese Celadon Wares*. London: Faber & Faber.

Goodman, J., P.E. Lovejoy, and A. Sherratt (eds.). 1995. *Consuming Habits: Drugs in History and Anthropology*. London: Routledge.

Gordon, G.J. 1835. "Journal of an Attempted Ascent of the Min River to Visit the Tea Plantations of the Fuh-kin Province of China," *Journal of the Asiatic Society of Bengal*, 4, 553–64.

Graham, P.J. 1998. *Tea of the Sages: The Art of Sencha*. Honolulu: University of Hawai'i Press.

Griffiths, P. 1967. *The History of the Indian Tea Industry*. London: Weidenfeld and Nicolson.

Gronewold, S.E. 1984. "Yankee Doodle Went to China," *Natural History*, 93.2, 62–74.

Hanes, W.T., and F. Sanello. 2002. *Opium Wars: The Addiction of One Empire and the Corruption of Another*. Naperville: Sourcebooks.

Hanway, J. 1756. *A Journal of Eight Days Journey from Portsmouth to Kingston upon Thames. . . . To which is added, An Essay on Tea. . . .* London: Printed by H. Woodfall.

Harler, C.R. 1956 (2nd ed.). *The Culture and Marketing of Tea*. London: Oxford University Press.

Herlihy, P. 2002. *The Alcoholic Empire: Vodka & Politics in Late Imperial Russia*. Oxford: Oxford University Press.

Hill, A.F. 1952. *Economic Botany: A Textbook of Useful Plants and Plant Products*. New York: McGraw-Hill.

Hirota, D. (ed.). 1995. *Winds in the Pines: Classic Writings of the Way of Tea as a Buddhist Path*. Freemont, CA: Asian Humanities.

Hirth, F., and W.W. Rockhill (tr. and annot.). 1911. *Chau Ju-kua: His Work on the Chinese and Arab Trade in the Twelfth and Thirteenth Centuries, entitled Chu-fan-chï*. St. Petersburg: Imperial Academy of Science.

Hobhouse, H. 1999. *Seeds of Change: Six Plants that Transformed Mankind*. London: Papermac.

Holes, C. 1996. "The Dispute of Coffee and Tea. A Debate-poem from the Gulf." In J.R. Smart (ed.), *Tradition and Modernity in Arabic Language and Literature*, Richmond: Curzon, 302–15.

Holtzman, J.D. 2003. "In A Cup Of Tea: Commodities and history among Samburu pastoralists in northern Kenya," *American Ethnologist*, 30.1, 136–55.

Honey, W.B. 1946. *Dresden China: An Introduction to the Study of Meissen Porcelain*. London: Adam and Charles Black.

Houssaye, J.G. 1843. *Monographie du thé: Description botanique, torréfaction, composition chimique, propriétés hygiéniques de cette feuille*. Paris: Chez l'auteur.

Huang, H.T. 2000. "Tea Processing and Utilisation." In *Science and Civilisation in China*. Volume 6, part 5. Cambridge: Cambridge University Press, 503–70.

Huc, É.R. 1925 (2 vols.). *Souvenirs d'un voyage dans la Tartarie, le Thibet et la Chine*. Paris: Plon-Nourrit.

Hudson, C.M. 1979. *Black Drink: A Native American Tea.* Athens, Georgia: University of Georgia Press.

Israel, J.I. 1989. *Dutch Primacy in World Trade 1585–1740.* Oxford: Clarendon.

Ivanov, M. 2001. "Steeped in Tradition," *Russian Life*, 58–63.

Izikowitz, K.G. 1951. *Lamet Hill Peasants in French Indochina.* Gothenburg: Etnografiska Museet.

Jacob, H.E. 1935. *Coffee: The Epic of a Commodity.* New York: Viking.

Jacobs, E.M. 1991. *In Pursuit of Pepper and Tea: The Story of the Dutch East India Company.* Amsterdam: Netherlands Maritime Museum.

Jagchid, S., and C.R. Bowden. 1965. "Some Notes on the Horse Policy of the Mongol Dynasty," *Central Asiatic Journal*, 10, 246–68.

Jarring, G. 1993. *Stimulants Among the Turks of Eastern Turkestan. An Eastern Turki Text Edited with Translation, Notes and Glossary.* Scripta Minora. Lund: Kungl. Humanistiska Vetenskapssamfundet.

Jenkins, G.L. 1941. *The Chemistry of Organic Medicinal Products.* New York: John Wiley and Sons.

Johnson, S. 1757. "Review of 'A Journal of Eight Days Journey'...," *Literary Magazine*, Vol II, No. xiii, 333–48.

Kato, E. 2004. *The Tea Ceremony and Women's Empowerment in Modern Japan: Bodies Re-Presenting the Past.* London: RoutledgeCurzon.

Kaufmann, T. 1989. *Un Drint'n Koppte Tee... Zur Socialgeschichte des Teetrinkens in Ostfriesland.* Aurich: Museumfachstelle Mobile der Ostfriesischen Landschaft.

Keene, D. 2003. *Yoshimasa and the Silver Pavilion: The Creation of the Soul of Japan.* New York: Columbia University Press.

Khamis, S. 2006. "A Taste for Tea: How Tea Travelled to (and Through) Australian Culture," *The Journal of the History of Culture in Australia*, 24, 57–80.

Kieschnick, J. 2003. *The Impact of Buddhism on Chinese Material Culture.* Princeton: Princeton University Press.

Koerner, L. 1999. *Linnaeus: Nature and Nation.* Cambridge, Massachusetts: Harvard University Press.

Labaree, B.W. 1964. *The Boston Tea Party.* Oxford: Oxford University Press.

Lai, S. 1971. "Tea in the Tenth Century: A Study of its Place in Social Life and the Development of its Trade." University of Hong Kong: M.A. thesis.

Lancaster, O. 1944. *The Story of Tea.* London: Tea Centre.

Lane, G. 2006. *Daily Life in the Mongol Empire.* Westport, Connecticut: Greenwood.

Lao, S. 1980. *Teahouse: A Play in Three Acts.* John Howard-Gibbon (tr.). Beijing: Foreign Languages Press.

Lattimore, O. 1928. *The Desert Road to Turkestan.* London: Methuen & Co.

Lau, Y. 1972. "The Patent Laws of Tea and its Impact on the Economy and Society of the Song Dynasty." University of Hong Kong: M.A. thesis.

Laufer, B. 1919. *Chinese Contributions to the History of Civilization in Ancient Iran. With Special Reference to the History of Cultivated Plants and Products.* Publication 201, Anthropological Series, Vol. XV, No. 3. Chicago: Field Museum of Natural History.

Lempriere, W. 1791. *A Tour from Gibraltar to Tangier, Sallee, Mogodore, Santa Cruz, Tarudant, and Thence over Mount Atlas to Morocco: including a particular account of the royal harem, &c.* London: Printed for the author, and sold by J. Walter, J. Johnson, and J. Sewell.

Lettsom, J.C. 1772. *The Natural History of the Tea-tree.* London.

Lewis, W.H., and M.P.F. Lewis. 2003. *Medical Botany. Plants Affecting Human Health.* Hoboken, N.J.: John Wiley & Sons.

Li, S. 2003. *Compendium of Materia Medica.* Beijing: Foreign Languages Press.

Liao, B. 2002. *Vessels, Replenished Minds: The Culture, Practice and Art of Tea.* Taipei: National Palace Museum.

Lipton, T.J. 1931. *Leaves from the Lipton Logs.* London: Hutchinson & Co.

Liu, Y. 2007. *The Dutch East India Company's Tea Trade with China, 1757–1781.* Leiden: Brill.

Lubbock, B. 1919 (4th ed.). *The China Clippers.* Glasgow: J. Brown and Son.

Ludwig, T.M. 1974. "The Way of Tea: A Religio-Aesthetic Mode of Life," *History of Religions*, 14.1, 28–50.

———1981. "Before Rikyū: Religious and Aesthetic Influences in the Early History of the Tea Ceremony," *Monumenta Nipponica*, 36.4, 367–90.

Macfarlane, A. 2004. *Green Gold: The Empire of Tea.* London: Ebury.

MacGregor, D.R. 1983 (2nd ed.). *The Tea Clippers: Their History and Development 1833–1875.* London: Conway Maritime Press.

Mack, G.R., and A. Surina. 2005. *Food Culture in Russia and Central Asia.* Westport: Greenwood.

Mackerras, C. 1972. *The Uighur Empire According to the T'ang Dynasty Histories: A Study in Sino-Uighur Relations 744–840.* Canberra: Australian National University Press.

Mair, V.H., ed. 1994. *The Columbia Anthology of Traditional Chinese Literature.* New York: Columbia University Press.

Mason, S. 1745. *The Good and Bad Effects of Tea Consider'd.* London: Printed for M. Cooper.

Mather, R.B. (tr., intro., and annot.). 1976. *Shih-shuo Hsin-yü. A New Account of Tales of the World.* By Liu I-ching, with commentary by Liu Chün. Minneapolis: University of Minneapolis Press.

Matthee, R. 1996. "From Coffee to Tea: Shifting Patterns of Consumption in Qajar Iran," *Journal of World History*, 7.2.

Medley, M. 1976. *The Chinese Potter: A Practical History of Chinese Ceramics.* Oxford: Phaidon.

Miege, J.-L. 1957. "Origine et Developpement de la Consommation du Thé au Maroc," *Bulletin Économique et Social du Maroc*, 20.71.

Mills, J.V.G. (tr. and annot.). 1970. *Ying-yai sheng-lan: "The Overall Survey of the Ocean's Shores."* By Ma Huan. Hakluyt Society, Extra Series, no. 42. London: Cambridge University Press.

Millward, J.A. 1998. *Beyond the Pass. Economy, Ethnicity and Empire in Qing Central Asia, 1759–1864.* Stanford: Stanford University Press.

Mintz, S.W. 1985. *Sweetness and Power: The Place of Sugar in Modern History.* New York: Viking Penguin.

Morton, W.S. 1994 (3rd ed.). *Japan: Its History and Culture.* New York: McGraw-Hill.

Mote, F.W. 1999. *Imperial China 900–1800.* Cambridge, MA: Harvard University Press.

Moxham, R. 2003. *Tea: Addiction, Exploitation and Empire.* New York: Carroll & Graf.

Mui, H., and L.H. Mui (eds.). 1973. *William Melrose in China 1845–1855: The Letters of a Scottish Tea Merchant.* Edinburgh: T. and A. Constable.

Murdoch, J. 1903–26. *A History of Japan.* Yokohama: Kelly & Walsh.

Nathanson, J.A. 1984. "Caffeine and Related Methylxanthines: Possible Naturally Occurring Pesticides," *Science,* 226:4671, 184–87.

Okakura, K. 1989. *The Book of Tea.* Tokyo: Kodansha International.

Ovington, J. 1699. *An Essay Upon the Nature and Qualities of Tea.* London: Printed by R. Roberts.

Painter, G.D. 1989. *Marcel Proust.* London: Chatto & Windus.

Parkes, H. 1854. "Report on the Russian Caravan Trade with China," *Journal of the Royal Geographical Society of London,* 24, 306–12.

Parmentier, J. 1996. *Tea Time in Flanders: The Maritime Trade Between the Southern Netherlands and China in the 18th Century.* Bruges-Zeebrugge: Ludion.

Paulli, S. 1746. *A Treatise On Tobacco, Tea, Coffee, and Chocolate: In which the advantages and disadvantages attending the use of these commodities are... considered.... The Whole Illustrated with Copper Plates, exhibiting the Tea Utensils of the Chinese and Persians.* Dr. James (tr.). London: T. Osborne.

Perdue, P. 2005. *China Marches West: The Qing Conquest of Central Eurasia.* Cambridge, MA: Harvard University Press.

Pettigrew, J. 2001. *A Social History of Tea.* London: The National Trust.

Pitelka, M. (ed.). 2003. *Japanese Tea Culture: Art, History and Practice.* New York: RoutledgeCurzon.

Plutschow, H.E. 1986. *Historical Chanoyu.* Tokyo: The Japan Times.

——2003. *Rediscovering Rikyū and the Beginnings of the Japanese Tea Ceremony.* Kent: Global Oriental.

Pomet, P. 1694 (3 vols. in 1). *Histoire Générale des Drogues, Traitant des Plantes, des Animaux & des Mineraux....* Paris: J.-B Loyson.

Pregadio, F. 2006. *Great Clarity: Daoism and Alchemy in Early Medieval China.* Stanford: Stanford University Press.

Purseglove, J.W. 1968 (2 vols.). *Tropical Crops: Dicotyledons.* New York: John Wiley and Sons.

Raji, N.K. 2003. *L'Art du Thé au Maroc: Traditions, Rituels, Symboles.* Paris: ACR Édition.

Reppler, A. 1932. *To Think of Tea.* Boston: Houghton Mifflin.

Richardson, H. 1962. *Tibet and Its History.* London: Oxford University Press.

——1998. *High Peaks, Pure Earth: Collected Writings on Tibetan History and Culture.* London: Serindia.

Robbins, M. 1974. "The Inland Fukien Tea Industry: Five Dynasties to the Opium War," *Transactions of the International Conference of Orientalists in Japan,* 19, 121–42.

Rockhill, W.W. 1891. *The Land of the Lamas.* London: Longman, Green and Co.

Rossabi, M. 1970. "The Tea and Horse Trade with Inner Asia during the Ming," *Journal of Asian History,* 4, 136–68.

——(ed.). 1983. *China Among Equals: The Middle Kingdom and Its Neighbors, 10th–14th Centuries.* Berkeley: University of California Press.

Rosthorn, A. de. 1895. *On the Tea Cultivation in Western Ssŭch'uan and the Tea Trade with Tibet viâ Tachienlu.* London: Luzac & Co.

Royle, J.F. 1850. "Report on the Progress of the Culture of the Chinese Tea Plant in the Himalayas from 1835 to 1847," *Journal of the Agricultural and Horticultural Society of India,* 7, 11–41.

Sadler, A.L. 1934. *Cha-No-Yu: The Japanese Tea Ceremony.* Kobe: J.L. Thompson; London: Kegan, Paul, Trench, Trubner & Co.

Sage, S.F. 1992. *Ancient Sichuan and the Unification of China.* Albany: State University of New York Press.

Schafer, E.H. 1967. *The Vermilion Bird: T'ang Images of the South.* Berkeley and Los Angeles: University of California Press.

Sealy, R.J. 1958. *A Revision of the Genus Camellia.* London: The Royal Horticultural Society.

Sen Sōshitsu XV. 1998. *The Japanese Way of Tea: From Its Origins in China to Sen Rikyū.* V. Dixon Morris (tr.); P.H. Varley (foreword). Honolulu: University of Hawai'i Press.

Serruys, H. 1963. "Early Lamaism in Mongolia," *Oriens Extremus,* Jahrgang 10, 181–216.

——1975. "Sino-Mongol Trade during the Ming," *Journal of Asian History,* 9.1, 34–55.

Shaw, R. 1871. *Visits to High Tartary, Yârkand, and Kâshgar (Formerly Chinese Tartary), and Return Journey over the Karakoram Pass.* London: John Murray.

Shaw, S. 1900. *History of the Staffordshire Potteries.* London: Scott, Greenwood & Co.

Shewan, A. 1927. *The Great Days of Sail: Some Reminiscences of a Tea-Clipper Captain.* London: Heath Cranton.

Short, T. 1730. *A Dissertation Upon Tea, Explaining Its Nature and Properties by Many New Experiments, and Demonstrating from Philosophical Principles, the Various Effects It Has on Different Constitutions.* London: W. Bowyer, for Fletcher Gyles.

Sladkovskii, M.I. 1966. *History of Economic Relations Between Russia and China.* Jerusalem: Israel Program for Scientific Translations.

Smith, P.J. 1991. *Taxing Heaven's Storehouse: Horses, Bureaucrats, and the Destruction of the Sichuan Tea Industry 1074–1224.*

Cambridge, MA: Council on East Asian Studies, Harvard University.

Smith, R.E.F., and D. Christian. 1984. *Bread and Salt: A Social and Economic History of Food and Drink in Russia.* Cambridge: Cambridge University Press.

Spengen, W. van. 1992. "Tibetan Border Worlds: A Geo-historical Analysis of Trade and Traders." University of Amsterdam: Ph.D. thesis.

Standage, T. 2007. *A History of the World in Six Glasses.* London: Atlantic Books.

Staunton, G.T. 1821. *Narrative of the Chinese Embassy to the Khan of the Tourgouth Tartars.* London: John Murray.

Suzuki, D.T. 1970. *Zen and Japanese Culture.* Princeton: Princeton University Press.

Tapper, R., and S. Zubaida (eds.). 1994. *Culinary Cultures of the Middle East.* London: I.B. Tauris.

Tea on Service. 1947. Introduced by Admiral Lord Mountevans and Lord Woolton. London: The Tea Centre.

Teng, J. 2004. *Zhong-Ri Cha Wenhua Jiaoliu Shi* ("A History of Sino-Japanese Tea Culture Exchanges"). Beijing: Renmin.

Torniainen, M. 2000. *From Austere Wabi to Golden Wabi: Philosophical and Aesthetic Aspects of Wabi in the Way of Tea.* Helsinki: Finnish Oriental Society.

Trotzig, I. 1911. *Cha-No-Yu: Japanernas Teceremoni.* Stockholm: Rikmuseets Etnografiska Avdelning.

Twining, R. 1784. *Observations on the Tea and Window Act, and on the Tea Trade.* London.

Ukers, W. 1935 (2 vols.). *All About Tea.* New York: The Tea and Coffee Trade Journal Company.

Upton Tea Quarterly, 14.4 (2005) to 17.2 (2008).

Van Dyke, P. 2005. *The Canton Trade: Life and Enterprise on the China Coast 1700–1845.* Hong Kong: Hong Kong University Press.

Varley, P., and Kumakura I. (eds.). 1989. *Tea in Japan.* Honolulu: University of Hawai'i Press.

Waddell, L.A. 1939 (rptd.). *The Buddhism of Tibet.* Cambridge: W. Heffer & Sons, Ltd.

Wakeman, F. 1978. "The Canton Trade and the Opium War." In J. Fairbanks (ed.), *The Cambridge History of China,*

Volume 10, part 1. Cambridge: Cambridge University Press, 163–212.

Waldron, J. 1733. *A Satyr Against Tea. Or, Ovington's Essay Upon the Nature and Qualities of Tea, &c. Dissected and Burlesq'd.* Dublin: Printed by Sylvanus Pepyat.

Waley, A. 1958. *The Opium War Through Chinese Eyes.* London: Allen & Unwin.

Wang, L. 2005. *Tea and Chinese Culture.* San Francisco: Long River Press.

Wang, Y. (tr.). 1984. *A Record of Buddhist Monasteries in Lo-yang.* By Yang Hsüan-chih. Princeton: Princeton University Press.

Waugh, M. 1985. *Smuggling in Kent & Sussex 1700–1840.* Newbury, Berkshire: Countryside Books.

Weatherstone, J. 1986. *The Pioneers, 1825–1900: The Early British Tea and Coffee Planters and Their Way of Life.* London: Quiller.

Wesley, J. 1825. *A Letter to a Friend, Concerning Tea.* London: Printed by A. Macintosh.

Wong, H. 1966. "A Historical Analysis of Tibet's Tea Trade with Szechuan and Other Regions in the Ch'ing Dynasty." University of Hong Kong: M.A. thesis.

Wood, F. 1995. *Did Marco Polo Go To China?* London: Martin Secker & Warburg.

Wu, C. 1996. *Zhongguo Nongye Shi* ("A History of Chinese Agriculture"). Beijing: Jingguan Jiaoyu.

Yuan, J.H. 1981. "English Words of Chinese Origin," *Journal of Chinese Linguistics,* 9, 244–86.

———1982. "An Anglo-Chinese Glossary," *Journal of Chinese Linguistics,* 10, 108–65.

Yule, H., and A. Coke Burnell. 1886. *Hobson-Jobson: being a glossary of Anglo-Indian colloquial words and phrases, and of kindred terms: etymological, historical, geographical and discursive.* London: John Murray, 1886.

Zhu, Z. 1996. *Chashi Chutan* ("An Initial Investigation into the History of Tea"). Beijing: Zhongguo Nongye.

Zhuang, G. 1993. *Tea, Silver, Opium and War: The International Tea Trade and Western Commercial Expansion into China in 1740–1840.* Xiamen: Xiamen University Press.

INDEX